maranGraphics'™ Simplified Computer Guide

WordPerfect® for DOS Version 5.1
Expanded Edition

Ruth Maran

maranGraphics Inc.
Mississauga, Ontario, Canada

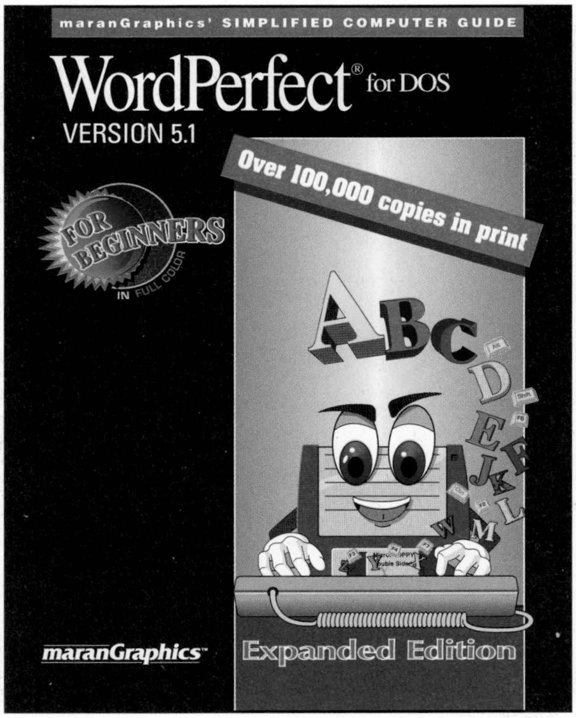

Distributed in United States
by Regents/Prentice Hall

Telephone: 1-800-223-1360
Fax: 1-800-445-6991

Distributed in Canada
by Prentice Hall Canada

Telephone: 1-800-567-3800
Fax: 416-299-2529

Distributed Internationally
by Simon & Schuster

Telephone: 201-767-4990
Fax: 201-767-5625

maranGraphics'™ Simplified Computer Guide
WordPerfect® for DOS Version 5.1
Expanded Edition

Published 1993.

Library of Congress Cataloging-in-Publication Data

Maran, Ruth, 1970-
maranGraphics' simplified computer guide:
WordPerfect version 5.1 / Ruth Maran. -- Expanded ed.
p. cm.
Includes index.
ISBN 0-13-106295-6
1. WordPerfect (Computer file) 2. Word processing.
I. Title. II. Title: WordPerfect version 5.1.
Z52.5.W65M273 1993
652.5'536--dc20 93-3098
CIP

Trademark Acknowledgments

WordPerfect is a registered trademark of WordPerfect Corporation.

MS-DOS is a registered trademark of Microsoft Corporation.

Hewlett-Packard, HP, LaserJet, and PCL are registered trademarks of Hewlett-Packard Company.

Cover Design and Graphic Consultant:
Jim C. Leung

Art Director:
Béla Korcsog

Production and Illustration:
Béla Korcsog
Dave Ross

Film generated on maranGraphics' Linotronic L-330 imagesetter at 2540 dpi resolution.

Acknowledgments

Special thanks to Wendi Blouin Ewbank for her patience, intelligence and good humor throughout the project. Also to Saverio C. Tropiano for his consultation and expert advice.

To the dedicated staff of maranGraphics Inc., including Maria Damiano, Monica DeVries, Eric Feistmantl, Béla Korcsog, Jim C. Leung, Maxine Maran, Robert Maran and David Ross.

And finally, to Richard Maran who originated the easy-to-use graphic format of this guide. Thank you for your inspiration and guidance.

Table of Contents

INTRODUCTION

What is a Word Processor?

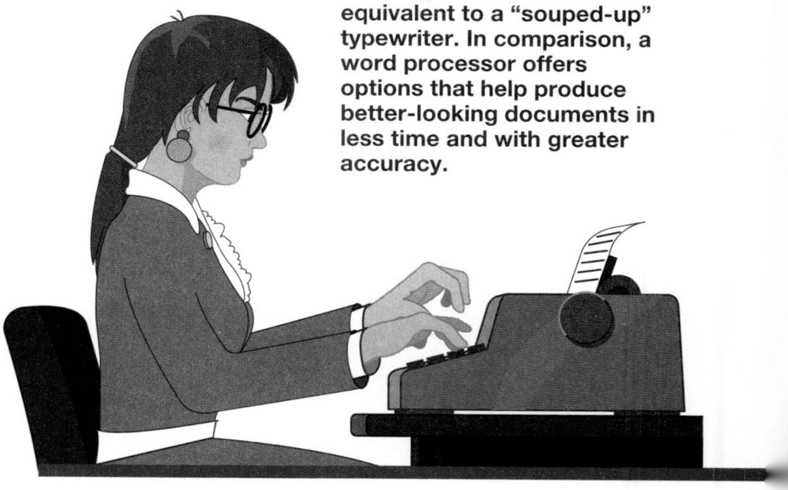

A word processor is the 90's equivalent to a "souped-up" typewriter. In comparison, a word processor offers options that help produce better-looking documents in less time and with greater accuracy.

What are Word Processors used for?

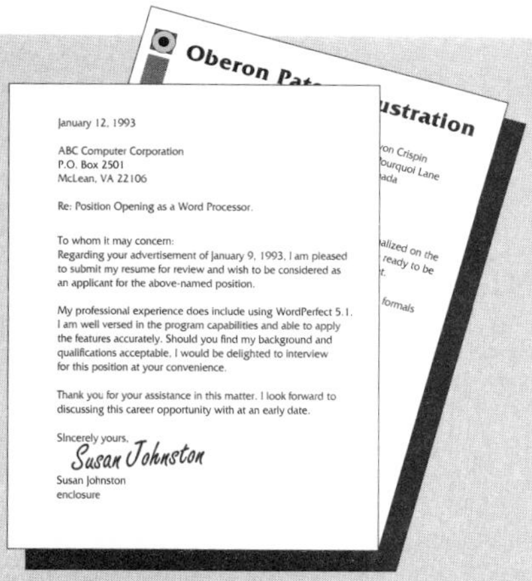

Oberon Pat
ustration
January 12, 1993
ABC Computer Corporation
P.O. Box 2501
McLean, VA 22106
Re: Position Opening as a Word Processor.
To whom it may concern:
Regarding your advertisement of January 9, 1993, I am pleased to submit my resume for review and wish to be considered as an applicant for the above-named position.
My professional experience does include using WordPerfect 5.1. I am well versed in the program capabilities and able to apply the features accurately. Should you find my background and qualifications acceptable, I would be delighted to interview for this position at your convenience.
Thank you for your assistance in this matter. I look forward to discussing this career opportunity with at an early date.
Sincerely yours,
Susan Johnston
Susan Johnston
enclosure

HOME AND BUSINESS LETTERS

Move, copy, spell check, undelete and alignment features make word processors easier, faster and more accurate than traditional typewriters.

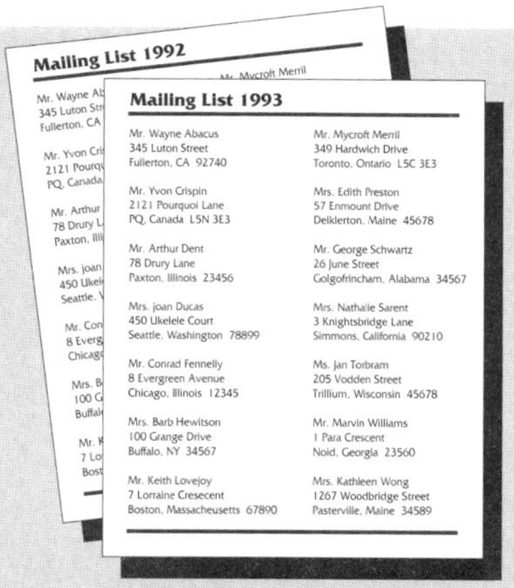

Mailing List 1992
Mailing List 1993
Mr. Wayne Abacus
345 Luton Street
Fullerton, CA 92740
Mr. Mycroft Merril
349 Hardwich Drive
Toronto, Ontario L5C 3E3
Mr. Yvon Crispin
2121 Pourquoi Lane
PQ, Canada L5N 3E3
Mrs. Edith Preston
57 Enmount Drive
Delklerton, Maine 45678
Mr. Arthur Dent
78 Drury Lane
Paxton, Illinois 23456
Mr. George Schwartz
26 June Street
Golgofrincham, Alabama 34567
Mrs. Joan Ducas
450 Ukelele Court
Seattle, Washington 78899
Mrs. Nathalie Sarent
3 Knightsbridge Lane
Simmons, California 90210
Mr. Conrad Fennelly
8 Evergreen Avenue
Chicago, Illinois 12345
Ms. Jan Torbram
205 Vodden Street
Trillium, Wisconsin 45678
Mrs. Barb Hewitson
100 Grange Drive
Buffalo, NY 34567
Mr. Marvin Williams
1 Para Crescent
Noid, Georgia 23560
Mr. Keith Lovejoy
7 Lorraine Cresecent
Boston, Massachuetts 67890
Mrs. Kathleen Wong
1267 Woodbridge Street
Pasterville, Maine 34589

MAILING LISTS

Documents can be merged with database records (example: a list of names and addresses) to quickly produce personalized letters.

Thesis on the Whereabouts of Pens I've Lost Since Birth
Jim Leung
M.B.A., B.I.C.
University of Seattle

REPORTS, MANUALS

Page numbering, indexing, table of contents, spell check, outlining and other features make a word processor ideal for longer documents such as reports or manuals.

- Using the word processor, you enter text and edit it as required.
- You can then check your document for spelling, save and print it.
- The printer produces a copy of the document you created on your screen.

Word Processor Basics

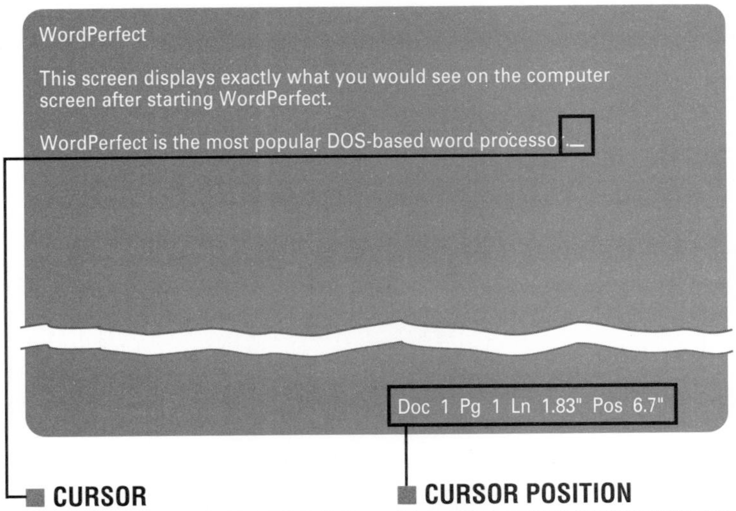

WordPerfect

This screen displays exactly what you would see on the computer screen after starting WordPerfect.

WordPerfect is the most popular DOS-based word processor.

Doc 1 Pg 1 Ln 1.83" Pos 6.7"

CURSOR

The cursor is the flashing line on your screen. This indicates where the text you type will appear.

CURSOR POSITION

The bottom of the screen indicates the current position of your cursor.

WORD WRAPPING

When typing a document, you do not press the Enter (or Return) key when reaching the end of a line. The word processor automatically moves you to the next line. This is called "word wrapping".

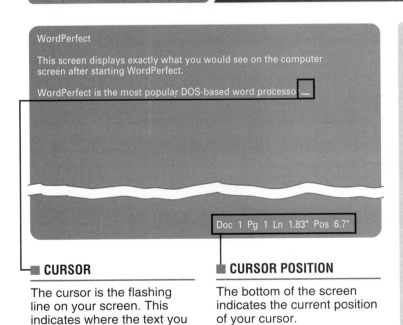

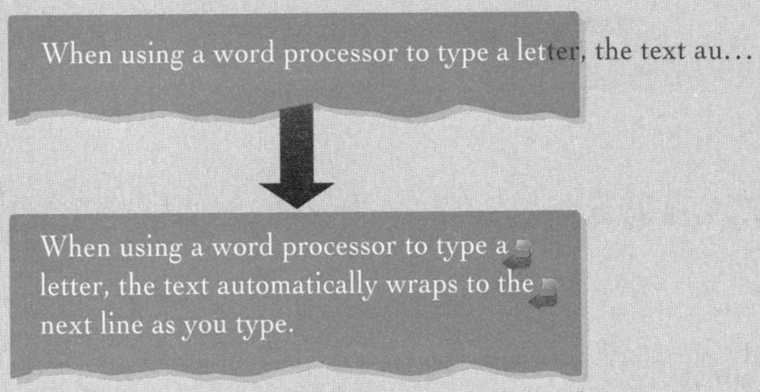

When using a word processor to type a letter, the text au…
When using a word processor to type a
letter, the text automatically wraps to the
next line as you type.

Press the Enter key only when you want to start a new line or paragraph.

START WORDPERFECT

ENTER TEXT

Let's Assume...

WordPerfect is installed on your hard drive in a directory named WP51. The default settings are used.

Start WordPerfect

C:\>wp

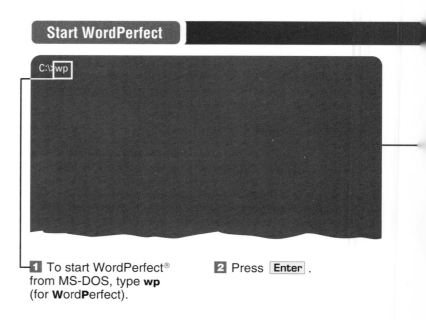

1 To start WordPerfect® from MS-DOS, type **wp** (for **W**ord**P**erfect).

2 Press Enter .

Enter Text

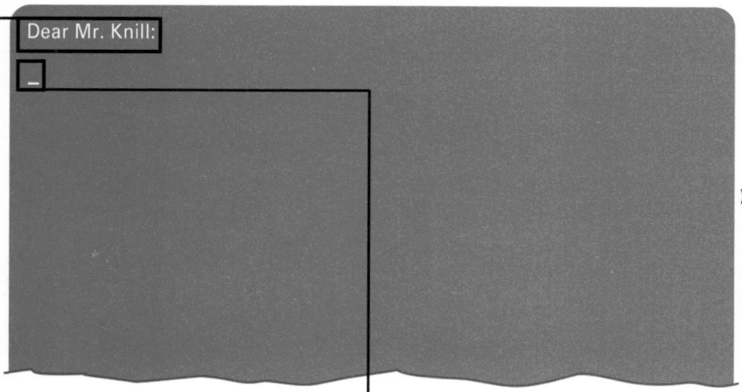
Dear Mr. Knill:
_

The cursor (flashing underline _) indicates where the text you type will appear in the document.

1 Type the first line of text.

2 To start a new paragraph, press Enter twice.

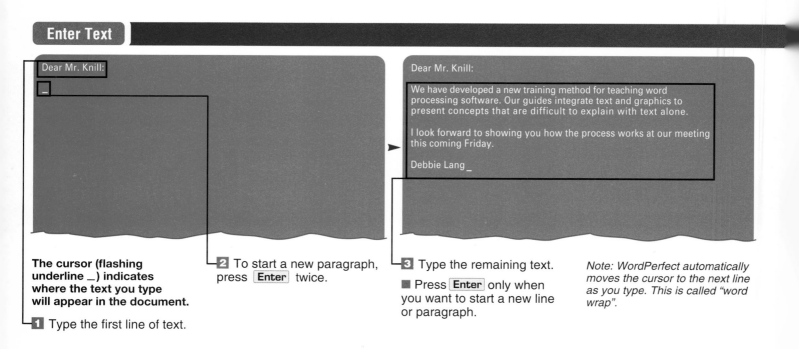

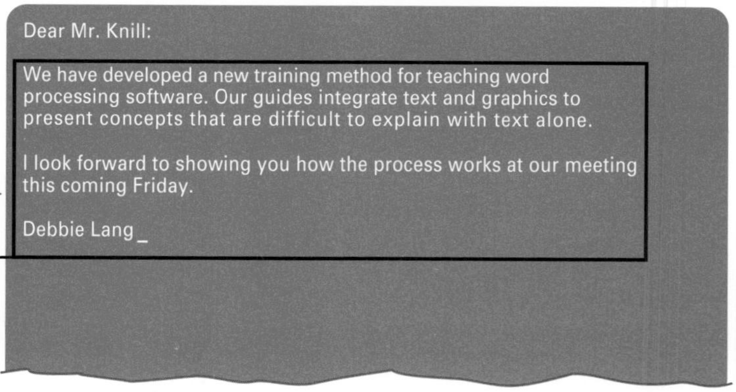
Dear Mr. Knill:
We have developed a new training method for teaching word processing software. Our guides integrate text and graphics to present concepts that are difficult to explain with text alone.
I look forward to showing you how the process works at our meeting this coming Friday.
Debbie Lang _

3 Type the remaining text.

- Press Enter only when you want to start a new line or paragraph.

Note: WordPerfect automatically moves the cursor to the next line as you type. This is called "word wrap".

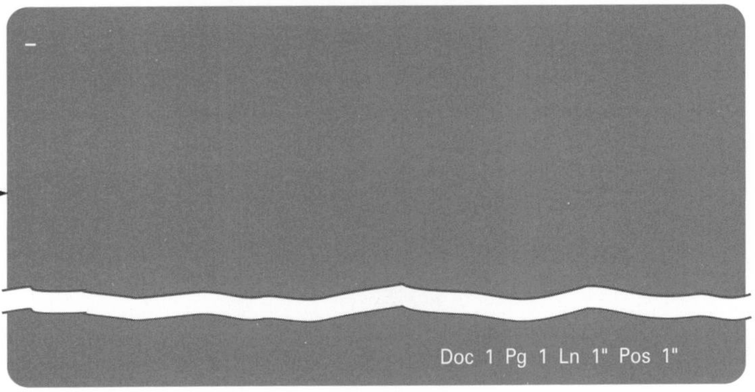
Doc 1 Pg 1 Ln 1" Pos 1"

■ WordPerfect displays a blank screen.

USING THE KEYBOARD

■ If key names are separated by a hyphen (-), press and hold down the first key before pressing the second key (example: Shift - F2).

■ If key names are separated by a comma (,), press and release the first key before pressing the second key (example: Ctrl , Home).

When you start a new document, WordPerfect automatically sets a one-inch margin around the page. Although margins are not displayed on the computer screen, they are in effect when the document is printed.

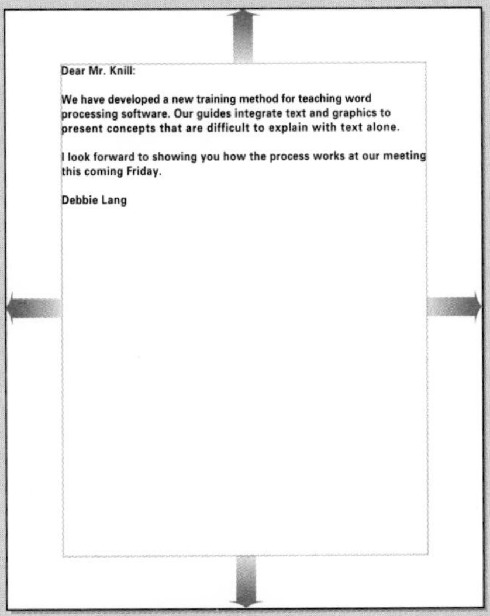
Dear Mr. Knill:
We have developed a new training method for teaching word processing software. Our guides integrate text and graphics to present concepts that are difficult to explain with text alone.
I look forward to showing you how the process works at our meeting this coming Friday.
Debbie Lang

Note: Later in this guide you will learn how to change the margins and print a document.

The position of the cursor is indicated at the bottom of the screen.

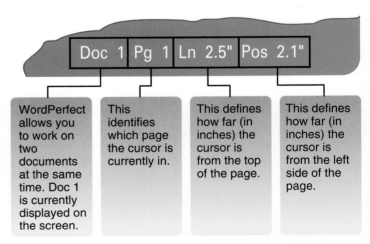

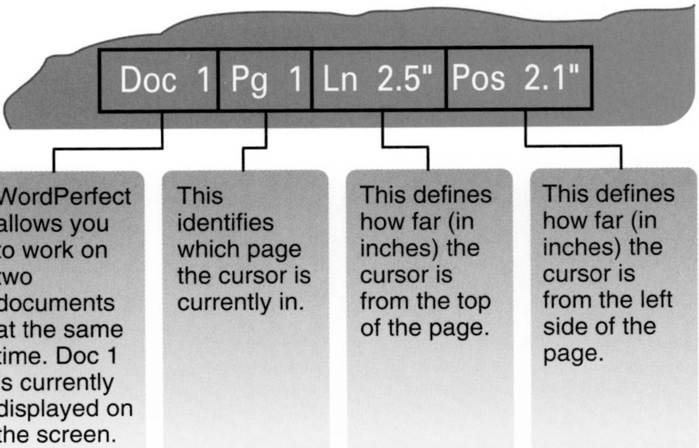
Doc 1 Pg 1 Ln 2.5" Pos 2.1"

WordPerfect allows you to work on two documents at the same time. Doc 1 is currently displayed on the screen.

This identifies which page the cursor is currently in.

This defines how far (in inches) the cursor is from the top of the page.

This defines how far (in inches) the cursor is from the left side of the page.

MOVE THE CURSOR

Move the Cursor

Press this key to move the cursor one line up.

Press this key to move the cursor one line down.

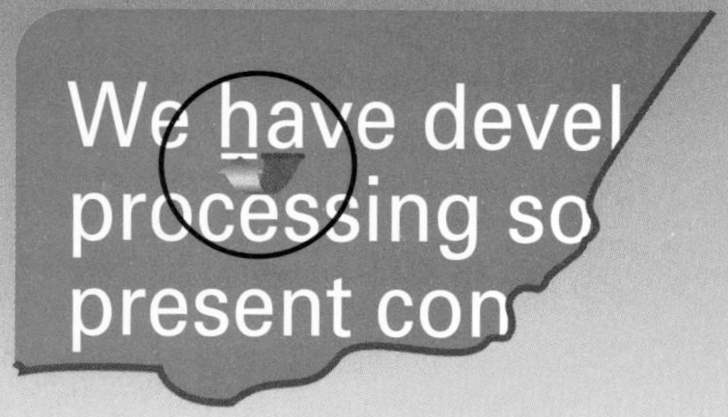

Press this key to move the cursor left one character.

Press this key to move the cursor right one character.

Press these keys to move left one word.

Press these keys to move right one word.

Page Up Press this key to move to the top of the previous page.

Page Down Press this key to move to the top of the next page.

Note: If there is only one page in your document, **Page Up** *will move the cursor to the top of the screen and* **Page Down** *will move it to the last character in the document.*

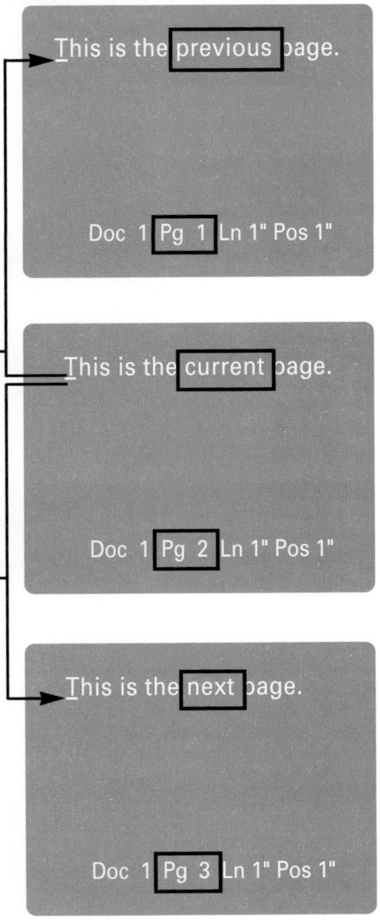
This is the previous page.
Doc 1 Pg 1 Ln 1" Pos 1"
This is the current page.
Doc 1 Pg 2 Ln 1" Pos 1"
This is the next page.
Doc 1 Pg 3 Ln 1" Pos 1"

Ctrl - **Home**

MOVE TO ANY PAGE IN THE DOCUMENT

Press these keys and **Go to** appears at the bottom of the screen. Type the page number you want to move to. Then press **Enter**.

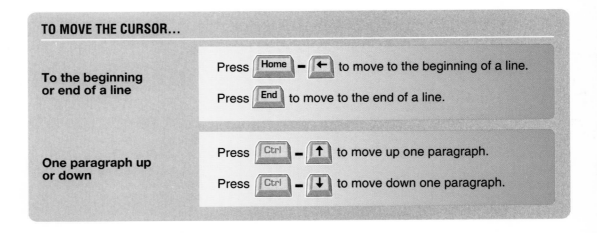

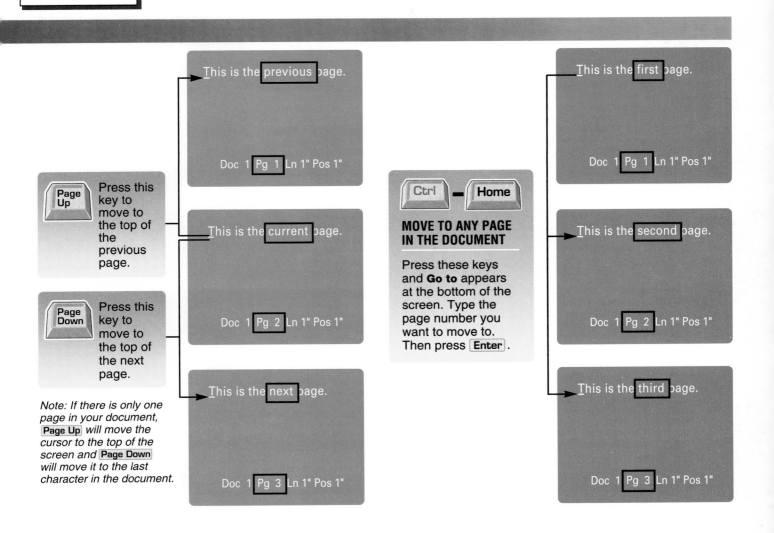

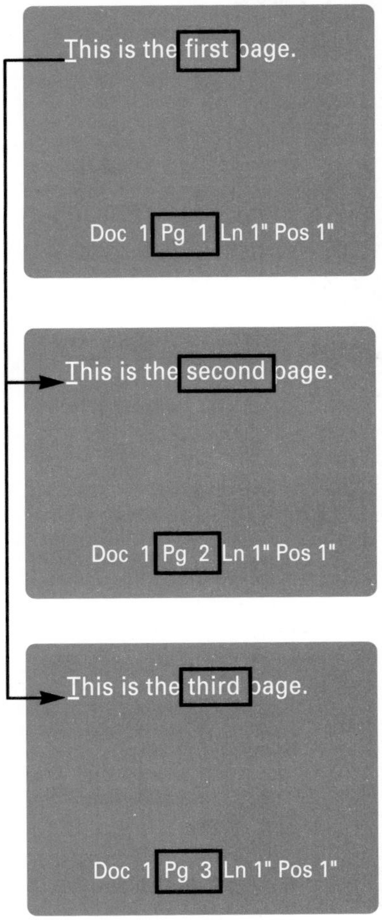
This is the first page.
Doc 1 Pg 1 Ln 1" Pos 1"
This is the second page.
Doc 1 Pg 2 Ln 1" Pos 1"
This is the third page.
Doc 1 Pg 3 Ln 1" Pos 1"

TO MOVE THE CURSOR...

To the beginning or end of a line

Press **Home** - **←** to move to the beginning of a line.

Press **End** to move to the end of a line.

One paragraph up or down

Press **Ctrl** - **↑** to move up one paragraph.

Press **Ctrl** - **↓** to move down one paragraph.

INSERT OR TYPEOVER TEXT

INSERT OR TYPEOVER TEXT

You can easily insert (add) or typeover (replace) text without using correction fluid or having to retype a letter. You can also insert blank lines and split and join paragraphs with ease.

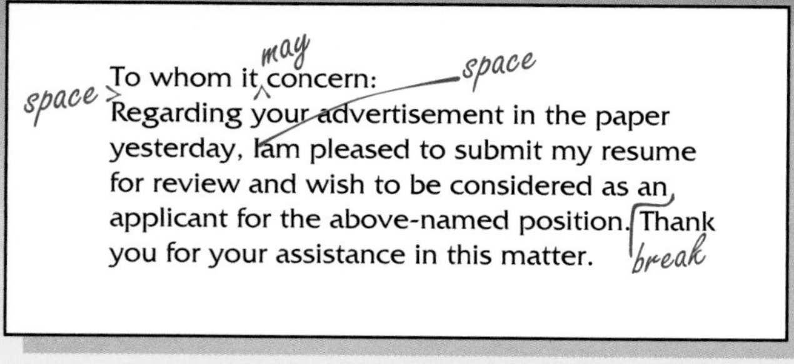

To whom it may concern:
space
space
Regarding your advertisement in the paper yesterday, I am pleased to submit my resume for review and wish to be considered as an applicant for the above-named position. Thank you for your assistance in this matter.
break

Insert a Blank Line

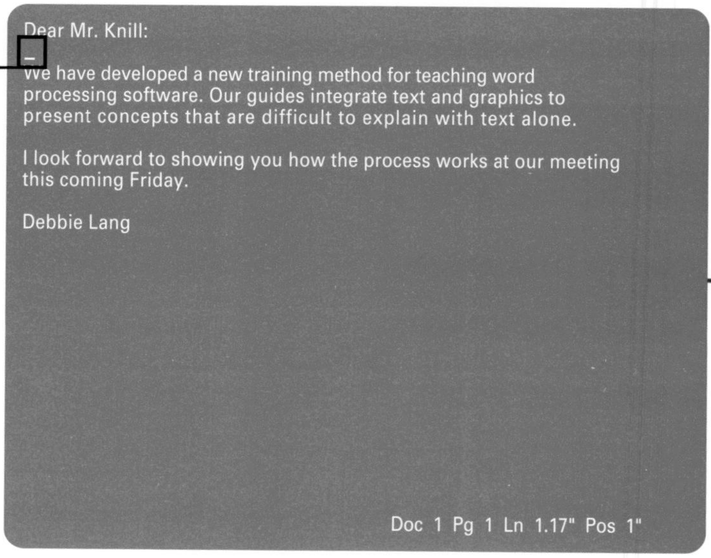

Dear Mr. Knill:
We have developed a new training method for teaching word processing software. Our guides integrate text and graphics to present concepts that are difficult to explain with text alone.
I look forward to showing you how the process works at our meeting this coming Friday.
Debbie Lang
Doc 1 Pg 1 Ln 1.17" Pos 1"

1 Position the cursor where you want to insert a blank line.

Split and Join Paragraphs

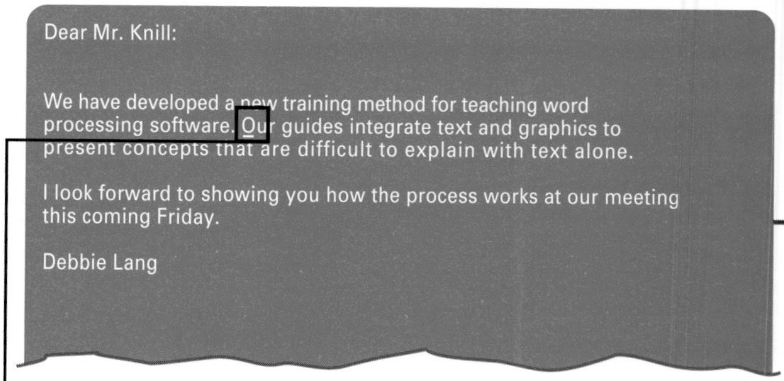

Split a Paragraph

1 Position the cursor where you want to split a paragraph in two.

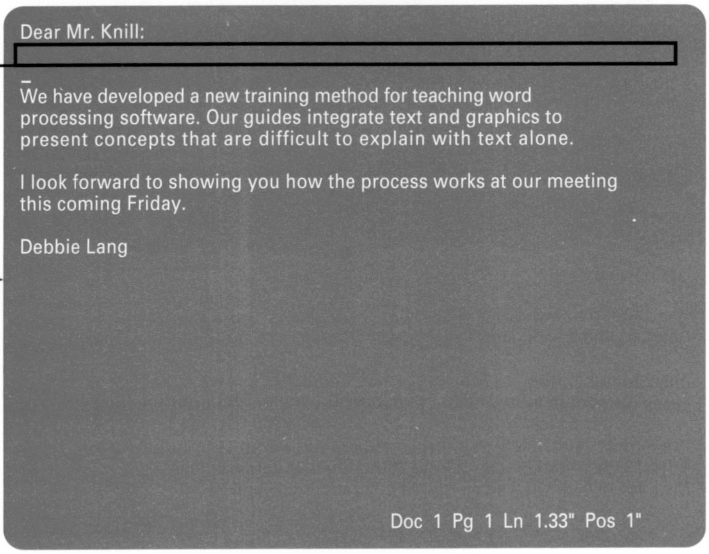

Dear Mr. Knill:
We have developed a new training method for teaching word processing software. Our guides integrate text and graphics to present concepts that are difficult to explain with text alone.
I look forward to showing you how the process works at our meeting this coming Friday.
Debbie Lang
Doc 1 Pg 1 Ln 1.33" Pos 1"

2 Press **Enter** to insert a blank line.

Note: The line the cursor is on, as well as all lines below, are shifted downward.

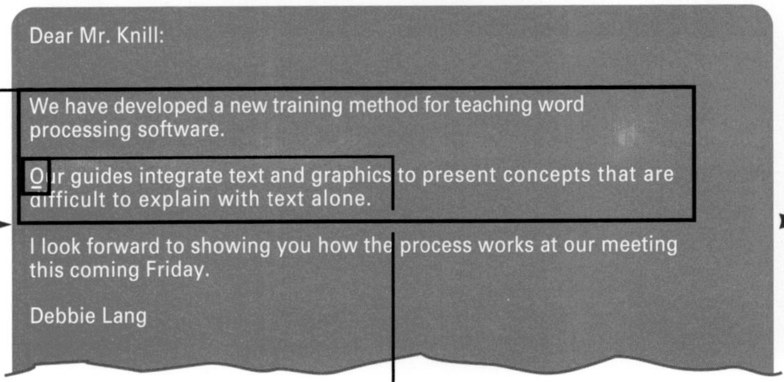

2 Press **Enter** and the paragraph is split in two.

3 To leave a blank line between the two paragraphs, press **Enter** again.

Join Two Paragraphs

1 Position the cursor at the beginning of the second paragraph.

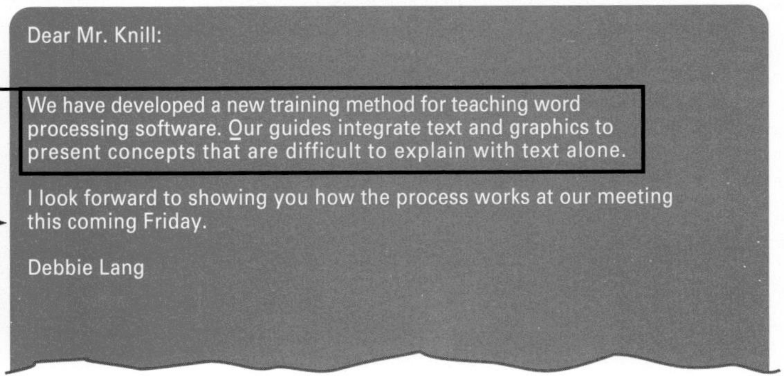

2 Press **←Backspace** until the paragraphs are joined.

INSERT OR TYPEOVER TEXT

Insert Text

When in the Insert mode, any text you type appears at the current cursor position. Any existing text is pushed to the right to make room for the new text.

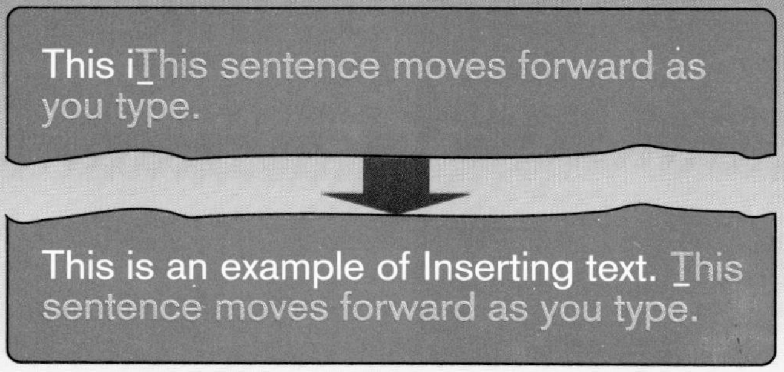
This iThis sentence moves forward as you type.
This is an example of Inserting text. This sentence moves forward as you type.

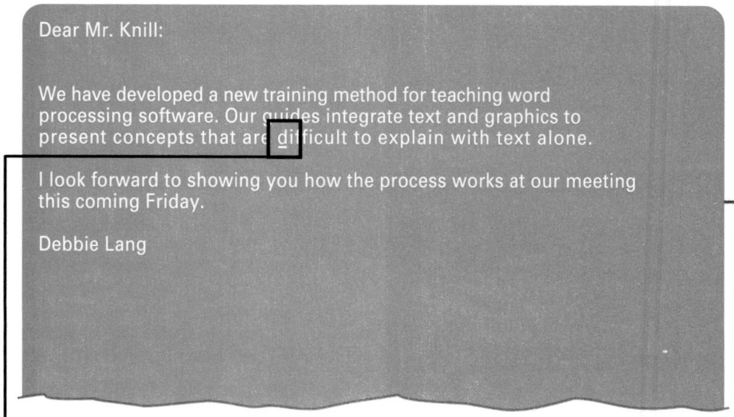
Dear Mr. Knill:
We have developed a new training method for teaching word processing software. Our guides integrate text and graphics to present concepts that are difficult to explain with text alone.
I look forward to showing you how the process works at our meeting this coming Friday.
Debbie Lang

1 Position the cursor where you want to insert new text.

*Note: If **Typeover** is displayed at the bottom left corner of the screen, press* Insert*. This turns off the Typeover mode.*

Typeover Text

When in the Typeover mode, any text you type appears at the current cursor position. The new text replaces (types over) any existing text.

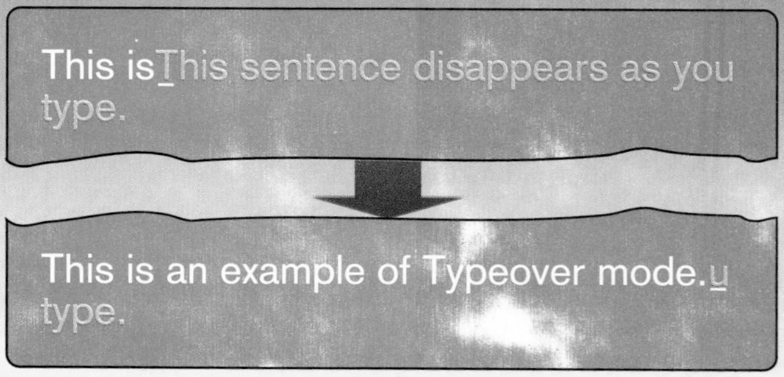
This isThis sentence disappears as you type.
This is an example of Typeover mode.u type.

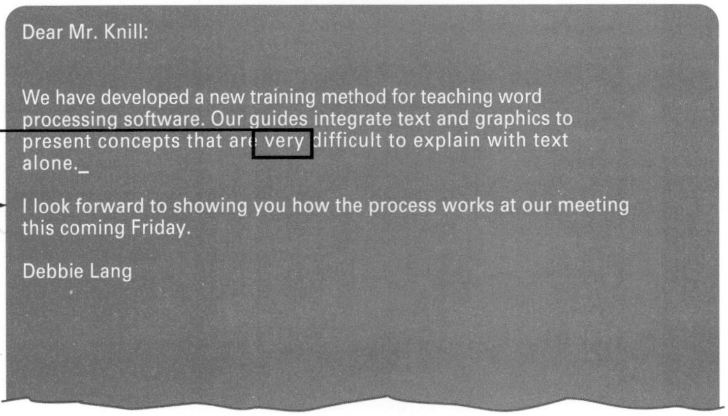

Dear Mr. Knill:
We have developed a new training method for teaching word processing software. Our guides integrate text and graphics to present concepts that are very difficult to explain with text alone.
I look forward to showing you how the process works at our meeting this coming Friday.
Debbie Lang

2 Type the text you want to insert (example: **very**).

3 To insert a blank space, press the **Spacebar**.

Note: The words to the right of the inserted text are pushed forward.

To refresh the screen display after a text change, press ↓.

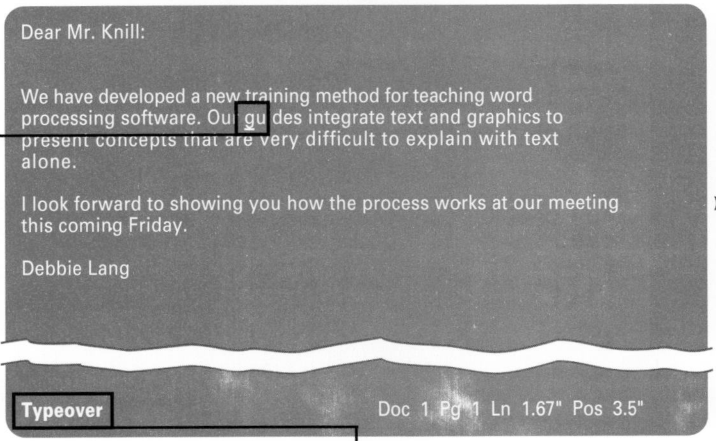

Dear Mr. Knill:
We have developed a new training method for teaching word processing software. Our guides integrate text and graphics to present concepts that are very difficult to explain with text alone.
I look forward to showing you how the process works at our meeting this coming Friday.
Debbie Lang
Typeover
Doc 1 Pg 1 Ln 1.67" Pos 3.5"

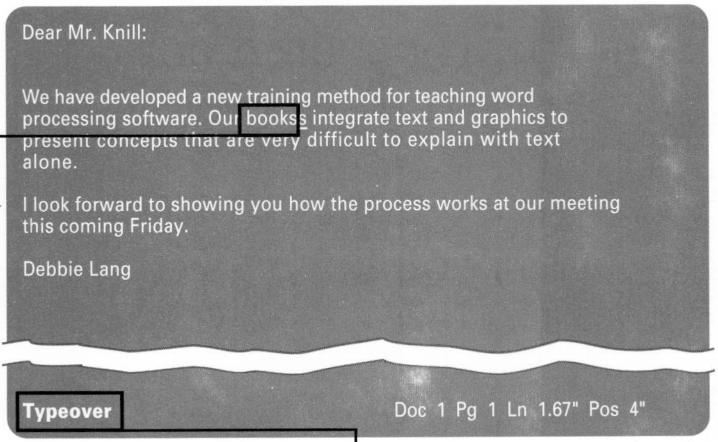

Dear Mr. Knill:
We have developed a new training method for teaching word processing software. Our bookss integrate text and graphics to present concepts that are very difficult to explain with text alone.
I look forward to showing you how the process works at our meeting this coming Friday.
Debbie Lang
Typeover
Doc 1 Pg 1 Ln 1.67" Pos 4"

1 Position the cursor where you want to replace existing text with new text.

2 Press Insert to turn on the Typeover mode. The word **Typeover** appears at the bottom left corner of the screen.

3 Type the text you want to replace existing text (example: **books**).

*Note: The method for deleting the extra "**s**" at the end of **bookss** will be shown on page 12.*

4 Press Insert to turn off the Typeover mode. The word **Typeover** disappears from the bottom of the screen.

DELETE TEXT

Delete Characters

When you press Delete, WordPerfect removes the character above the cursor.

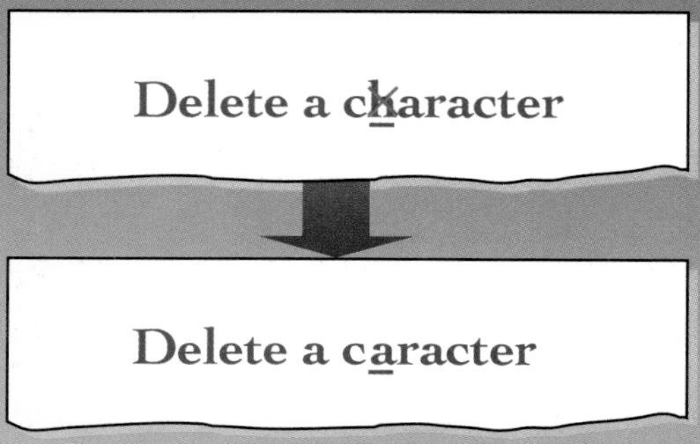

When you press ←Backspace, WordPerfect removes the character to the left of the cursor.

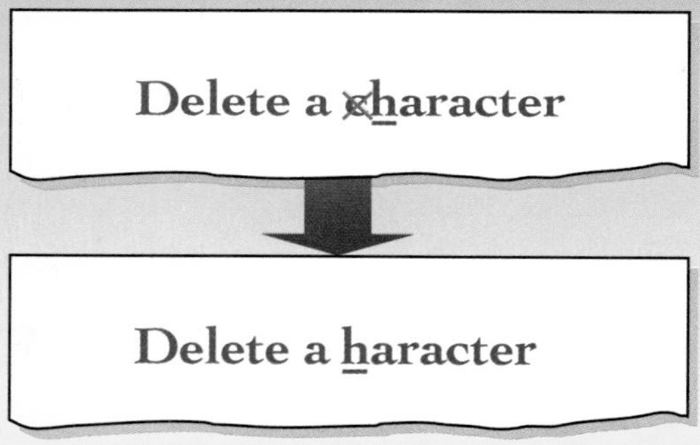

Delete a character
Delete a haracter

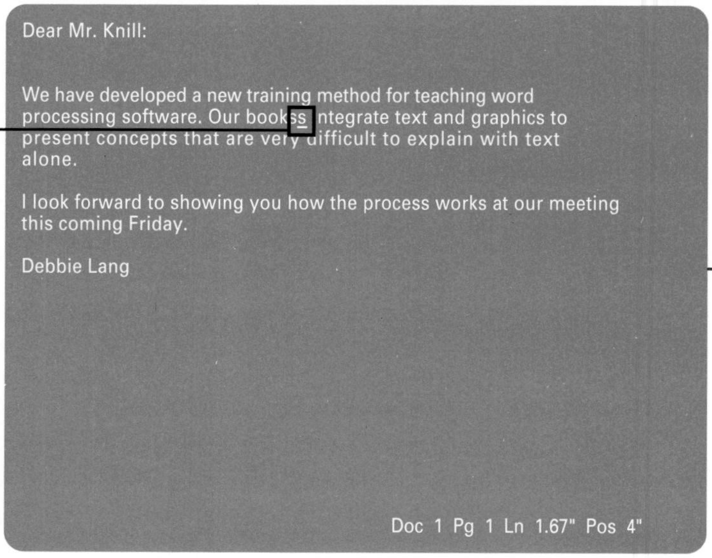

Dear Mr. Knill:
We have developed a new training method for teaching word processing software. Our bookss integrate text and graphics to present concepts that are very difficult to explain with text alone.
I look forward to showing you how the process works at our meeting this coming Friday.
Debbie Lang
Doc 1 Pg 1 Ln 1.67" Pos 4"

1 Position the cursor on the character you want to delete (example: **s** in **bookss**).

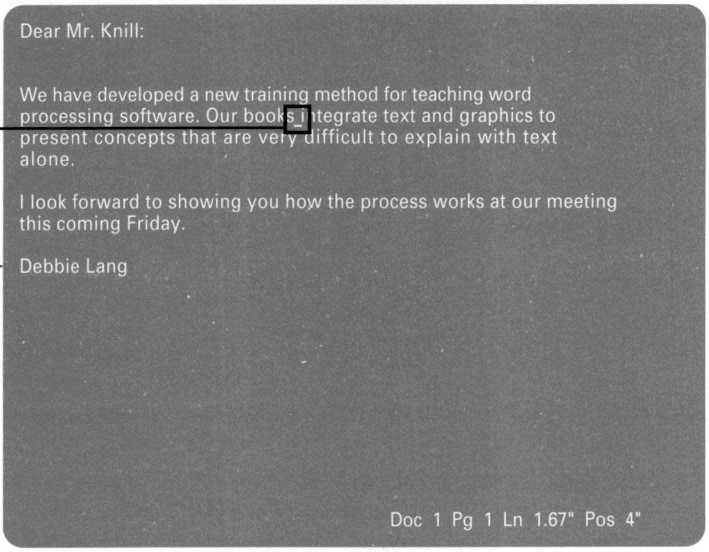
Dear Mr. Knill:
We have developed a new training method for teaching word processing software. Our books integrate text and graphics to present concepts that are very difficult to explain with text alone.
I look forward to showing you how the process works at our meeting this coming Friday.
Debbie Lang
Doc 1 Pg 1 Ln 1.67" Pos 4"

2 Press Delete to delete the character.

Note: You can also delete a character by positioning the cursor to the right of that character. Then press **←Backspace**.

Ctrl
←Backspace

Delete Words

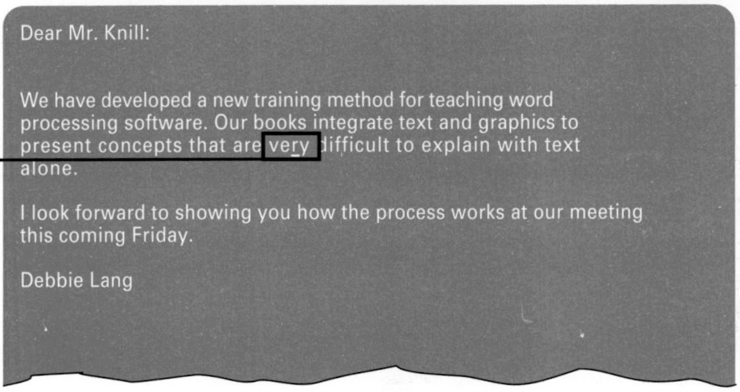
Dear Mr. Knill:
We have developed a new training method for teaching word processing software. Our books integrate text and graphics to present concepts that are very difficult to explain with text alone.
I look forward to showing you how the process works at our meeting this coming Friday.
Debbie Lang

1 Position the cursor under any letter of the word you want to delete (example: **very**).

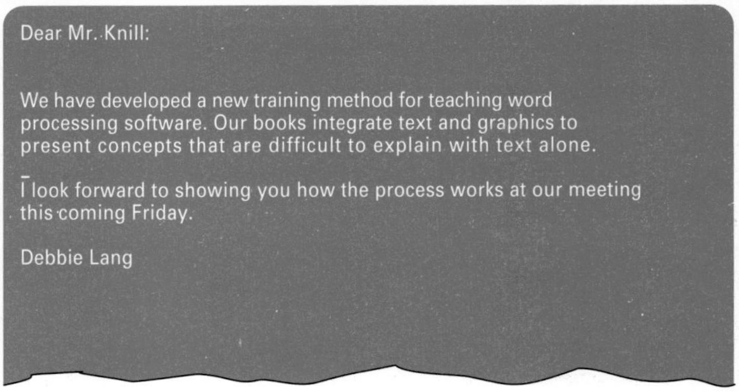
Dear Mr. Knill:
We have developed a new training method for teaching word processing software. Our books integrate text and graphics to present concepts that are difficult to explain with text alone.
I look forward to showing you how the process works at our meeting this coming Friday.
Debbie Lang

2 Press Ctrl - ←Backspace to delete the word.

To refresh the screen display after a text change, press ↓.

DELETE TEXT

Delete Delete Lines

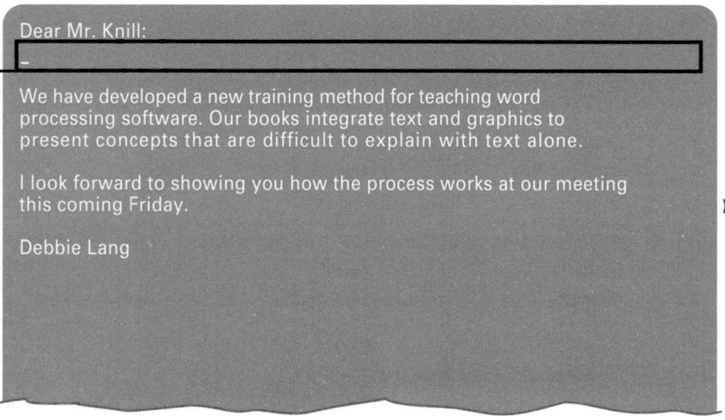

Dear Mr. Knill:
We have developed a new training method for teaching word processing software. Our books integrate text and graphics to present concepts that are difficult to explain with text alone.
I look forward to showing you how the process works at our meeting this coming Friday.
Debbie Lang

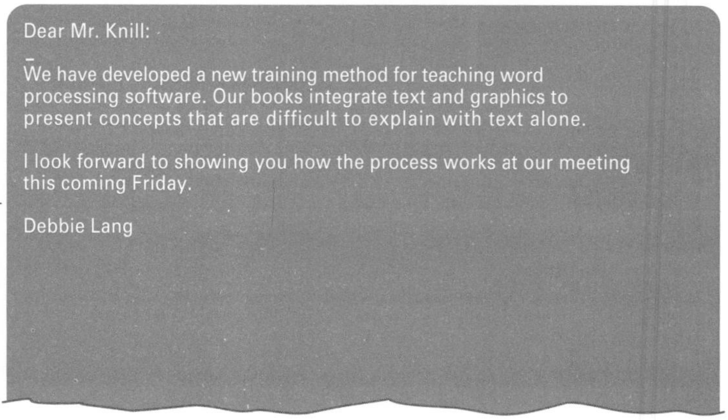

Dear Mr. Knill:
We have developed a new training method for teaching word processing software. Our books integrate text and graphics to present concepts that are difficult to explain with text alone.
I look forward to showing you how the process works at our meeting this coming Friday.
Debbie Lang

Delete a blank line

1 Position the cursor on the blank line you want to delete.

2 Press Delete to remove the blank line.

Ctrl Page Down Delete Remainder of Page

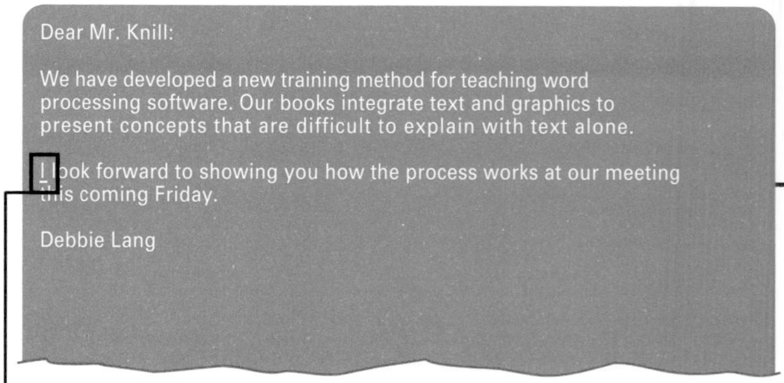

Dear Mr. Knill:
We have developed a new training method for teaching word processing software. Our books integrate text and graphics to present concepts that are difficult to explain with text alone.
I look forward to showing you how the process works at our meeting this coming Friday.
Debbie Lang

1 Position the cursor where you want the deletion to start.

Delete remainder of a line

1 Position the cursor where you want the deletion to start.

2 Press Ctrl - End to delete all text from the cursor to the end of the line.

TIP

WordPerfect remembers the last few changes you made to your document. If you accidentally erase text, you can reverse this using the "Undelete" feature. For more information, refer to page 16.

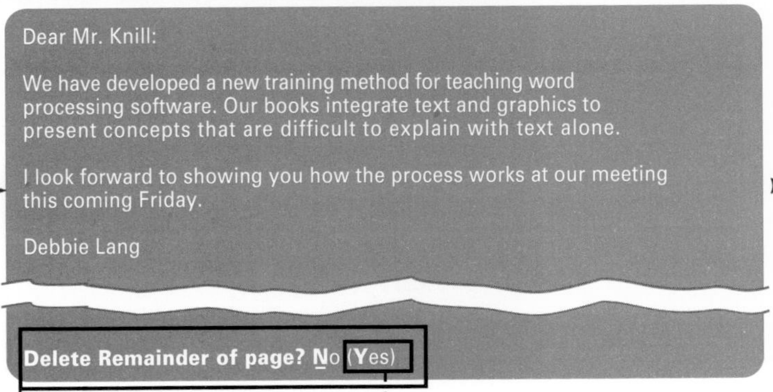
Dear Mr. Knill:
We have developed a new training method for teaching word processing software. Our books integrate text and graphics to present concepts that are difficult to explain with text alone.
I look forward to showing you how the process works at our meeting this coming Friday.
Debbie Lang
Delete Remainder of page? No (Yes)

2 Press Ctrl - Page Down and this message appears.

3 Press Y (for **Y**es) to delete all the text from the cursor to the bottom of the page.

*Note: Press N (for **N**o) to cancel the command.*

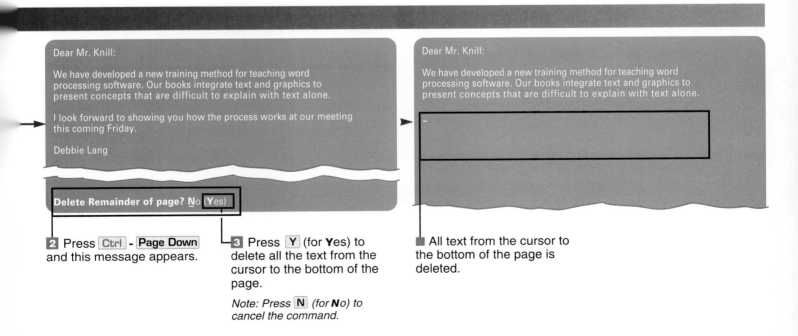

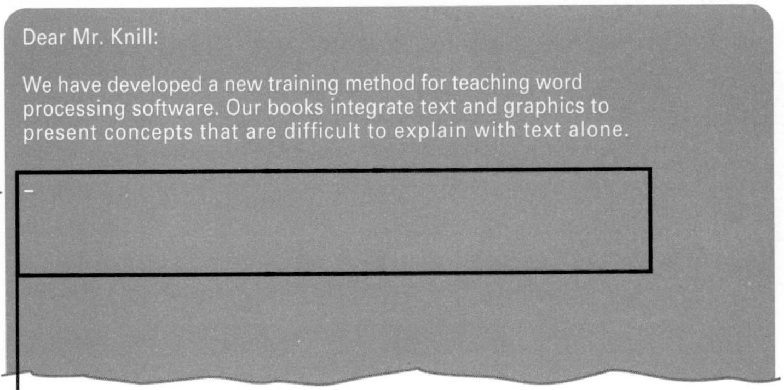
Dear Mr. Knill:
We have developed a new training method for teaching word processing software. Our books integrate text and graphics to present concepts that are difficult to explain with text alone.

■ All text from the cursor to the bottom of the page is deleted.

Ctrl F4 Delete a Sentence, Paragraph or Page

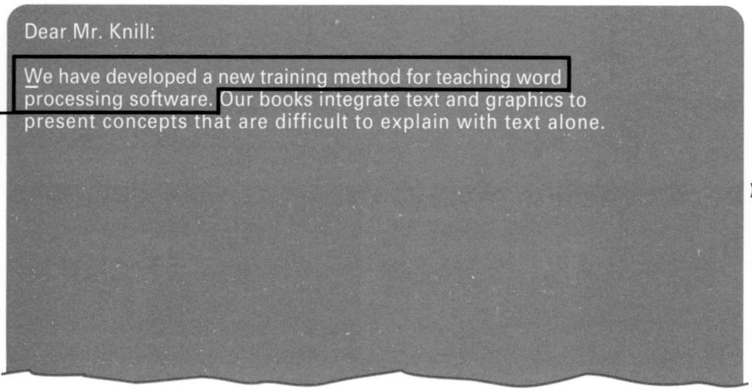
Dear Mr. Knill:
We have developed a new training method for teaching word processing software. Our books integrate text and graphics to present concepts that are difficult to explain with text alone.

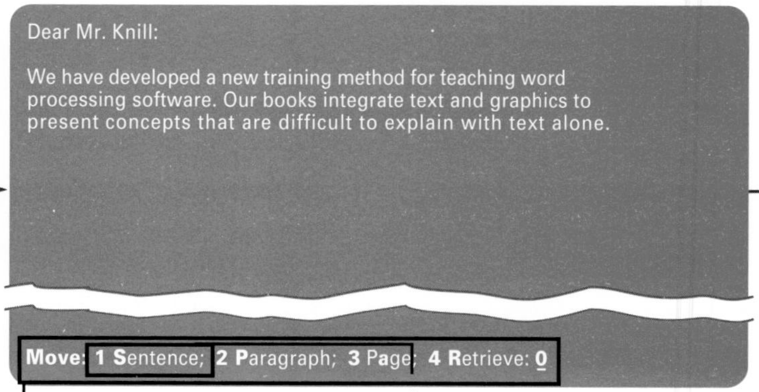
Dear Mr. Knill:
We have developed a new training method for teaching word processing software. Our books integrate text and graphics to present concepts that are difficult to explain with text alone.
Move: 1 Sentence; 2 Paragraph; 3 Page; 4 Retrieve: 0

1 Position the cursor anywhere in the sentence, paragraph or page you want to delete.

2 Press Ctrl - F4 and this message appears.

3 To delete a sentence, press S.

Note: To delete a paragraph, press P. To delete a page, press A.

F1 Undelete Text

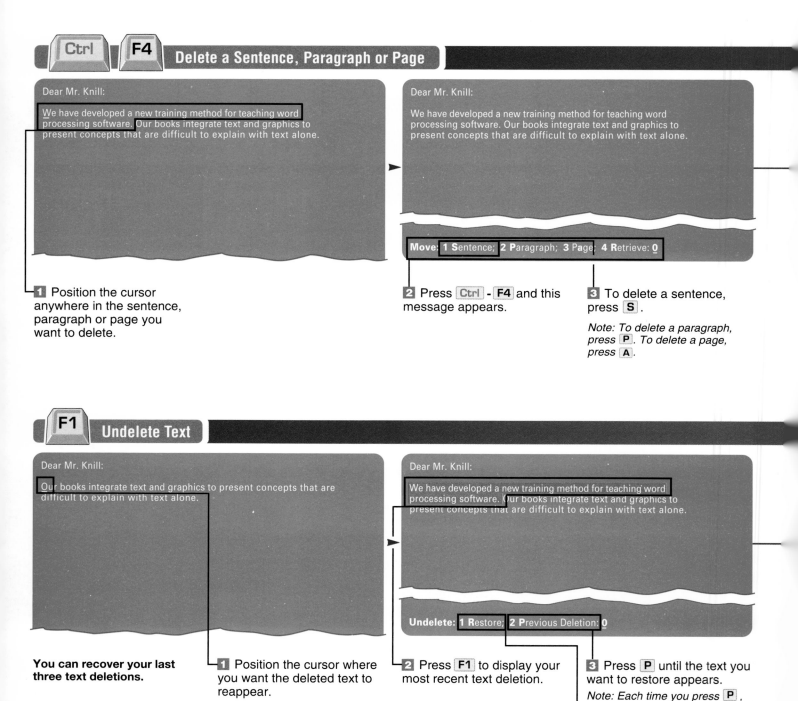

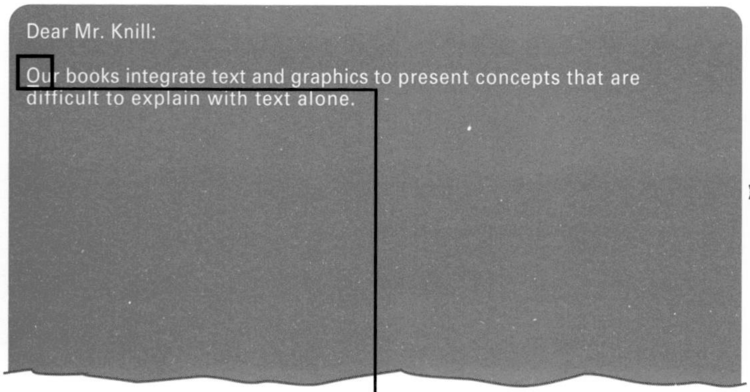
Dear Mr. Knill:
Our books integrate text and graphics to present concepts that are difficult to explain with text alone.

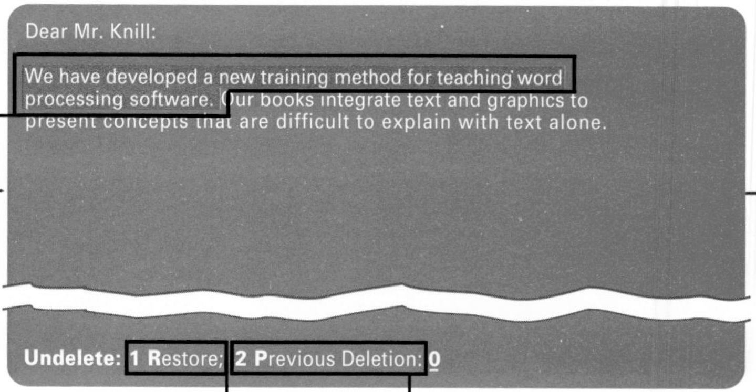
Dear Mr. Knill:
We have developed a new training method for teaching word processing software. Our books integrate text and graphics to present concepts that are difficult to explain with text alone.
Undelete: 1 Restore; 2 Previous Deletion: 0

You can recover your last three text deletions.

1 Position the cursor where you want the deleted text to reappear.

2 Press F1 to display your most recent text deletion.

3 Press P until the text you want to restore appears.

Note: Each time you press P, the screen will display one of your three most recent text deletions.

4 Press R to restore that text.

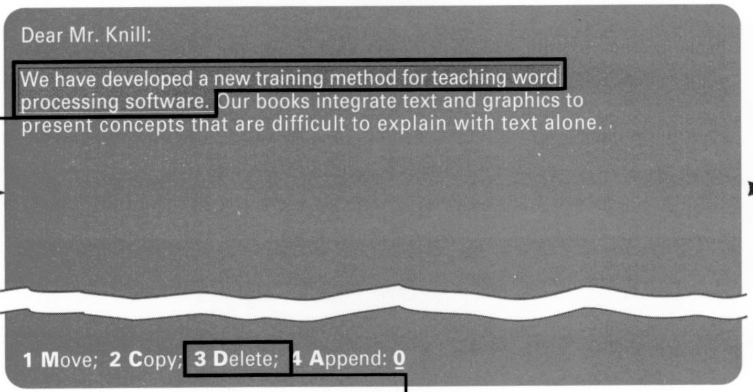
Dear Mr. Knill:
We have developed a new training method for teaching word processing software. Our books integrate text and graphics to present concepts that are difficult to explain with text alone.
1 Move; 2 Copy; 3 Delete; 4 Append: 0

■ WordPerfect highlights the text you want to delete.

4 Press D to delete the selected text.

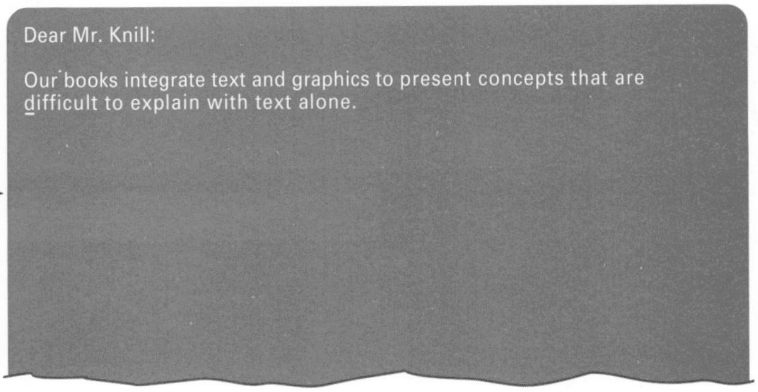
Dear Mr. Knill:
Our books integrate text and graphics to present concepts that are difficult to explain with text alone.

■ The text is deleted.

> To refresh the screen display after a text change, press ↓.

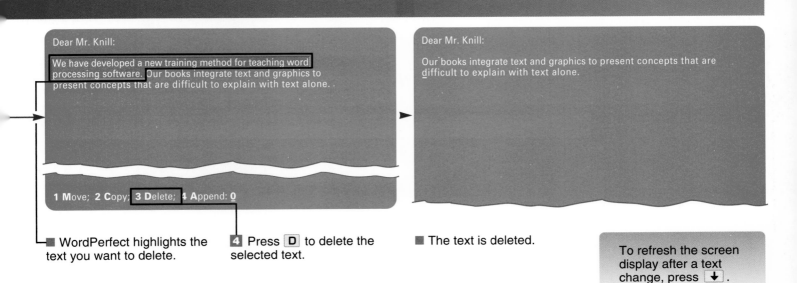

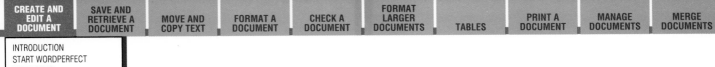

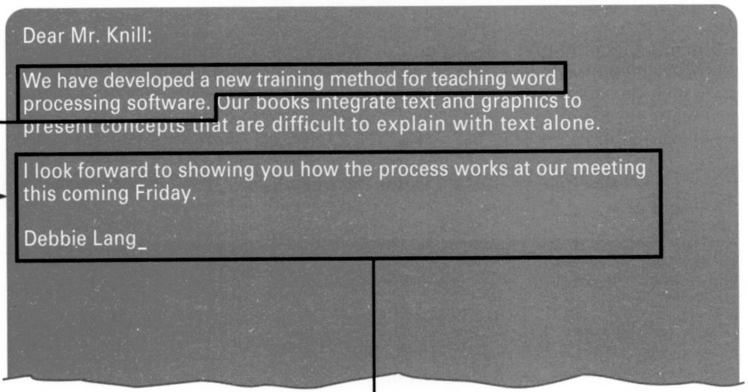
Dear Mr. Knill:
We have developed a new training method for teaching word processing software. Our books integrate text and graphics to present concepts that are difficult to explain with text alone.
I look forward to showing you how the process works at our meeting this coming Friday.
Debbie Lang_

■ The text is restored.

5 To restore another previous text deletion, repeat steps **1** to **4**.

REVEAL CODES

Alt F3 Display the WordPerfect Codes

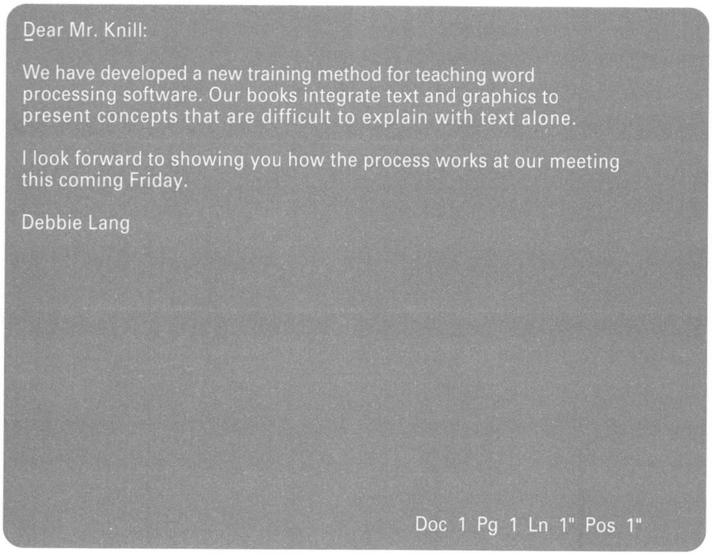
Dear Mr. Knill:
We have developed a new training method for teaching word processing software. Our books integrate text and graphics to present concepts that are difficult to explain with text alone.
I look forward to showing you how the process works at our meeting this coming Friday.
Debbie Lang
Doc 1 Pg 1 Ln 1" Pos 1"

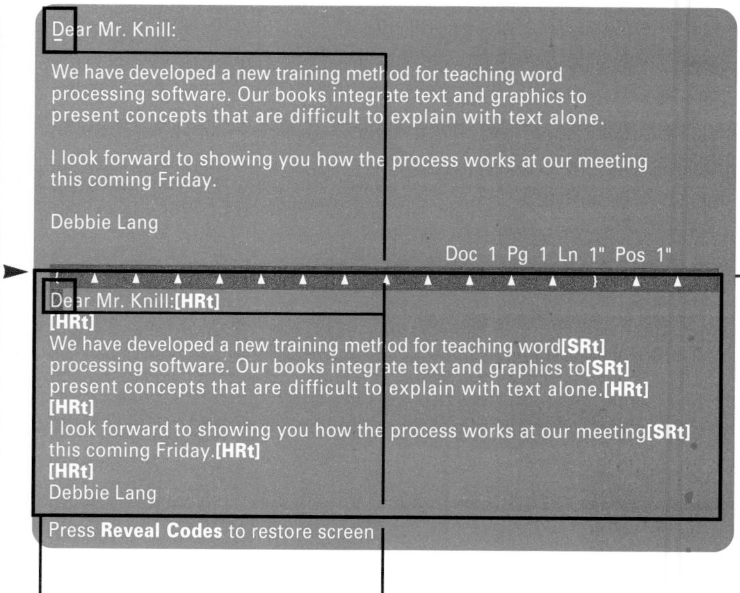
Dear Mr. Knill:
We have developed a new training method for teaching word processing software. Our books integrate text and graphics to present concepts that are difficult to explain with text alone.
I look forward to showing you how the process works at our meeting this coming Friday.
Debbie Lang
Doc 1 Pg 1 Ln 1" Pos 1"
Dear Mr. Knill:[HRt]
[HRt]
We have developed a new training method for teaching word[SRt]
processing software. Our books integrate text and graphics to[SRt]
present concepts that are difficult to explain with text alone.[HRt]
[HRt]
I look forward to showing you how the process works at our meeting[SRt]
this coming Friday.[HRt]
[HRt]
Debbie Lang
Press Reveal Codes to restore screen

WordPerfect records all your commands by inserting invisible codes into the document. By displaying these codes, you can visually see how the program is actually working. This can help solve formatting problems.

1 To display the WordPerfect codes, press F11 or Alt - F3.

■ The screen is split in half. In the bottom screen, a copy of the document appears, displaying the same text plus the WordPerfect codes.

2 Press the arrow keys (example: →, ↓, ↑ or ←) to move the cursor.

■ When you move the cursor in the top screen, the cursor in the bottom screen also moves.

Note: In the bottom screen, the cursor appears as a red block.

Insert or Delete a Code

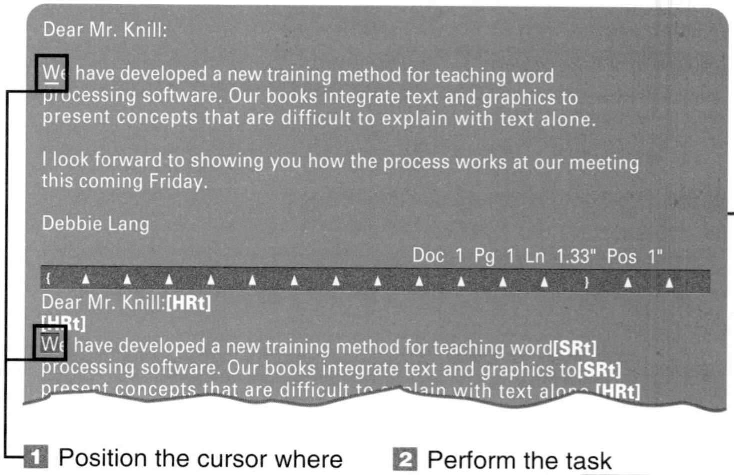
Dear Mr. Knill:
We have developed a new training method for teaching word processing software. Our books integrate text and graphics to present concepts that are difficult to explain with text alone.
I look forward to showing you how the process works at our meeting this coming Friday.
Debbie Lang
Doc 1 Pg 1 Ln 1.33" Pos 1"
Dear Mr. Knill:[HRt]
We have developed a new training method for teaching word[SRt]
processing software. Our books integrate text and graphics to[SRt]

1 Position the cursor where you want to insert a code.

2 Perform the task (example: press Enter to insert a hard return).

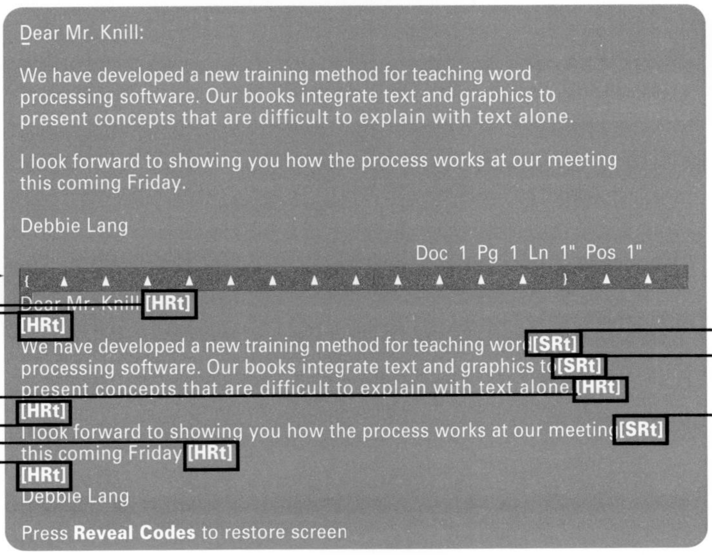
Dear Mr. Knill:
We have developed a new training method for teaching word processing software. Our books integrate text and graphics to present concepts that are difficult to explain with text alone.
I look forward to showing you how the process works at our meeting this coming Friday.
Debbie Lang
Doc 1 Pg 1 Ln 1" Pos 1"
Dear Mr. Knill:[HRt]
[HRt]
We have developed a new training method for teaching word[SRt]
processing software. Our books integrate text and graphics to[SRt]
present concepts that are difficult to explain with text alone.[HRt]
[HRt]
I look forward to showing you how the process works at our meeting[SRt]
this coming Friday.[HRt]
[HRt]
Debbie Lang
Press **Reveal Codes** to restore screen

HIDE THE WORDPERFECT CODES

Press F11 or Alt - F3.

■ **[HRt]** is the code for a hard return. This code appears whenever the Enter key is pressed.

■ **[SRt]** is the code for a soft return. This code appears when text automatically wraps to the next line.

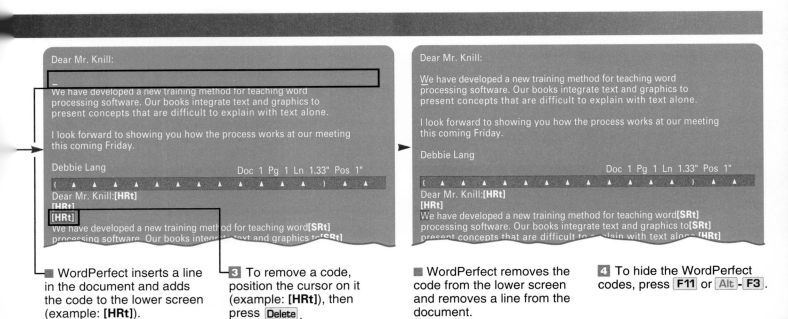

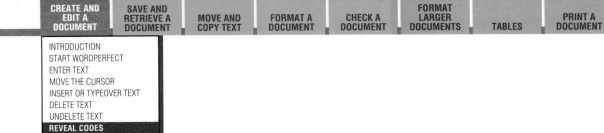

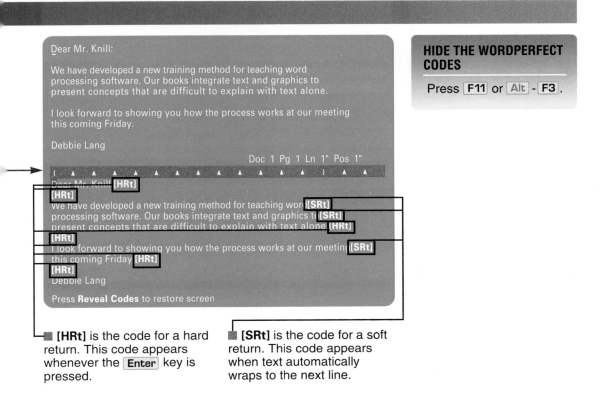

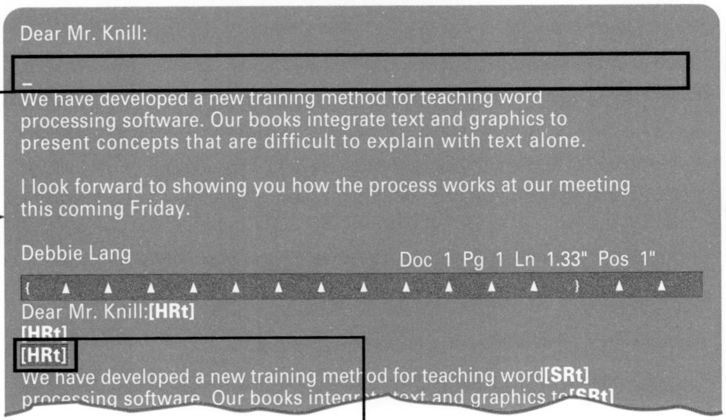
Dear Mr. Knill:
We have developed a new training method for teaching word processing software. Our books integrate text and graphics to present concepts that are difficult to explain with text alone.
I look forward to showing you how the process works at our meeting this coming Friday.
Debbie Lang
Doc 1 Pg 1 Ln 1.33" Pos 1"
Dear Mr. Knill:[HRt]
[HRt]
We have developed a new training method for teaching word[SRt]

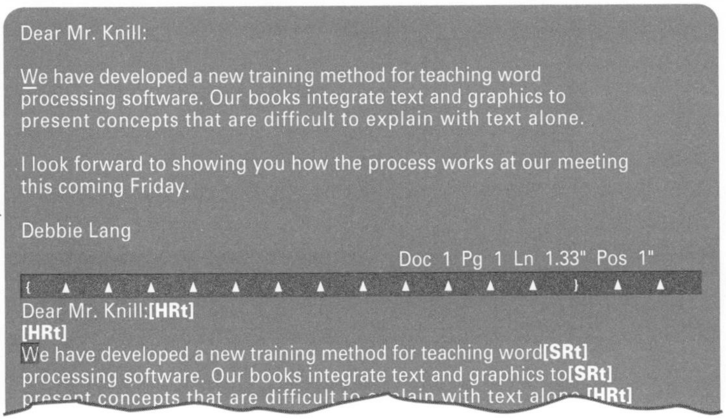
Dear Mr. Knill:
We have developed a new training method for teaching word processing software. Our books integrate text and graphics to present concepts that are difficult to explain with text alone.
I look forward to showing you how the process works at our meeting this coming Friday.
Debbie Lang
Doc 1 Pg 1 Ln 1.33" Pos 1"
Dear Mr. Knill:[HRt]
[HRt]
We have developed a new training method for teaching word[SRt]
processing software. Our books integrate text and graphics to[SRt]

■ WordPerfect inserts a line in the document and adds the code to the lower screen (example: **[HRt]**).

3 To remove a code, position the cursor on it (example: **[HRt]**), then press Delete.

■ WordPerfect removes the code from the lower screen and removes a line from the document.

4 To hide the WordPerfect codes, press F11 or Alt - F3.

SELECT COMMANDS

Alt = Using the Menus

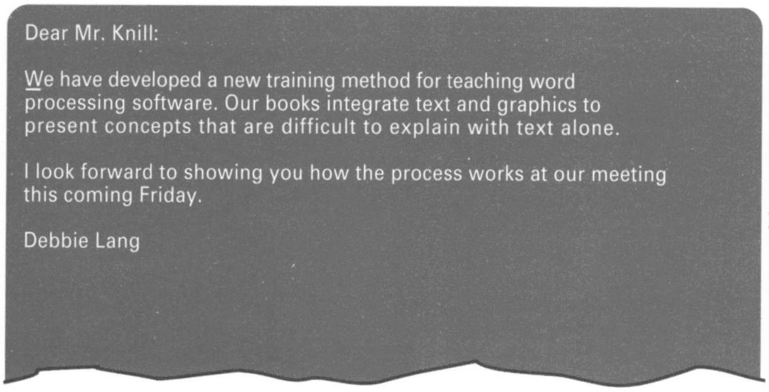
Dear Mr. Knill:
We have developed a new training method for teaching word processing software. Our books integrate text and graphics to present concepts that are difficult to explain with text alone.
I look forward to showing you how the process works at our meeting this coming Friday.
Debbie Lang

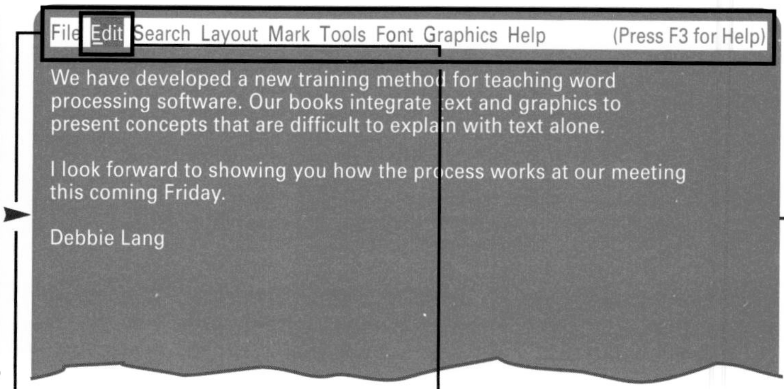
File Edit Search Layout Mark Tools Font Graphics Help (Press F3 for Help)
We have developed a new training method for teaching word processing software. Our books integrate text and graphics to present concepts that are difficult to explain with text alone.
I look forward to showing you how the process works at our meeting this coming Friday.
Debbie Lang

You can compare the WordPerfect menu with a menu used in a restaurant. Both present a list of options.

The WordPerfect menu helps you quickly find a command without having to remember which function keys to press.

1 While holding down Alt, press = to display the main menu.

■ The main menu appears.

Note: When the menu appears, it hides your first line of text. Don't worry. When you later remove this menu, the text will reappear.

2 Press → until you highlight the desired menu heading (example: **Edit**). Then press Enter.

or

Press the highlighted letter in the desired menu heading (example: E for **E**dit).

Using the Function Keys

This is an illustration of the WordPerfect template, which you can place above the function keys on your keyboard.

Although the template is not an essential tool for using WordPerfect, it can help you remember which tasks each key is responsible for.

Shell	Spell	Screen	Move	Text In/Out	Tab Align	Footnote	Font
Thesaurus	Replace	Reveal Codes	Block	Mark Text	Flush Right	Math/Columns	Style
Setup	← Search	Switch	→ Indent ←	Date/Outline	Center	Print	Format
Cancel	→ Search	Help	→ Indent	List Files	Bold	Exit	Underline
F1	F2	F3	F4	F5	F6	F7	F8

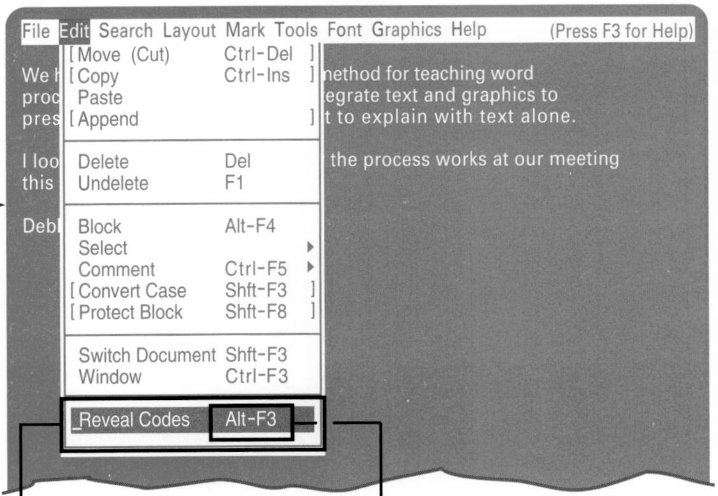

3 Press ↓ until you highlight the desired command (example: **Reveal Codes**). Then press Enter.

or

Press the highlighted letter in the command (example: R for **R**eveal Codes).

■ Some commands display the function key equivalent to select the same command (example: Alt - F3).

■ To return to the document screen without selecting a command, press F7.

Note: To hide the WordPerfect codes, press Alt - F3.

The ▷ marker beside a command indicates that a sub-menu is available for that command.

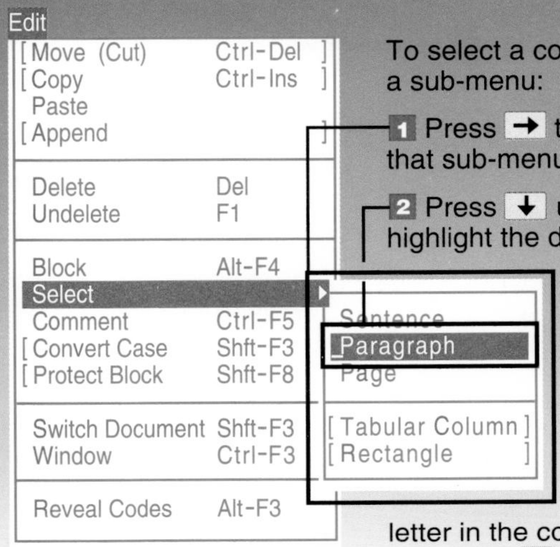

To select a command from a sub-menu:

1 Press → to move to that sub-menu.

2 Press ↓ until you highlight the desired command (example: **Paragraph**). Then press Enter.

or

Press the highlighted letter in the command (example: P for **P**aragraph).

Merge/Sort	Macro Define		
Graphics	Macro		
Merge Codes	Retrieve		
Merge R	Save	Reveal Codes	Block

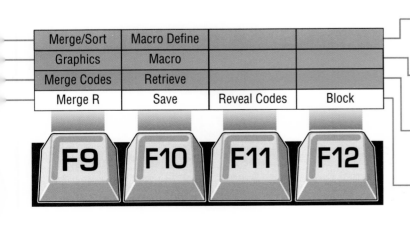

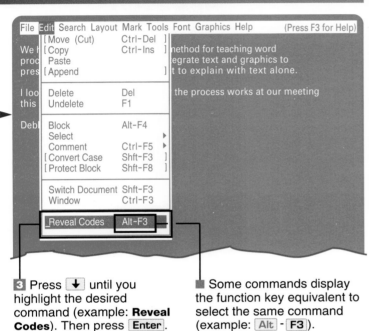

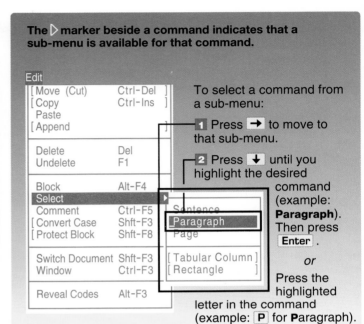

■ **To perform these tasks:**
While holding down Ctrl, press the function key (example: Ctrl - F3).

■ **To perform these tasks:**
While holding down Alt, press the function key (example: Alt - F3).

■ **To perform these tasks:**
While holding down Shift, press the function key (example: Shift - F3).

■ **To perform these tasks:**
Press the function key (example: F3).

HELP

F3 The Help Index

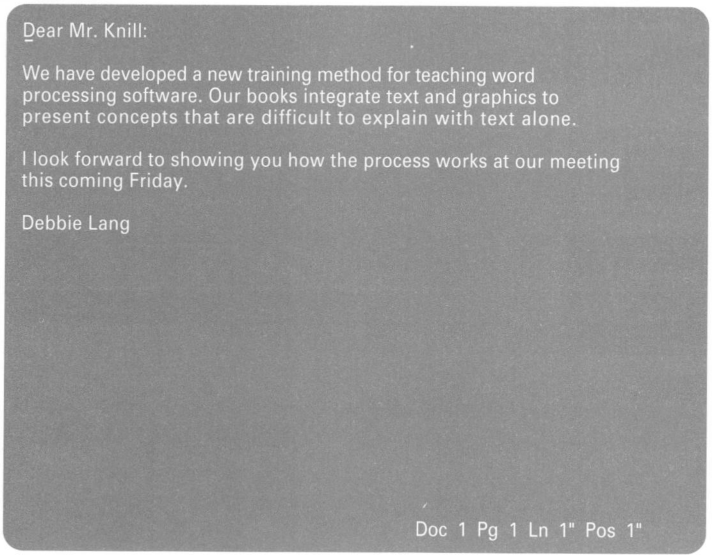
Dear Mr. Knill:

We have developed a new training method for teaching word processing software. Our books integrate text and graphics to present concepts that are difficult to explain with text alone.

I look forward to showing you how the process works at our meeting this coming Friday.

Debbie Lang

Doc 1 Pg 1 Ln 1" Pos 1"

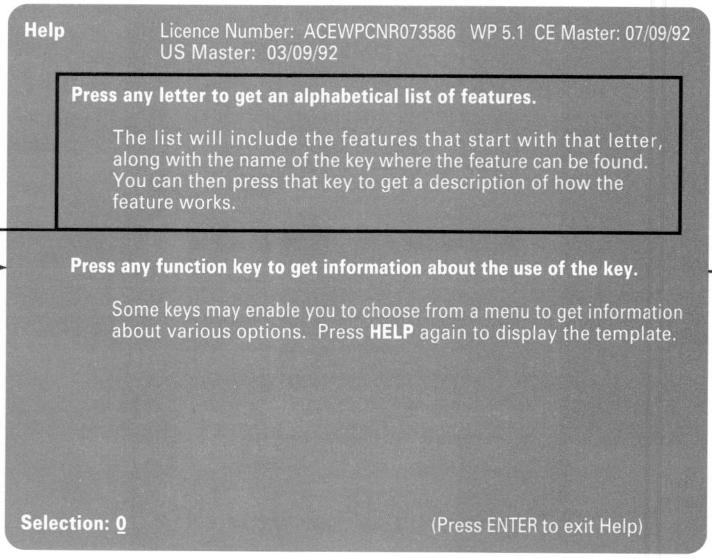
Help Licence Number: ACEWPCNR073586 WP 5.1 CE Master: 07/09/92 US Master: 03/09/92

Press any letter to get an alphabetical list of features.

The list will include the features that start with that letter, along with the name of the key where the feature can be found. You can then press that key to get a description of how the feature works.

Press any function key to get information about the use of the key.

Some keys may enable you to choose from a menu to get information about various options. Press **HELP** again to display the template.

Selection: 0 (Press ENTER to exit Help)

The WordPerfect Help index offers an alphabetical list of topics that you can receive help on.

1 Press F3 to access the **Help** screen.

2 To get help on a particular feature, press the first letter of that feature (example: B), and an alphabetical list of all features starting with that letter appears.

Note: To receive help on a function key, refer to page 24.

The Help feature provides a complete reference for using WordPerfect. This is extremely useful if you cannot remember exactly how to perform a task.

Features [B]	WordPerfect Key	Keystrokes
Backspace (Erase)	Backspace	Backspace
Backup Directory Location	Setup	Shft-F1,6
Backup Files, Automatic	Setup	Shft-F1,3,1,1
Backup Options	Setup	Shft-F1,3,1
Backward Search	<-Search	Shft-F2
Banners	Print	Shft-F7,a
Base Font	Font	Ctrl-F8,4
Base Font (Document)	Format	Shft-F8,3,3
Base Font (Printer)	Print	Shft-F7,s,3,5
Baseline Placement for Typesetters	Format	Shft-F8,4,6,5
Beep Options	Setup	Shft-F1,3,2
Binding Offset	Print	Shft-F7,b
Binding Offset (Default)	Setup	Shft-F1,4,8,1
Black and White, View Document In	Setup	Shft-F1,2,5,1
Block	Block	Alt-F4
Block, (Assign Variable w/Block On)	Macro Commands	Ctrl-PgUp
Block, Append (Block On)	Move	Ctrl-F4,1,4
Block, Center (Block On)	Center	Shft-F6
Block, Comment (Block On)	Text In/Out	Ctrl-F5
Block Copy (Block On)	Block Copy	Ctrl-Ins
More... Press B to continue.		
Selection: 0	(Press ENTER to exit Help)	

■ The Help index displays all features starting with that letter (example: **B**).

■ To view more topics starting with the same letter, press the letter again (example: **B**).

*Note: To view Help topics that start with another letter, press that letter (example: **L**).*

3 To exit Help, press **Enter**.

TIP

If you need help while performing a task, press **F3** to receive context sensitive help.

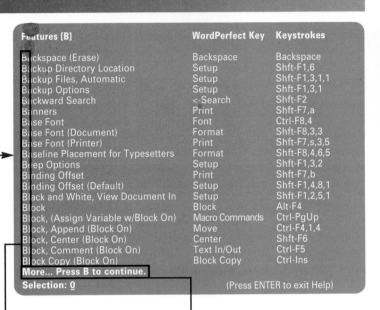

F3 Function Key Help

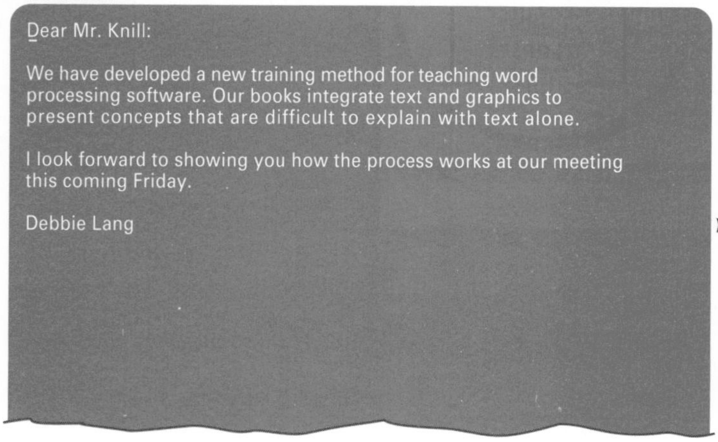
Dear Mr. Knill:

We have developed a new training method for teaching word processing software. Our books integrate text and graphics to present concepts that are difficult to explain with text alone.

I look forward to showing you how the process works at our meeting this coming Friday.

Debbie Lang

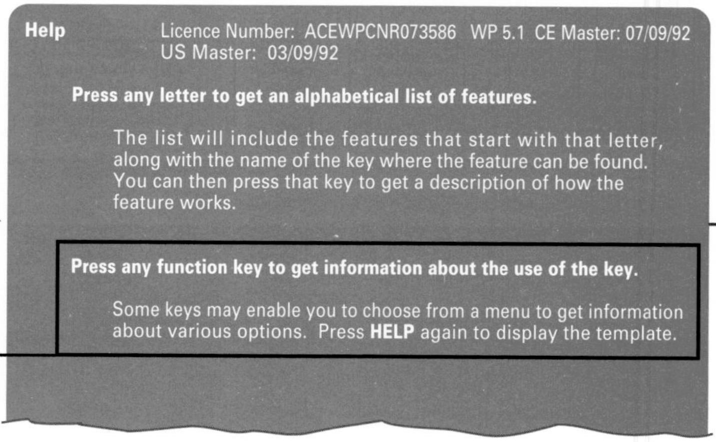
Help Licence Number: ACEWPCNR073586 WP 5.1 CE Master: 07/09/92 US Master: 03/09/92

Press any letter to get an alphabetical list of features.

The list will include the features that start with that letter, along with the name of the key where the feature can be found. You can then press that key to get a description of how the feature works.

Press any function key to get information about the use of the key.

Some keys may enable you to choose from a menu to get information about various options. Press **HELP** again to display the template.

WordPerfect offers information on all the function keys.

1 Press F3 to access the **Help** screen.

2 To receive information on a function key, press that key (example: F1).

Note: You can also receive information on key combinations (example: Alt - F3).

F3 Display the WordPerfect Template

At any time while using Help you can display the WordPerfect template. This template tells you what each function key is responsible for.

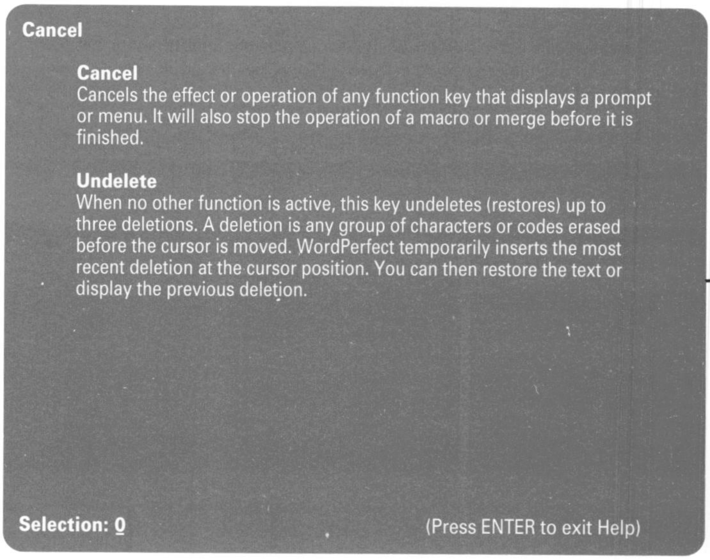
Cancel

Cancel
Cancels the effect or operation of any function key that displays a prompt or menu. It will also stop the operation of a macro or merge before it is finished.

Undelete
When no other function is active, this key undeletes (restores) up to three deletions. A deletion is any group of characters or codes erased before the cursor is moved. WordPerfect temporarily inserts the most recent deletion at the cursor position. You can then restore the text or display the previous deletion.

Selection: 0 (Press ENTER to exit Help)

1 Press F3 to display the WordPerfect template.

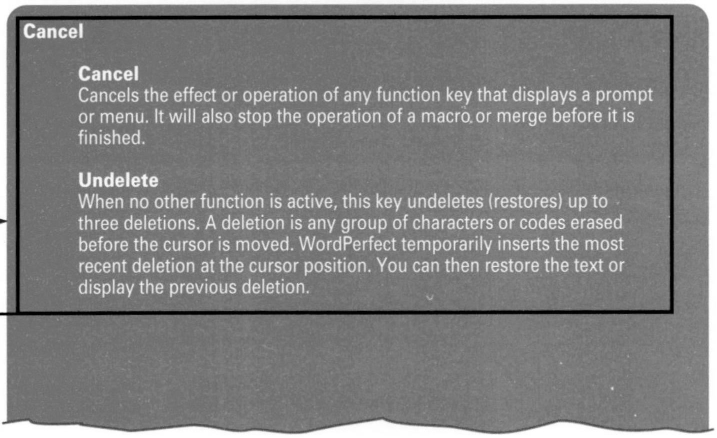

■ Help information for that function key appears.

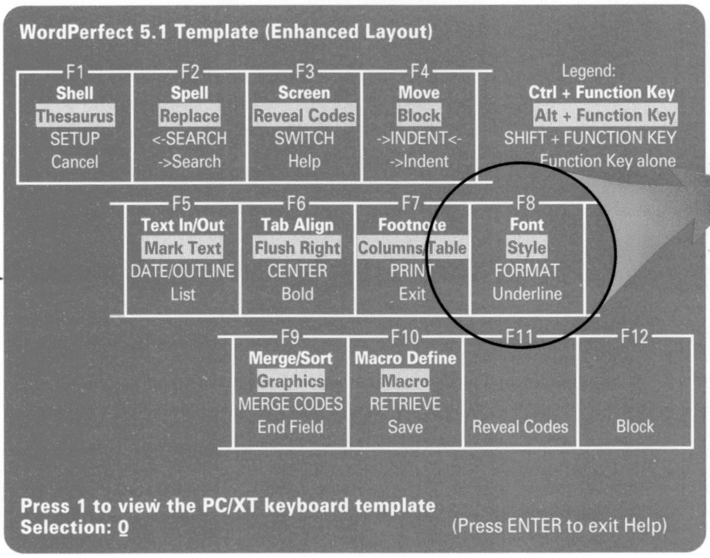

■ The WordPerfect template appears.

2 To exit Help, press Enter .

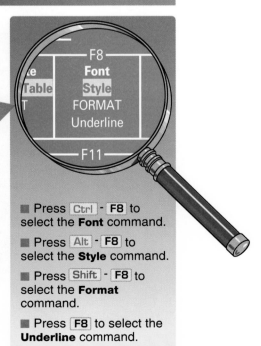

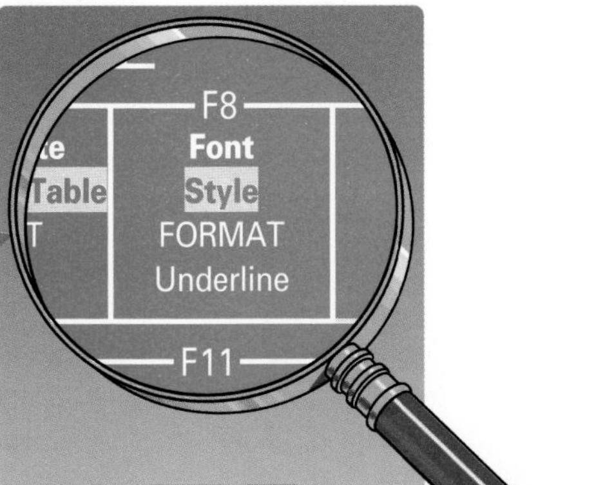

■ Press Ctrl - F8 to select the **Font** command.

■ Press Alt - F8 to select the **Style** command.

■ Press Shift - F8 to select the **Format** command.

■ Press F8 to select the **Underline** command.

FILES AND DIRECTORIES

HOW FILES ARE SPECIFIED

In an office environment, people create, edit, review and organize paper documents (example: letters, spreadsheets, reports, etc.). These documents are stored in folders, which in turn are placed in cabinets. To retrieve a specific document, you must identify it by location (cabinet and folder) and then by name.

Computers work the same way. After creating a document, you must name and save it. During this process, you must tell WordPerfect the drive (cabinet) and directory (folder) where you want to save the file.

WordPerfect uses a multilevel filing system to store and retrieve your files. The first level is called the root directory. From this directory, other subdirectories may be created. A typical multilevel filing system is illustrated on the next page.

Note: The terms "directory" and "subdirectory" are interchangeable. The "root directory" is the only directory that cannot be called a "subdirectory".

File Specification

A file is specified by describing its drive, path and name (filename and extension).

C: \WP51\MYWORK\ SALES .LET

DRIVE

Tells WordPerfect which drive the file is in.

PATH

Tells WordPerfect the path through the directory structure to get to the file location.

FILENAME

The filename can contain up to 8 characters.

EXTENSION

The extension can contain up to 3 characters. In some cases, it is omitted.

Note: The first backslash (\) specifies the path to the root directory. Subsequent backslashes (\) are used to separate directories and the filename.

The following characters are allowed:

- The letters A to Z, upper or lower case
- The numbers 0 through 9
- The symbols ! @ # $ % ^ & - ( ) _
- The filename cannot contain a . (period) or blank space

Using Directories to Organize Your Files

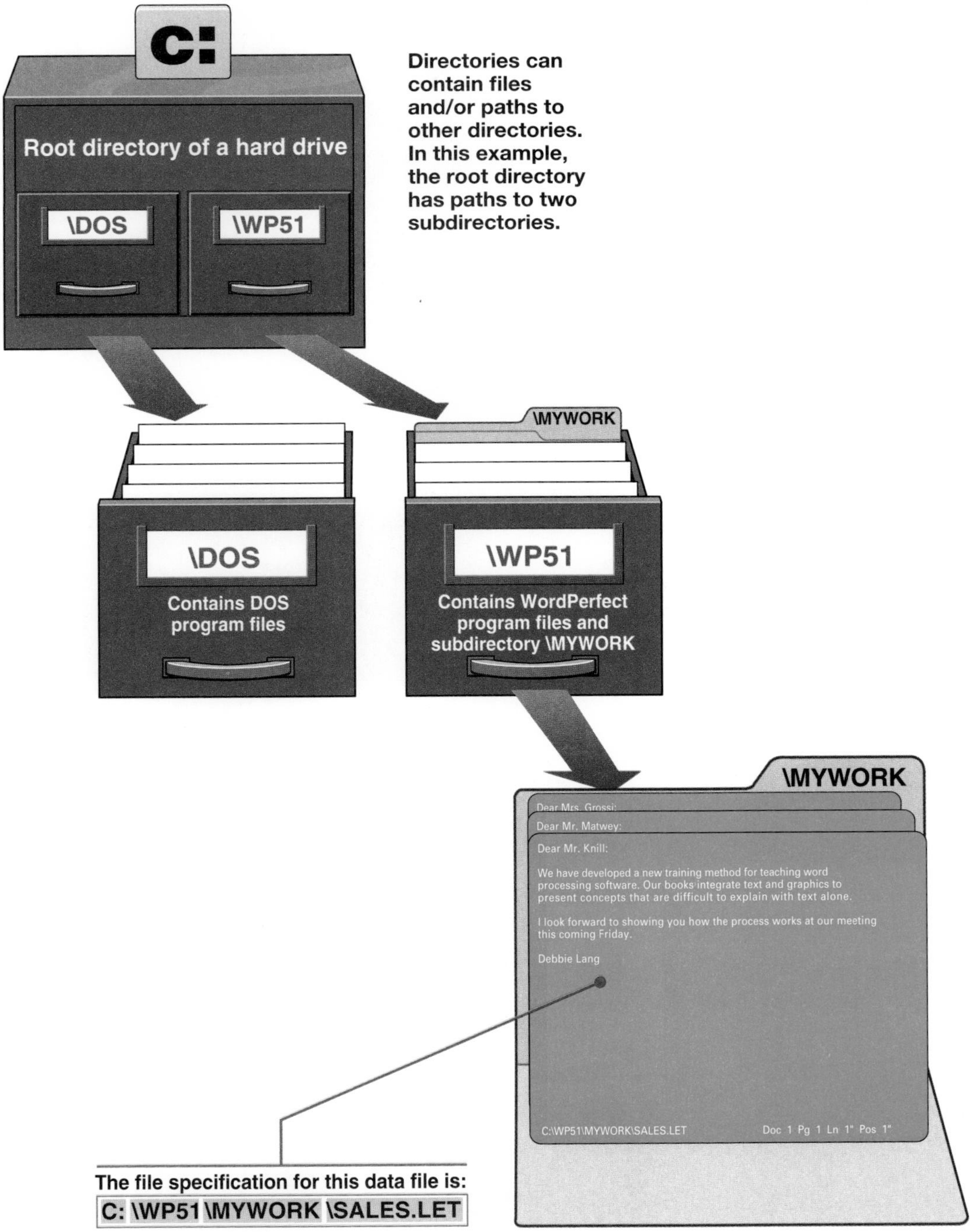
C:
Root directory of a hard drive
\DOS
\WP51
\MYWORK
\DOS
Contains DOS program files
\WP51
Contains WordPerfect program files and subdirectory \MYWORK
\MYWORK
Dear Mrs. Grossi:
Dear Mr. Matwey:
Dear Mr. Knill:
We have developed a new training method for teaching word processing software. Our books integrate text and graphics to present concepts that are difficult to explain with text alone.
I look forward to showing you how the process works at our meeting this coming Friday.
Debbie Lang
C:\WP51\MYWORK\SALES.LET
Doc 1 Pg 1 Ln 1" Pos 1"
The file specification for this data file is:
C: \WP51 \MYWORK \SALES.LET

Directories can contain files and/or paths to other directories. In this example, the root directory has paths to two subdirectories.

CREATE A NEW DIRECTORY

CHANGE THE DEFAULT DIRECTORY

C:
\MYWORK
\WP51

WordPerfect saves your files to the WP51 directory. This directory also contains the program files needed to run the WordPerfect program.

To organize your documents, separate them from the program files by placing them in a different directory. To do this, you will create a new directory (folder) and tell WordPerfect to store all your files in this directory.

DRIVE AND DIRECTORY SPECIFICATION

C: \WP51\MYWORK

C:	\WP51\MYWORK
Tells WordPerfect which drive the directory is in.	Tells WordPerfect the path through the directory structure to get to the "**MYWORK**" directory.

F5 Create a New Directory

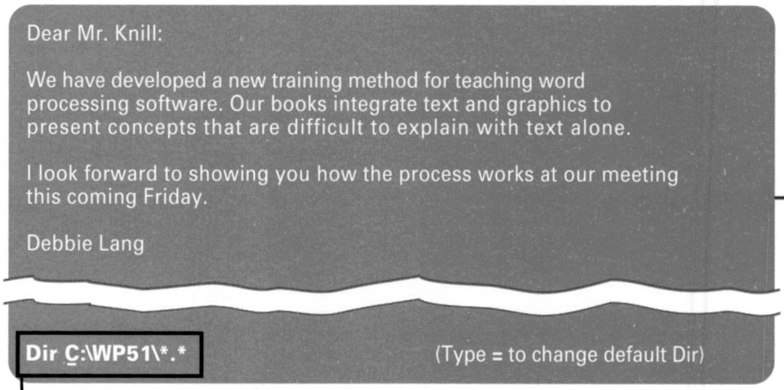

Dear Mr. Knill:
We have developed a new training method for teaching word processing software. Our books integrate text and graphics to present concepts that are difficult to explain with text alone.
I look forward to showing you how the process works at our meeting this coming Friday.
Debbie Lang
Dir C:\WP51*.*
(Type = to change default Dir)

1 Press F5 and this message appears.

Shift F1 Change the Default Directory

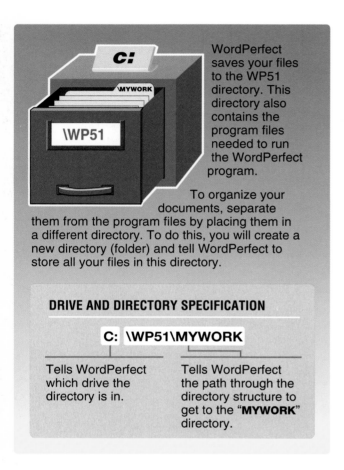

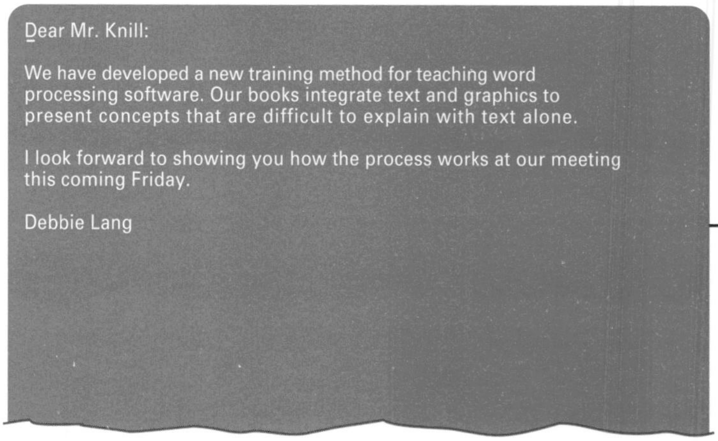

Dear Mr. Knill:
We have developed a new training method for teaching word processing software. Our books integrate text and graphics to present concepts that are difficult to explain with text alone.
I look forward to showing you how the process works at our meeting this coming Friday.
Debbie Lang

You can instruct WordPerfect to always save your files in a specific directory (folder).

1 Press Shift - F1 and the **Setup** screen appears.

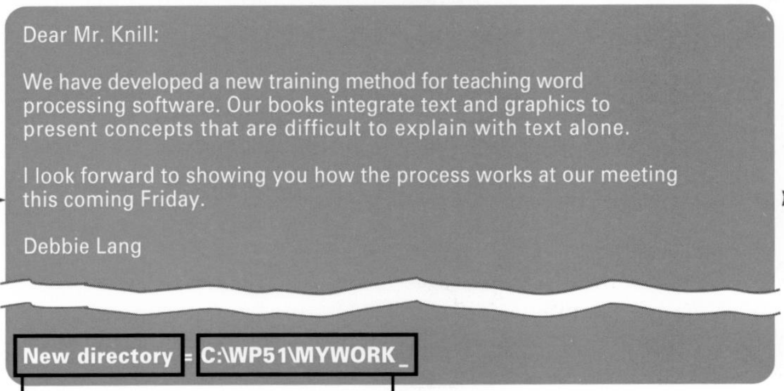
Dear Mr. Knill:
We have developed a new training method for teaching word processing software. Our books integrate text and graphics to present concepts that are difficult to explain with text alone.
I look forward to showing you how the process works at our meeting this coming Friday.
Debbie Lang
New directory = C:\WP51\MYWORK_

2 Press **=** to begin the process of creating a new directory. This message then appears.

3 Type the drive and path, followed by the name of the directory you want to create (example: **C:\WP51\MYWORK**).

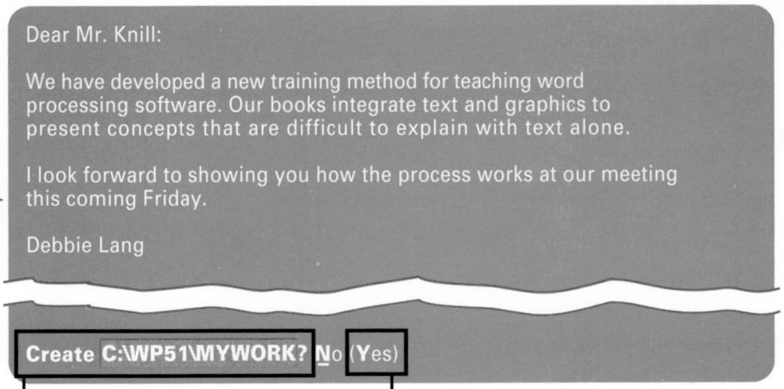
Dear Mr. Knill:
We have developed a new training method for teaching word processing software. Our books integrate text and graphics to present concepts that are difficult to explain with text alone.
I look forward to showing you how the process works at our meeting this coming Friday.
Debbie Lang
Create C:\WP51\MYWORK? No (Yes)

4 Press **Enter** and this message appears.

5 Press **Y** (for **Y**es) to create the directory.

Note: If you do not wish to create the directory, press **N** *(for* ***N****o).*

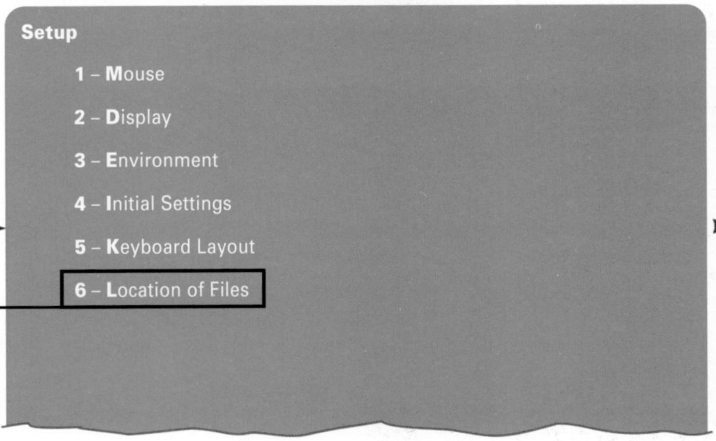
Setup
1 - Mouse
2 - Display
3 - Environment
4 - Initial Settings
5 - Keyboard Layout
6 - Location of Files

2 Press **L** (for **L**ocation of Files).

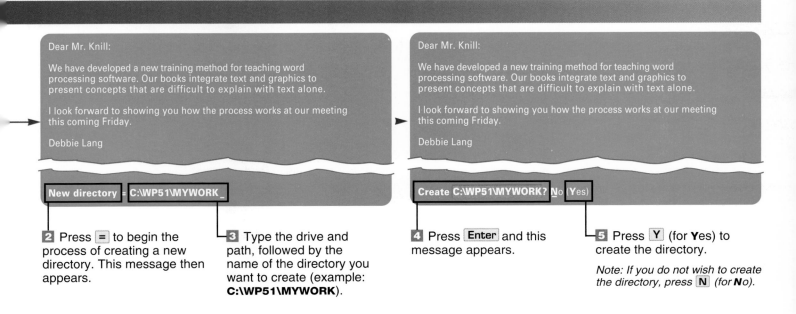

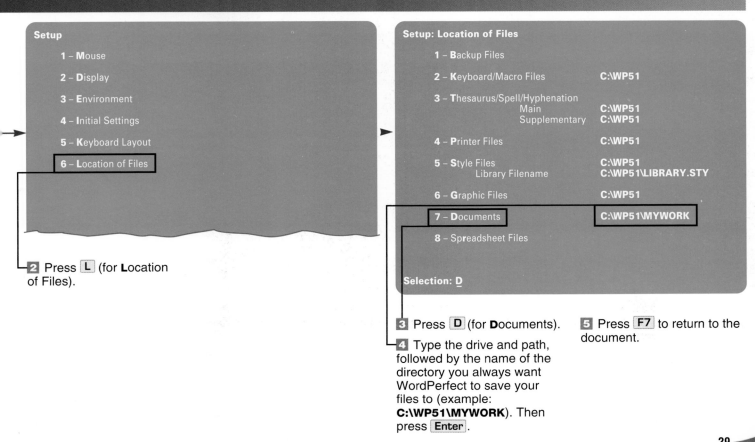

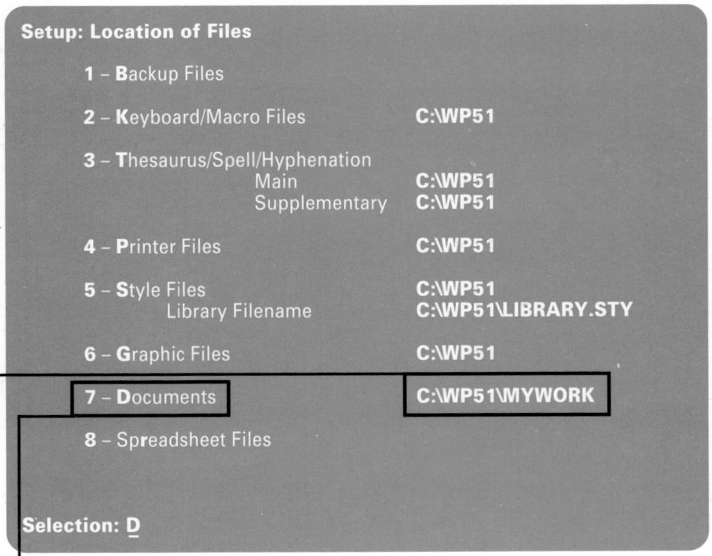
Setup: Location of Files
1 - Backup Files
2 - Keyboard/Macro Files C:\WP51
3 - Thesaurus/Spell/Hyphenation
Main C:\WP51
Supplementary C:\WP51
4 - Printer Files C:\WP51
5 - Style Files C:\WP51
Library Filename C:\WP51\LIBRARY.STY
6 - Graphic Files C:\WP51
7 - Documents C:\WP51\MYWORK
8 - Spreadsheet Files
Selection: D

3 Press **D** (for **D**ocuments).

4 Type the drive and path, followed by the name of the directory you always want WordPerfect to save your files to (example: **C:\WP51\MYWORK**). Then press **Enter**.

5 Press **F7** to return to the document.

SAVE A NEW DOCUMENT

SAVE A REVISED DOCUMENT

F10 Save a New Document

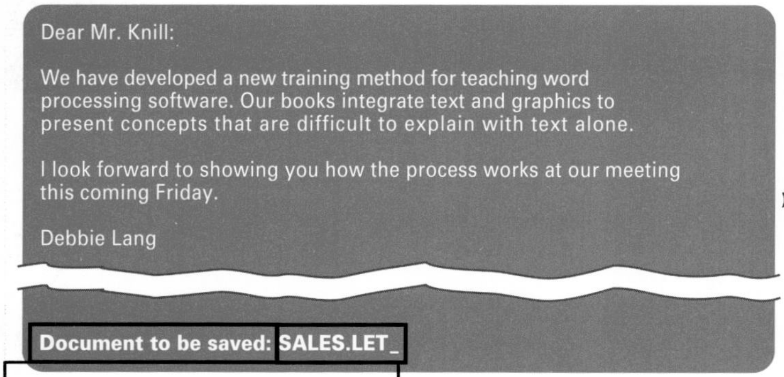
Dear Mr. Knill:
We have developed a new training method for teaching word processing software. Our books integrate text and graphics to present concepts that are difficult to explain with text alone.
I look forward to showing you how the process works at our meeting this coming Friday.
Debbie Lang
Document to be saved: SALES.LET_

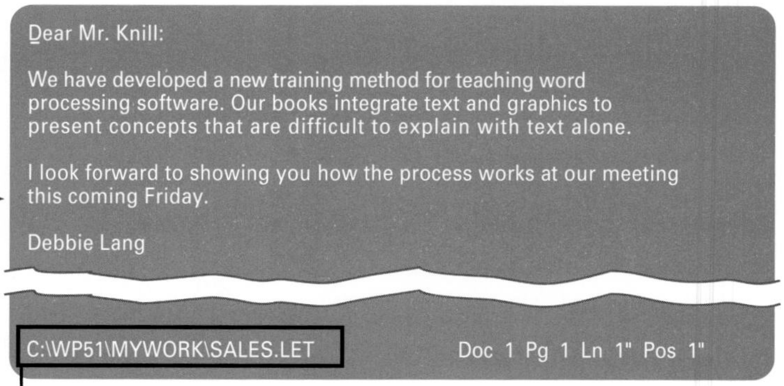
Dear Mr. Knill:
We have developed a new training method for teaching word processing software. Our books integrate text and graphics to present concepts that are difficult to explain with text alone.
I look forward to showing you how the process works at our meeting this coming Friday.
Debbie Lang
C:\WP51\MYWORK\SALES.LET
Doc 1 Pg 1 Ln 1" Pos 1"

To permanently retain a document, you must save it.

1 Press F10 and this message appears.

2 Type a name for your document (example: **SALES.LET**).

3 Press Enter and the document is saved in the current drive and directory.

F10 Save a Revised Document

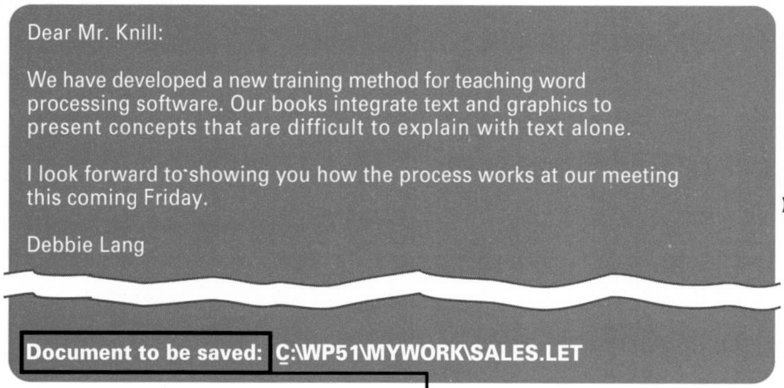
Dear Mr. Knill:
We have developed a new training method for teaching word processing software. Our books integrate text and graphics to present concepts that are difficult to explain with text alone.
I look forward to showing you how the process works at our meeting this coming Friday.
Debbie Lang
Document to be saved: C:\WP51\MYWORK\SALES.LET

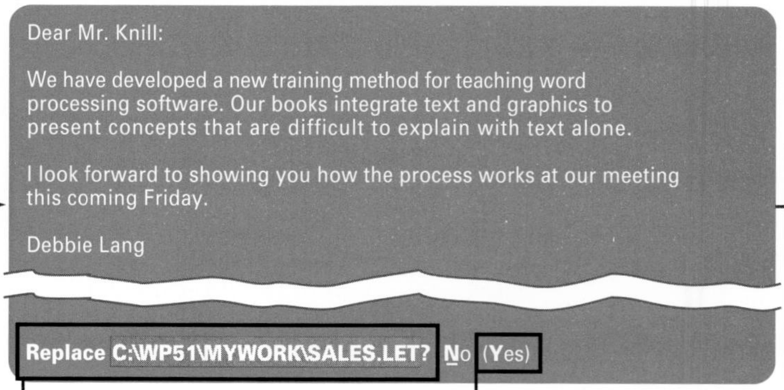
Dear Mr. Knill:
We have developed a new training method for teaching word processing software. Our books integrate text and graphics to present concepts that are difficult to explain with text alone.
I look forward to showing you how the process works at our meeting this coming Friday.
Debbie Lang
Replace C:\WP51\MYWORK\SALES.LET? No (Yes)

Save regularly to prevent losing work due to power failure or hardware malfunctions.

1 Press F10 and this message appears.

2 Press Enter and this message appears.

3 Press Y (for **Y**es) to replace the existing file with the new one.

NAME A FILE

SALES **.LET**

The filename can contain up to 8 characters.

The extension can contain up to 3 characters. In some cases, it is omitted.

The following characters are allowed:

- The letters A to Z, upper or lower case
- The numbers 0 through 9
- The symbols ! @ # $ % ^ & - ( ) _
- The filename cannot contain a . (period) or blank space

Dear Mr. Knill:

We have developed a new training method for teaching word processing software. Our books integrate text and graphics to present concepts that are difficult to explain with text alone.

I look forward to showing you how the process works at our meeting this coming Friday.

Debbie Lang

C:\WP51\MYWORK\SALES.LET   Doc 1 Pg 1 Ln 1" Pos 1"

- This document replaces the previously saved one.

SAVE DOCUMENT TO A FLOPPY DISK

Saving to a floppy disk protects your data in case of computer failure or accidental erasure of important files.

Backup your work regularly (daily or weekly).

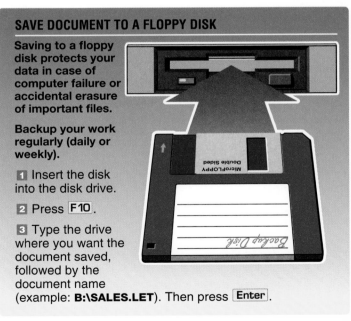

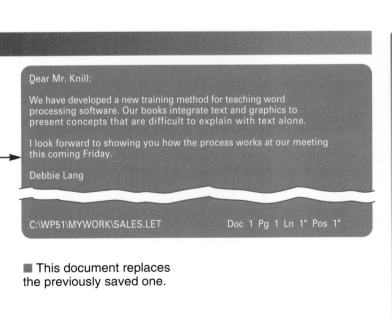

1. Insert the disk into the disk drive.
2. Press F10.
3. Type the drive where you want the document saved, followed by the document name (example: **B:\SALES.LET**). Then press Enter.

EXIT A DOCUMENT OR WORDPERFECT

RETRIEVE A DOCUMENT

F7 Exit a Document or WordPerfect

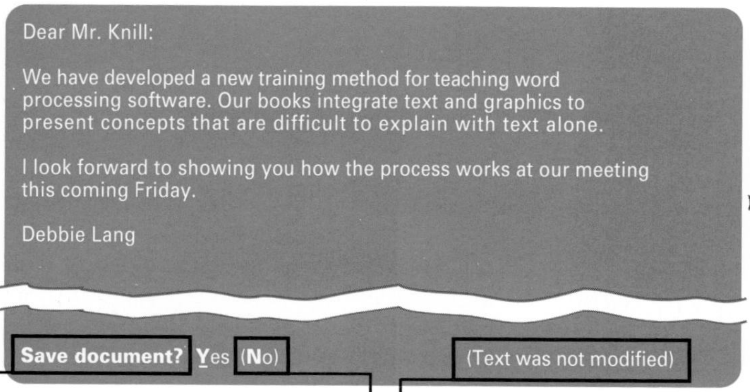
Dear Mr. Knill:
We have developed a new training method for teaching word processing software. Our books integrate text and graphics to present concepts that are difficult to explain with text alone.
I look forward to showing you how the process works at our meeting this coming Friday.
Debbie Lang
Save document? Yes (No)
(Text was not modified)

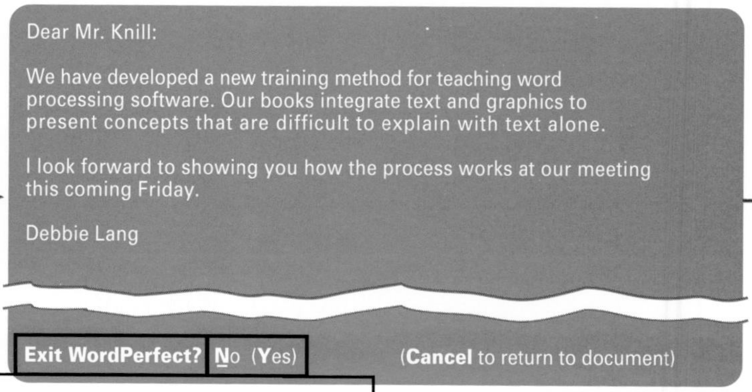
Dear Mr. Knill:
We have developed a new training method for teaching word processing software. Our books integrate text and graphics to present concepts that are difficult to explain with text alone.
I look forward to showing you how the process works at our meeting this coming Friday.
Debbie Lang
Exit WordPerfect? No (Yes)
(Cancel to return to document)

Exiting a document allows you to clear the screen and start a new document. Exiting the WordPerfect program returns you to MS-DOS.

1 Press F7 and this message appears.

■ This message appears if no changes were made since the last time you saved the document.

2 Press N (for **N**o) if you do not want to save the document.

*Note: Press Y (for **Y**es) if you want to save the document.*

■ This message appears.

3 To clear the screen and start a new document, press N (for **N**o).

or

To exit WordPerfect, press Y (for **Y**es).

Shift F10 Retrieve a Document

When you retrieve a document, WordPerfect inserts it into the current screen. If you do not want to retrieve a document into the current document, you must first clear the screen.

Note: This method is faster if you can remember the name of the file. If you do not remember the name of the file, refer to "View and Retrieve Documents" on page 34.

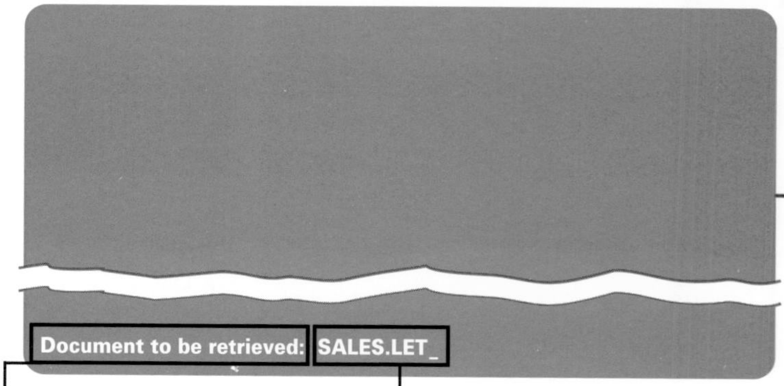
Document to be retrieved: SALES.LET_

1 Clear the screen.

Note: To clear the screen, refer to "Exit a Document" above.

2 Press Shift - F10 and this message appears.

3 If the document is in the current directory, just type the file name (example: **SALES.LET**).

OR

C:\>_

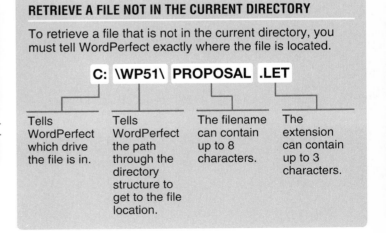

■ If you pressed N (for **N**o) in step 3, the screen is cleared. You can now start a new document.

■ If you pressed Y (for **Y**es) in step 3, you are returned to MS-DOS.

Note: To start the WordPerfect program from MS-DOS, refer to page 4.

IMPORTANT

You should always exit WordPerfect before turning off your computer.

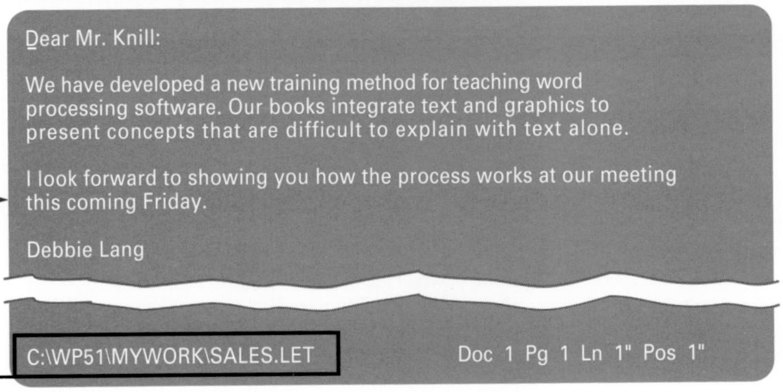
Dear Mr. Knill:
We have developed a new training method for teaching word processing software. Our books integrate text and graphics to present concepts that are difficult to explain with text alone.
I look forward to showing you how the process works at our meeting this coming Friday.
Debbie Lang
C:\WP51\MYWORK\SALES.LET
Doc 1 Pg 1 Ln 1" Pos 1"

4 Press Enter and the document is retrieved.

RETRIEVE A FILE NOT IN THE CURRENT DIRECTORY

To retrieve a file that is not in the current directory, you must tell WordPerfect exactly where the file is located.

C: \WP51\ PROPOSAL .LET

- **C:** — Tells WordPerfect which drive the file is in.
- **\WP51** — Tells WordPerfect the path through the directory structure to get to the file location.
- **PROPOSAL** — The filename can contain up to 8 characters.
- **.LET** — The extension can contain up to 3 characters.

VIEW AND RETRIEVE DOCUMENTS

F5 View Documents

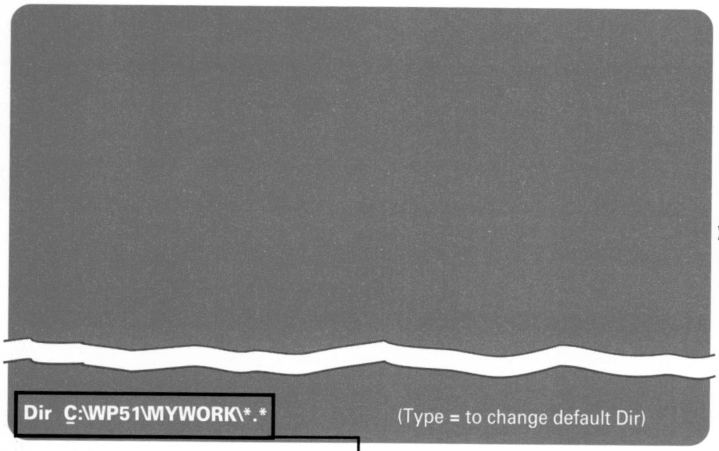

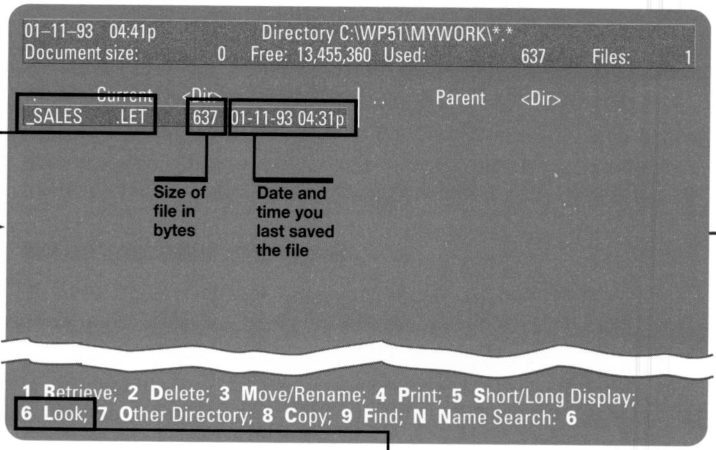

WordPerfect lets you quickly view the contents of files before retrieving a specific one.

1 Clear the screen.

Note: To clear the screen, refer to "Exit a Document" on page 32.

2 Press F5 and the drive and path of the current directory appear.

Note: To view the documents in a different directory, type the full directory name.

3 Press Enter and the List Files screen appears.

4 Press ↑, ↓, → or ← until you highlight the file you want to retrieve.

5 To view the file before retrieving it, press L (for **L**ook).

Retrieve a Document from List Files Screen

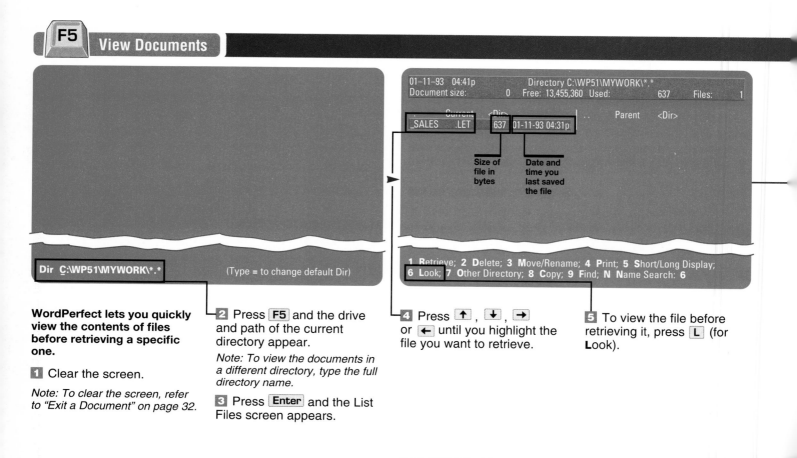

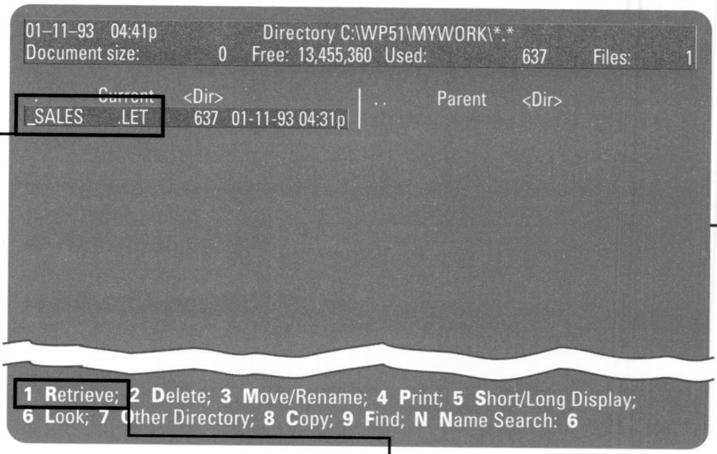

1 Press ↑, ↓, → or ← until you highlight the file you want to retrieve.

2 To retrieve the file, press R (for **R**etrieve).

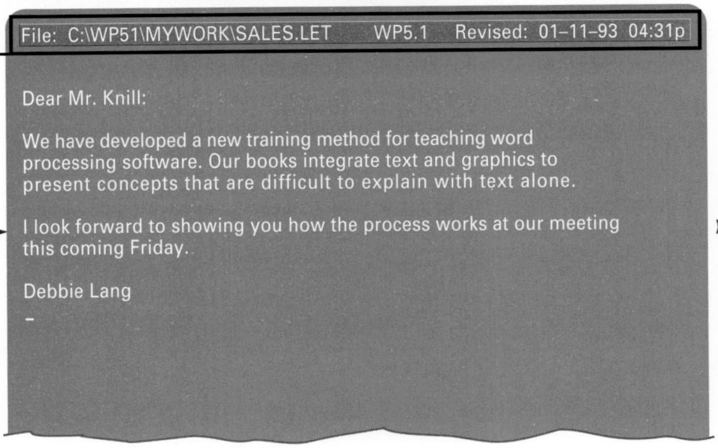
File: C:\WP51\MYWORK\SALES.LET WP5.1 Revised: 01-11-93 04:31p
Dear Mr. Knill:
We have developed a new training method for teaching word processing software. Our books integrate text and graphics to present concepts that are difficult to explain with text alone.
I look forward to showing you how the process works at our meeting this coming Friday.
Debbie Lang

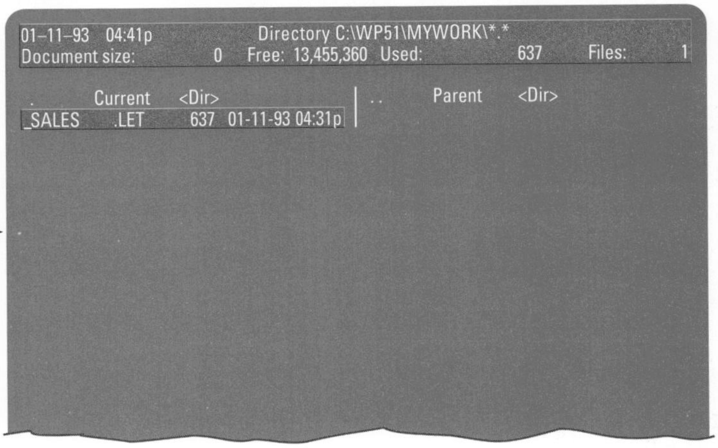
01-11-93 04:41p Directory C:\WP51\MYWORK*.*
Document size: 0 Free: 13,455,360 Used: 637 Files: 1
. Current <Dir>
.. Parent <Dir>
SALES .LET 637 01-11-93 04:31p

■ Notice the document information bar across the top of the screen. This lets you know you are merely viewing the document. You cannot edit the document.

6 To return to the List Files screen, press **F7**.

■ You are returned to the List Files screen.

Note: If you have another file to view, repeat steps **4** *to* **6**.

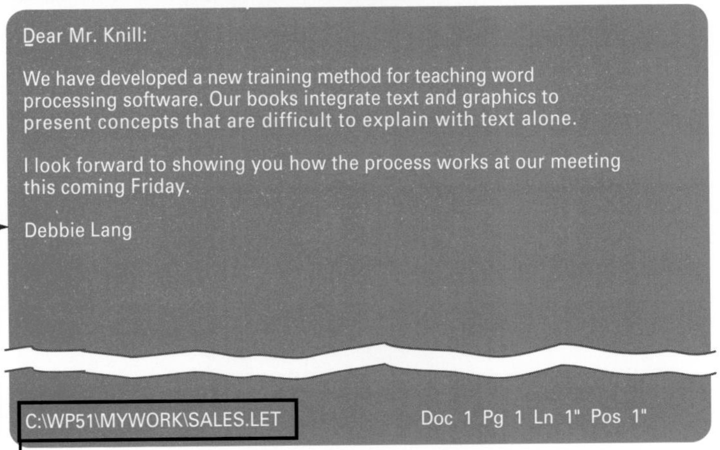
Dear Mr. Knill:
We have developed a new training method for teaching word processing software. Our books integrate text and graphics to present concepts that are difficult to explain with text alone.
I look forward to showing you how the process works at our meeting this coming Friday.
Debbie Lang
C:\WP51\MYWORK\SALES.LET
Doc 1 Pg 1 Ln 1" Pos 1"

■ The file is retrieved.

BLOCK TEXT

A text block is a group of characters that you highlight to perform a command. After you highlight a block of text, you then tell WordPerfect what you would like done to that text.

F12 Block any Amount of Text

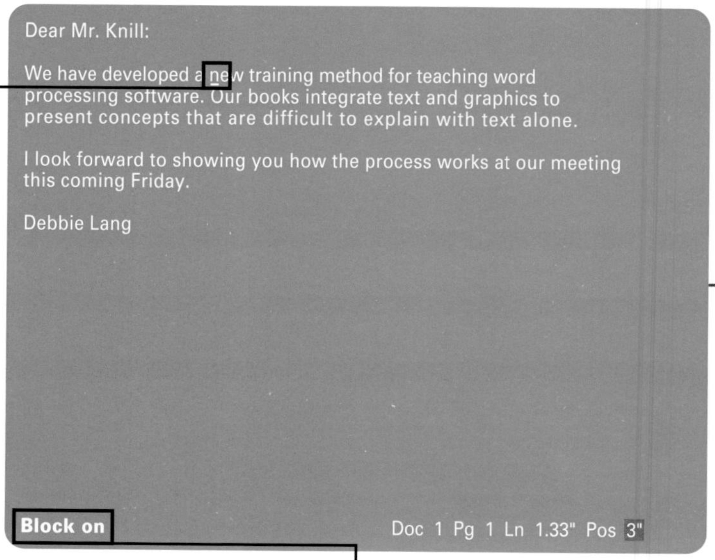

Dear Mr. Knill:
We have developed a new training method for teaching word processing software. Our books integrate text and graphics to present concepts that are difficult to explain with text alone.
I look forward to showing you how the process works at our meeting this coming Friday.
Debbie Lang
Block on
Doc 1 Pg 1 Ln 1.33" Pos 3"

1. Position the cursor at the beginning of the text you want to block.
2. Press F12 or Alt - F4. **Block on** flashes in the bottom left corner of the screen.

F12 Block a Sentence

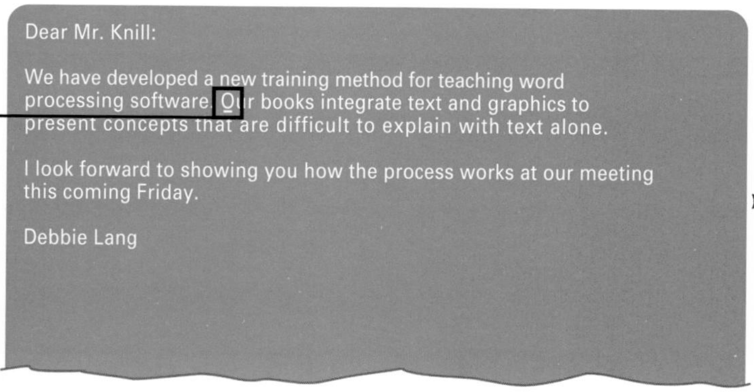

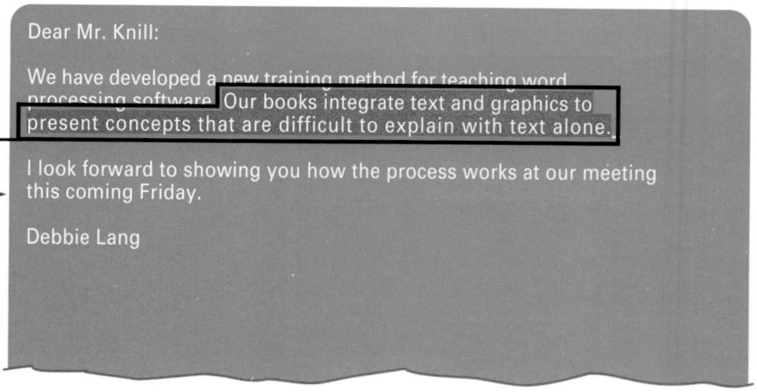

1. Position the cursor at the beginning of the sentence you want to block.
2. Press F12 or Alt - F4.
3. Press . (period) to block the text to the end of that sentence.

TO CANCEL

Press F1.

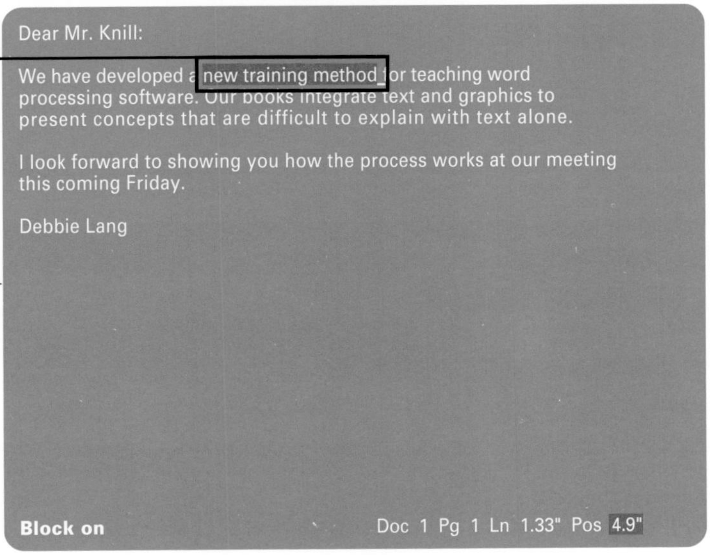
Dear Mr. Knill:
We have developed a new training method for teaching word processing software. Our books integrate text and graphics to present concepts that are difficult to explain with text alone.
I look forward to showing you how the process works at our meeting this coming Friday.
Debbie Lang
Block on
Doc 1 Pg 1 Ln 1.33" Pos 4.9"

3 Press →, ↓, ↑ or ← until you highlight the text you want to block.

Note: You may block text using any of the movement keys discussed on pages 6 and 7.

TO CANCEL

Press F1.

F12 BLOCK A LINE OF TEXT

1 Position the cursor at the beginning of the line you want to block.

2 Press F12 or Alt - F4.

3 Press End to block the text to the end of that line.

F12 Block a Paragraph

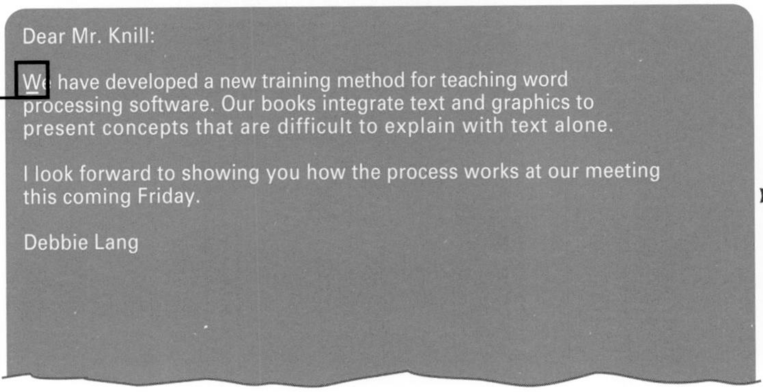
Dear Mr. Knill:
We have developed a new training method for teaching word processing software. Our books integrate text and graphics to present concepts that are difficult to explain with text alone.
I look forward to showing you how the process works at our meeting this coming Friday.
Debbie Lang

1 Position the cursor at the beginning of the paragraph you want to block.

2 Press F12 or Alt - F4.

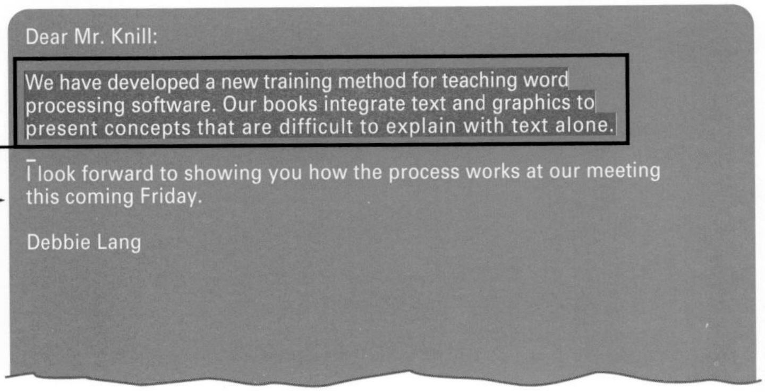
Dear Mr. Knill:
We have developed a new training method for teaching word processing software. Our books integrate text and graphics to present concepts that are difficult to explain with text alone.
I look forward to showing you how the process works at our meeting this coming Friday.
Debbie Lang

3 Press Enter to block the entire paragraph.

TO CANCEL

Press F1.

WORK WITH TWO DOCUMENTS

WordPerfect lets you work on two separate documents at the same time. This is a useful feature when copying or moving text between documents.

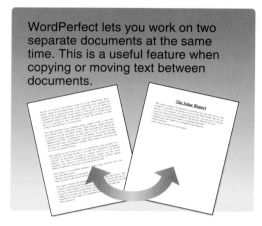

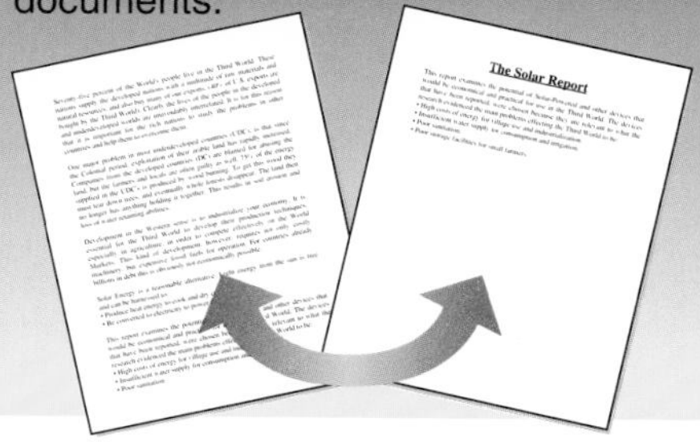

Shift F3 Switch Between Documents

Dear Mr. Knill:

We have developed a new training method for teaching word processing software. Our books integrate text and graphics to present concepts that are difficult to explain with text alone.

I look forward to showing you how the process works at our meeting this coming Friday.

Debbie Lang

C:\WP51\MYWORK\SALES.LET Doc 1 Pg 1 Ln 1.83" Pos 1"

- The current document number is displayed at the bottom of the screen.

1 To switch to the second document, press Shift - F3.

Ctrl F3 Display Two Documents

Dear Mr. Knill:

We have developed a new training method for teaching word processing software. Our books integrate text and graphics to present concepts that are difficult to explain with text alone.

I look forward to showing you how the process works at our meeting this coming Friday.

Debbie Lang

1 Window; **2 L**ine Draw; **3 R**ewrite: 3

You can view two documents at the same time by splitting the screen into two "windows".

1 Press Ctrl - F3 and this message appears.

2 Press W (for **W**indow).

Dear Mr. Knill:

We have developed a new training method for teaching word processing software. Our books integrate text and graphics to present concepts that are difficult to explain with text alone.

I look forward to showing you how the process works at our meeting this coming Friday.

Debbie Lang

Number of lines in this window: 11_

3 Type the number of lines you want the current document to display (example: **11**).

4 Press Enter.

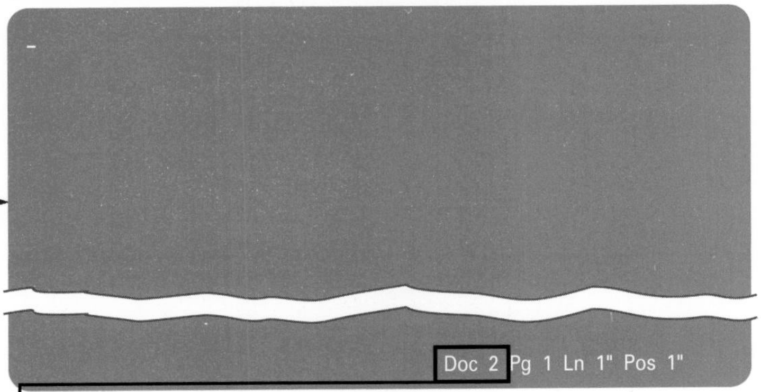
Doc 2 Pg 1 Ln 1" Pos 1"

The second document appears.

Note: ***Doc 1*** *is hidden behind* ***Doc 2****.*

2 To return to the first document, press Shift - F3.

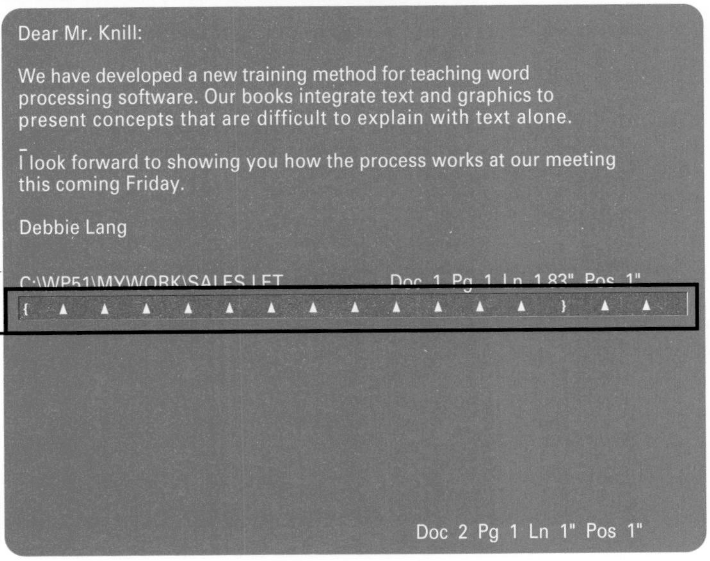
Dear Mr. Knill:
We have developed a new training method for teaching word processing software. Our books integrate text and graphics to present concepts that are difficult to explain with text alone.
I look forward to showing you how the process works at our meeting this coming Friday.
Debbie Lang
Doc 2 Pg 1 Ln 1" Pos 1"

The line in the middle separates the two documents. The triangles point to the active document.

Note: You can only edit the active document.

5 To switch between the documents, press Shift - F3.

TO RESTORE THE ACTIVE DOCUMENT TO FULL SCREEN SIZE

1 Press Ctrl - F3.

2 Press W (for **W**indow).

3 Type **24**.

4 Press Enter.

Indicates the top document is active.

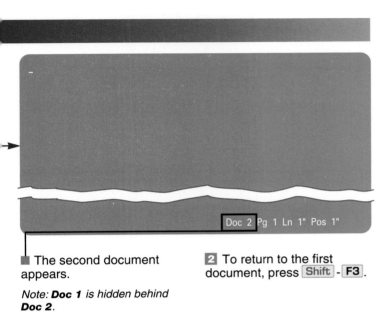

Indicates the bottom document is active.

MOVE AND COPY TEXT

Ctrl F4 Move Text (within the same document)

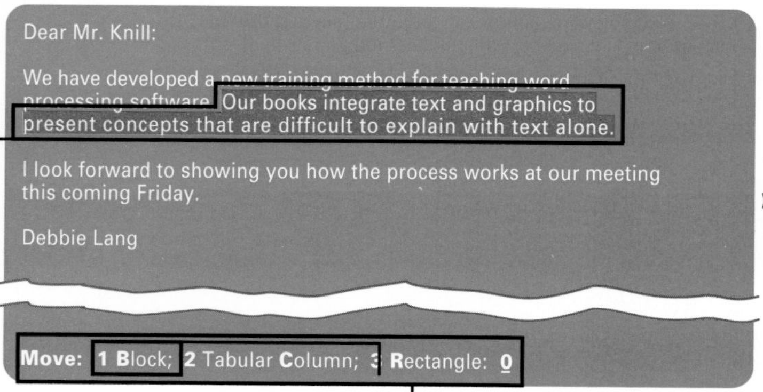
Dear Mr. Knill:
We have developed a new training method for teaching word processing software. Our books integrate text and graphics to present concepts that are difficult to explain with text alone.
I look forward to showing you how the process works at our meeting this coming Friday.
Debbie Lang
Move: 1 Block; 2 Tabular Column; 3 Rectangle: 0

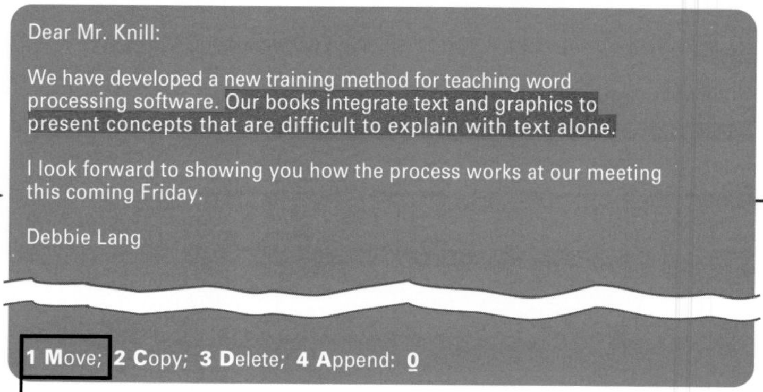
Dear Mr. Knill:
We have developed a new training method for teaching word processing software. Our books integrate text and graphics to present concepts that are difficult to explain with text alone.
I look forward to showing you how the process works at our meeting this coming Friday.
Debbie Lang
1 Move; 2 Copy; 3 Delete; 4 Append: 0

1 Position the cursor at the beginning of the text you want to move.

2 Press F12 or Alt - F4.

3 Press →, ↓, ↑ or ← until you highlight the text you want to move.

4 Press Ctrl - F4 and this message appears.

5 Press B (for **B**lock).

6 Press M (for **M**ove) and the text disappears from the screen.

Ctrl F4 Copy Text (within the same document)

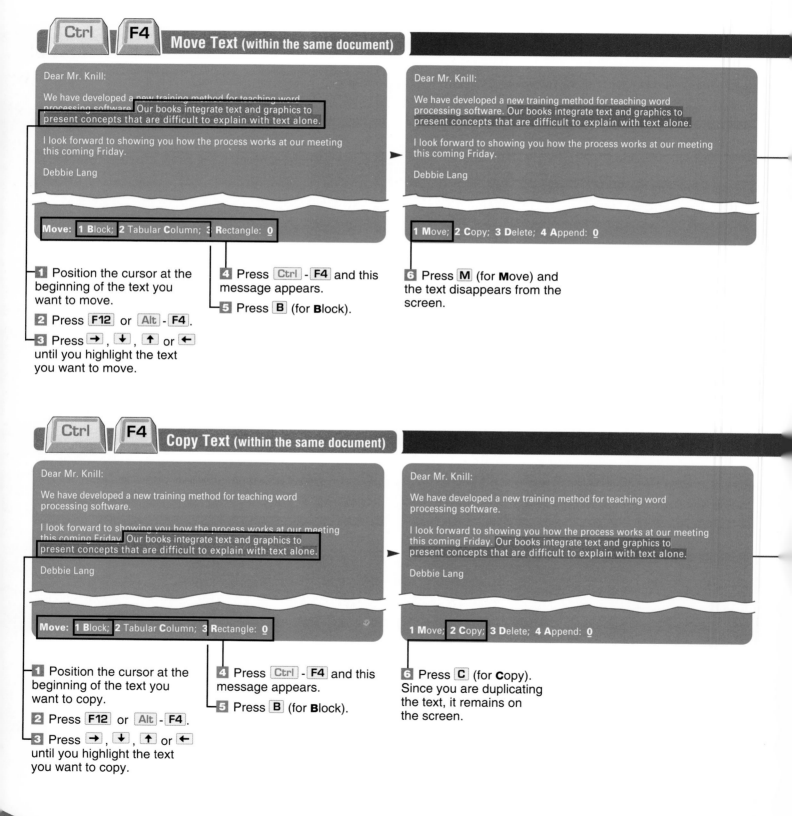

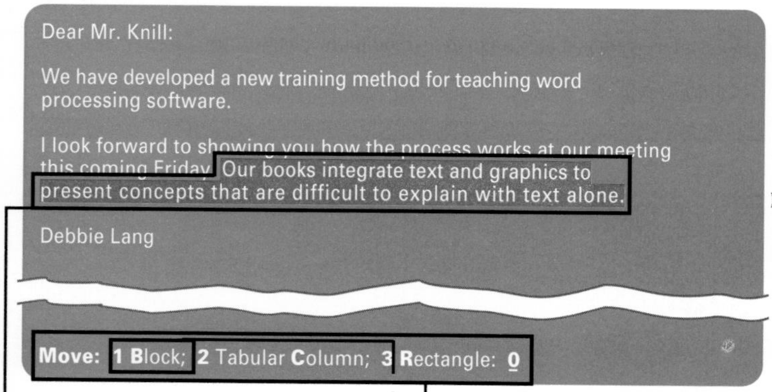
Dear Mr. Knill:
We have developed a new training method for teaching word processing software.
I look forward to showing you how the process works at our meeting this coming Friday. Our books integrate text and graphics to present concepts that are difficult to explain with text alone.
Debbie Lang
Move: 1 Block; 2 Tabular Column; 3 Rectangle: 0

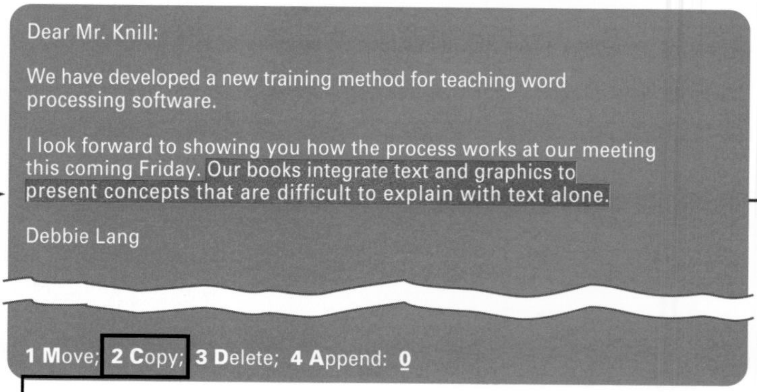
Dear Mr. Knill:
We have developed a new training method for teaching word processing software.
I look forward to showing you how the process works at our meeting this coming Friday. Our books integrate text and graphics to present concepts that are difficult to explain with text alone.
Debbie Lang
1 Move; 2 Copy; 3 Delete; 4 Append: 0

1 Position the cursor at the beginning of the text you want to copy.

2 Press F12 or Alt - F4.

3 Press →, ↓, ↑ or ← until you highlight the text you want to copy.

4 Press Ctrl - F4 and this message appears.

5 Press B (for **B**lock).

6 Press C (for **C**opy). Since you are duplicating the text, it remains on the screen.

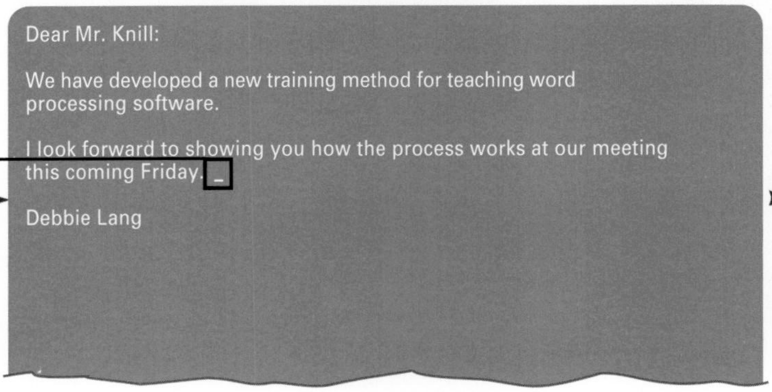
Dear Mr. Knill:
We have developed a new training method for teaching word processing software.
I look forward to showing you how the process works at our meeting this coming Friday. _
Debbie Lang

7 Position the cursor where you want the text moved.

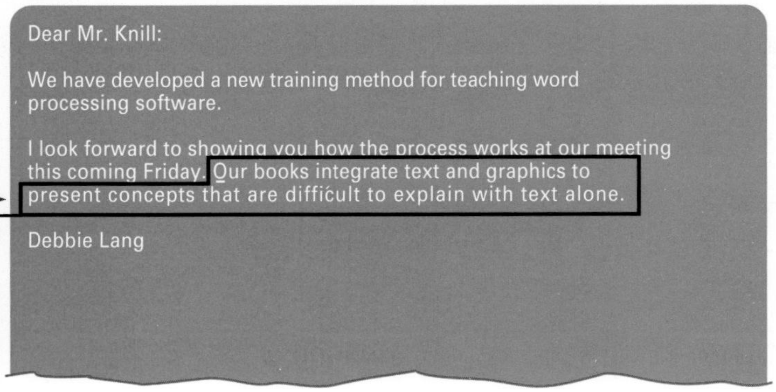
Dear Mr. Knill:
We have developed a new training method for teaching word processing software.
I look forward to showing you how the process works at our meeting this coming Friday. Our books integrate text and graphics to present concepts that are difficult to explain with text alone.
Debbie Lang

8 Press Enter to paste the text into its new location.

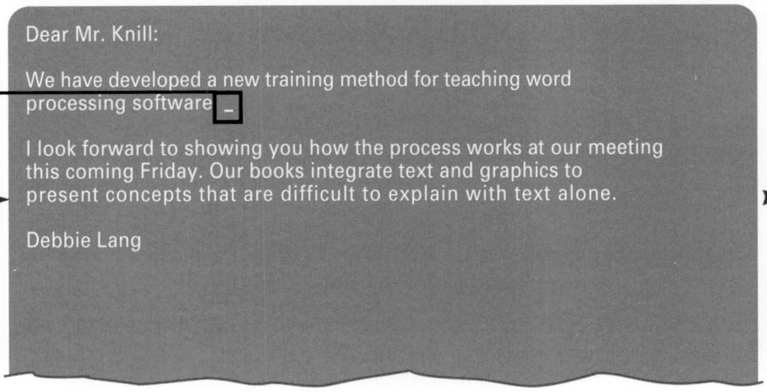
Dear Mr. Knill:
We have developed a new training method for teaching word processing software. _
I look forward to showing you how the process works at our meeting this coming Friday. Our books integrate text and graphics to present concepts that are difficult to explain with text alone.
Debbie Lang

7 Position the cursor where you want the text copied.

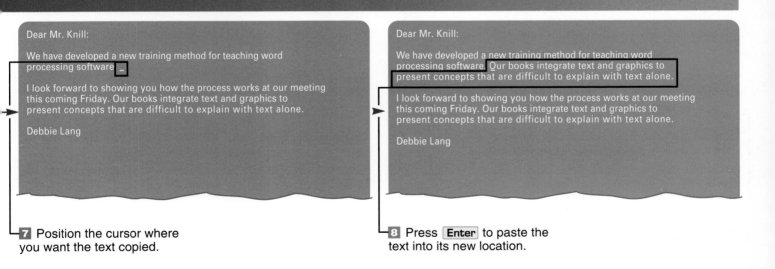

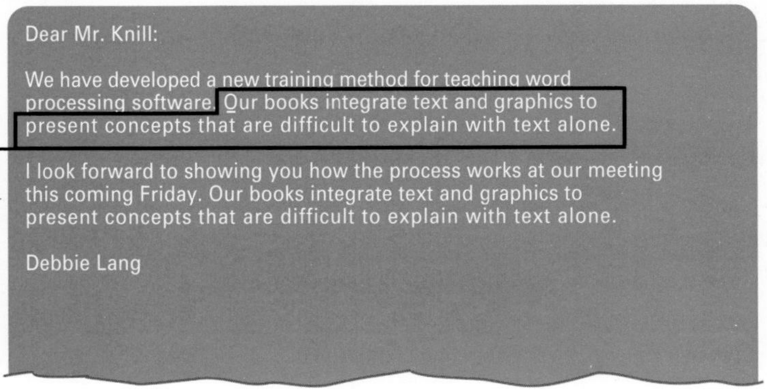
Dear Mr. Knill:
We have developed a new training method for teaching word processing software. Our books integrate text and graphics to present concepts that are difficult to explain with text alone.
I look forward to showing you how the process works at our meeting this coming Friday. Our books integrate text and graphics to present concepts that are difficult to explain with text alone.
Debbie Lang

8 Press Enter to paste the text into its new location.

MOVE AND COPY TEXT

Ctrl F3 Display Two Documents

Before copying or moving text between documents, display both documents on the screen.

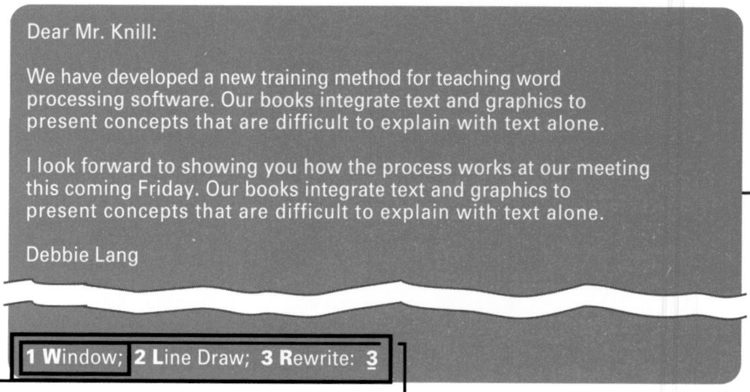
Dear Mr. Knill:
We have developed a new training method for teaching word processing software. Our books integrate text and graphics to present concepts that are difficult to explain with text alone.
I look forward to showing you how the process works at our meeting this coming Friday. Our books integrate text and graphics to present concepts that are difficult to explain with text alone.
Debbie Lang
1 Window; 2 Line Draw; 3 Rewrite: 3

1 Press Ctrl - F3 and this message appears.

2 Press W (for **W**indow).

Ctrl F4 Move or Copy Text (to another document)

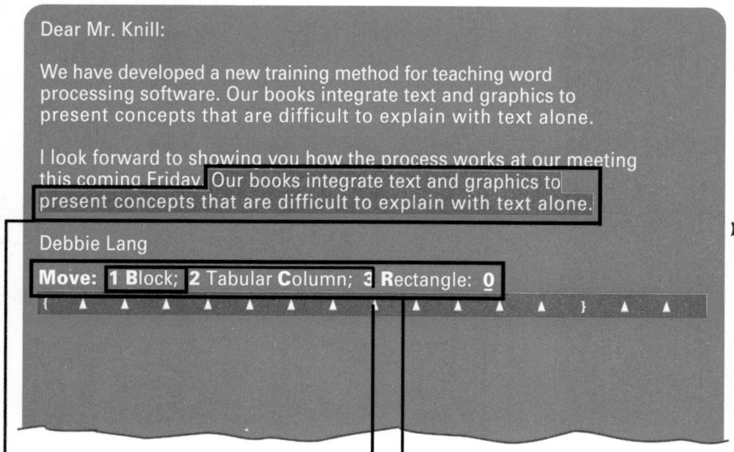
Dear Mr. Knill:
We have developed a new training method for teaching word processing software. Our books integrate text and graphics to present concepts that are difficult to explain with text alone.
I look forward to showing you how the process works at our meeting this coming Friday. Our books integrate text and graphics to present concepts that are difficult to explain with text alone.
Debbie Lang
Move: 1 Block; 2 Tabular Column; 3 Rectangle: 0

1 Position the cursor at the beginning of the text you want to move or copy.

2 Press F12 or Alt - F4.

3 Press →, ↓, ↑ or ← until you highlight the text you want to move or copy.

4 Press Ctrl - F4 and this message appears.

5 Press B (for **B**lock).

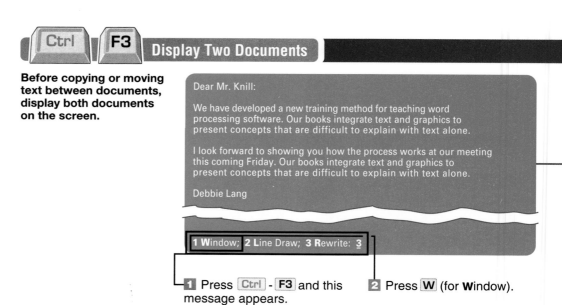

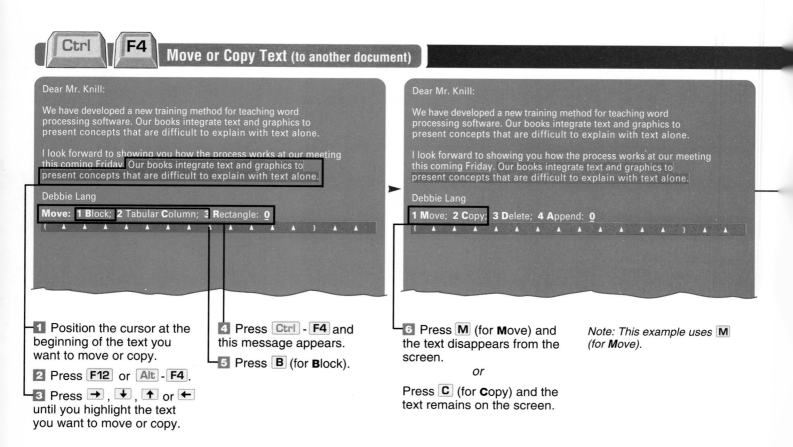

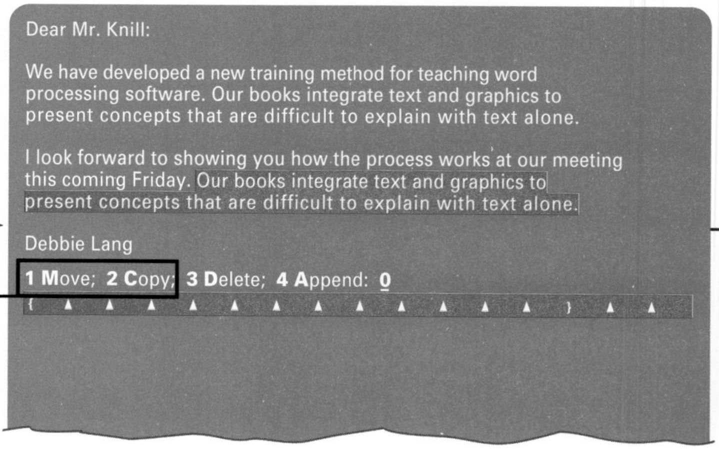
Dear Mr. Knill:
We have developed a new training method for teaching word processing software. Our books integrate text and graphics to present concepts that are difficult to explain with text alone.
I look forward to showing you how the process works at our meeting this coming Friday. Our books integrate text and graphics to present concepts that are difficult to explain with text alone.
Debbie Lang
1 Move; 2 Copy; 3 Delete; 4 Append: 0

6 Press M (for **M**ove) and the text disappears from the screen.

or

Press C (for **C**opy) and the text remains on the screen.

*Note: This example uses M (for **M**ove).*

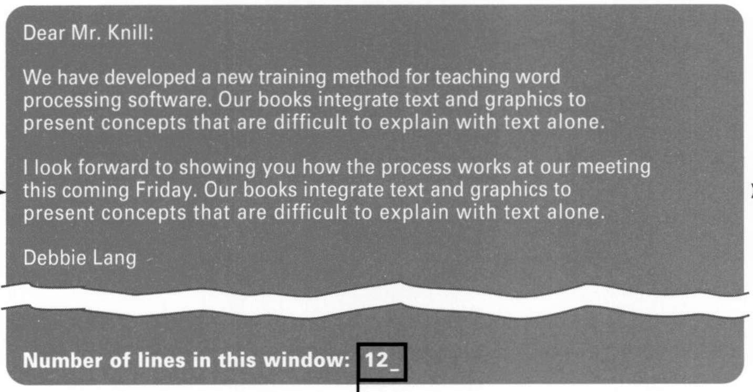
Dear Mr. Knill:
We have developed a new training method for teaching word processing software. Our books integrate text and graphics to present concepts that are difficult to explain with text alone.
I look forward to showing you how the process works at our meeting this coming Friday. Our books integrate text and graphics to present concepts that are difficult to explain with text alone.
Debbie Lang
Number of lines in this window: 12_

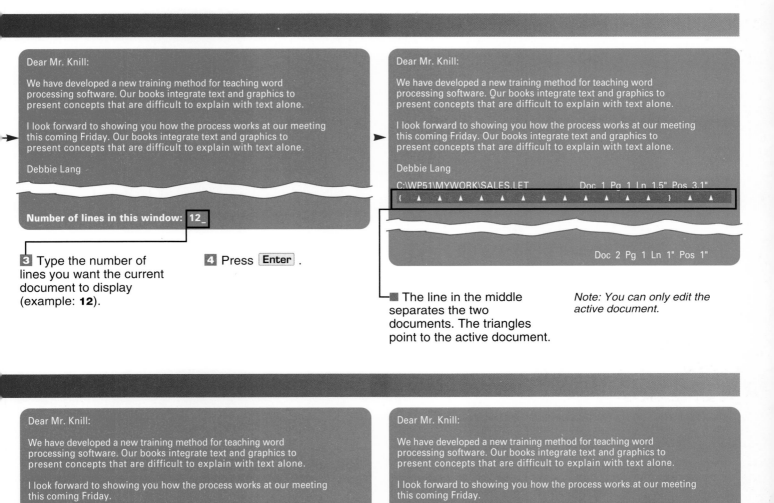

3 Type the number of lines you want the current document to display (example: **12**).

4 Press Enter .

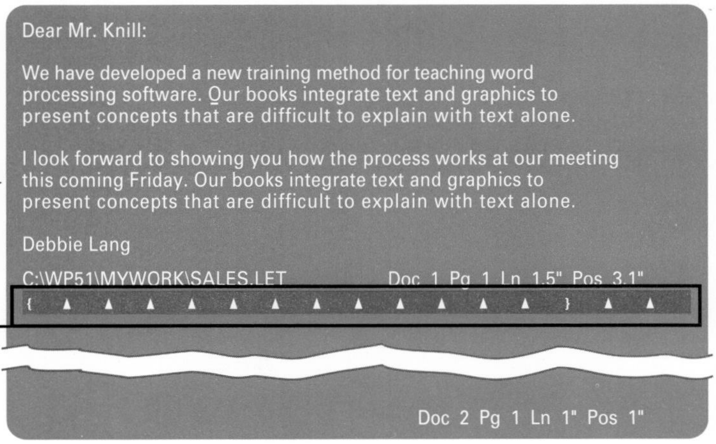
Dear Mr. Knill:
We have developed a new training method for teaching word processing software. Our books integrate text and graphics to present concepts that are difficult to explain with text alone.
I look forward to showing you how the process works at our meeting this coming Friday. Our books integrate text and graphics to present concepts that are difficult to explain with text alone.
Debbie Lang
C:\WP51\MYWORK\SALES.LET
Doc 1 Pg 1 Ln 1.5" Pos 3.1"
Doc 2 Pg 1 Ln 1" Pos 1"

■ The line in the middle separates the two documents. The triangles point to the active document.

Note: You can only edit the active document.

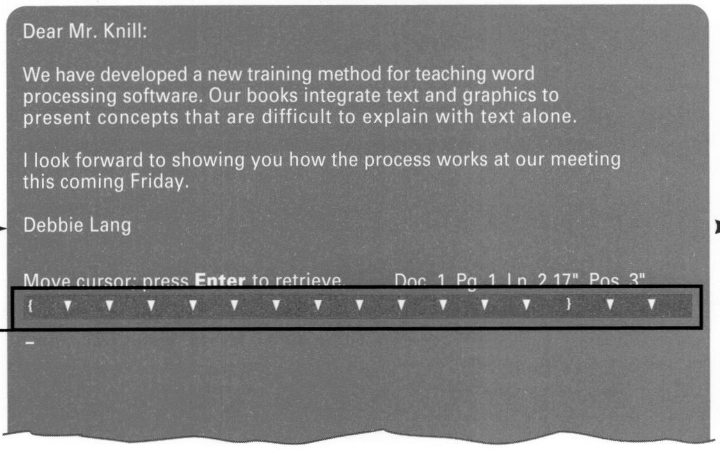
Dear Mr. Knill:
We have developed a new training method for teaching word processing software. Our books integrate text and graphics to present concepts that are difficult to explain with text alone.
I look forward to showing you how the process works at our meeting this coming Friday.
Debbie Lang
Move cursor; press Enter to retrieve.
Doc 1 Pg 1 Ln 2.17" Pos 3"

7 To switch to the other document, press Shift - F3 .

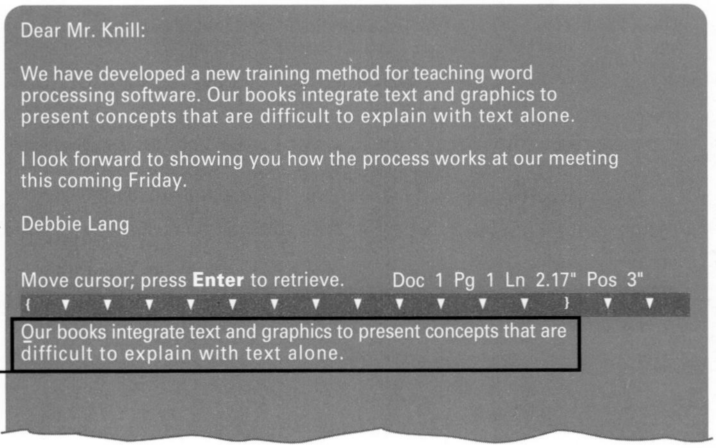
Dear Mr. Knill:
We have developed a new training method for teaching word processing software. Our books integrate text and graphics to present concepts that are difficult to explain with text alone.
I look forward to showing you how the process works at our meeting this coming Friday.
Debbie Lang
Move cursor; press Enter to retrieve.
Doc 1 Pg 1 Ln 2.17" Pos 3"
Our books integrate text and graphics to present concepts that are difficult to explain with text alone.

8 Press Enter to paste the text into its new location.

Note: To restore the active document to full screen size, refer to page 39.

SET MARGINS

Setting Margins

Margins define the distance between the text and the edges of the paper. You can lengthen or shorten the size of a document by changing its margins.

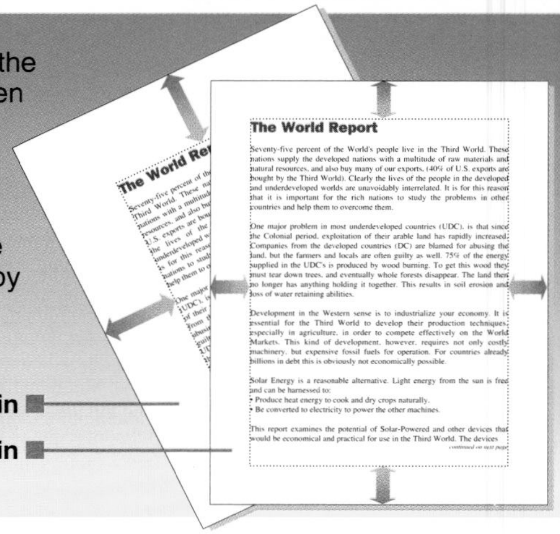

2 inch margin

1 inch margin

Shift F8 Set Left and Right Margins

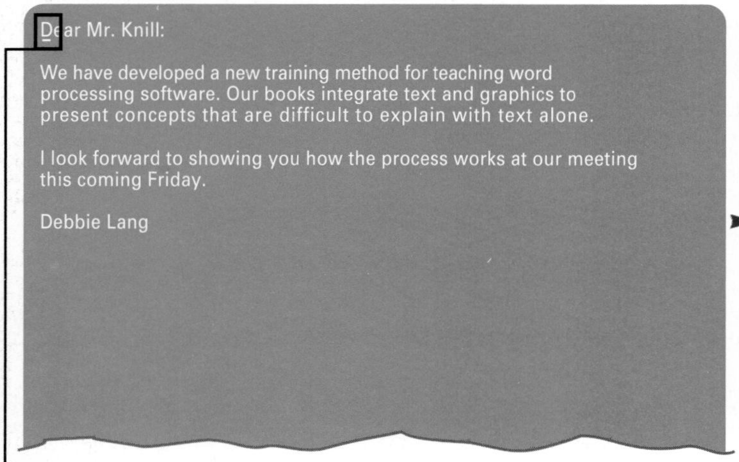

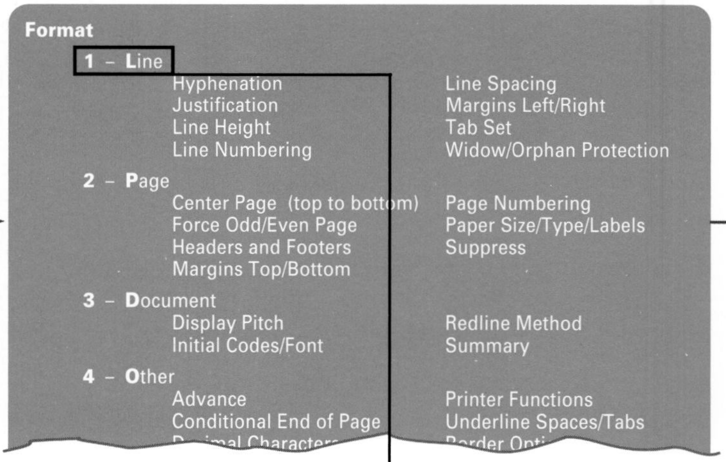

1 Position the cursor where you want the new margins to begin.

2 Press Shift - F8 and the **Format** screen appears.

3 Press L (for **L**ine).

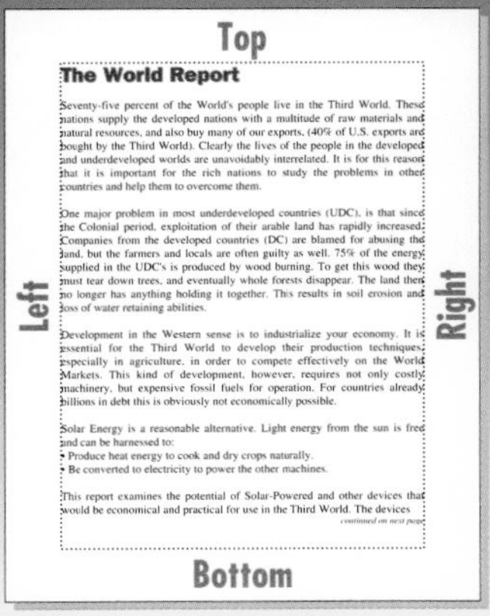
Top
Left
Right
Bottom

The World Report

Seventy-five percent of the World's people live in the Third World. These nations supply the developed nations with a multitude of raw materials and natural resources, and also buy many of our exports. (40% of U.S. exports are bought by the Third World). Clearly the lives of the people in the developed and underdeveloped worlds are unavoidably interrelated. It is for this reason that it is important for the rich nations to study the problems in other countries and help them to overcome them.

One major problem in most underdeveloped countries (UDC), is that since the Colonial period, exploitation of their arable land has rapidly increased. Companies from the developed countries (DC) are blamed for abusing the land, but the farmers and locals are often guilty as well. 75% of the energy supplied in the UDC's is produced by wood burning. To get this wood they must tear down trees, and eventually whole forests disappear. The land then no longer has anything holding it together. This results in soil erosion and loss of water retaining abilities.

Development in the Western sense is to industrialize your economy. It is essential for the Third World to develop their production techniques, especially in agriculture, in order to compete effectively on the World Markets. This kind of development, however, requires not only costly machinery, but expensive fossil fuels for operation. For countries already billions in debt this is obviously not economically possible.

Solar Energy is a reasonable alternative. Light energy from the sun is free and can be harnessed to:
- Produce heat energy to cook and dry crops naturally.
- Be converted to electricity to power the other machines.

This report examines the potential of Solar-Powered and other devices that would be economical and practical for use in the Third World. The devices

continued on next page

When you start a new document, WordPerfect automatically sets a one inch **Left**, **Right**, **Top** and **Bottom** margin on every page. You can change these settings.

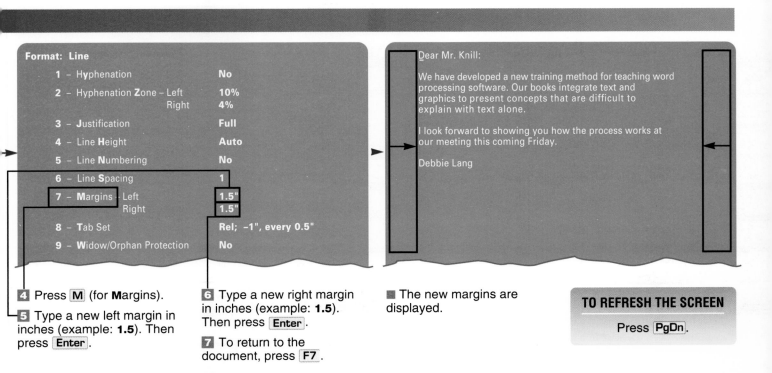

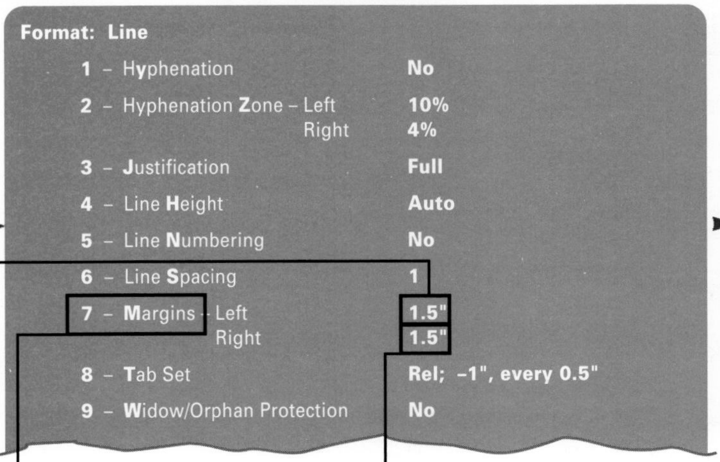
Format: Line
1 - Hyphenation No
2 - Hyphenation Zone - Left 10%
Right 4%
3 - Justification Full
4 - Line Height Auto
5 - Line Numbering No
6 - Line Spacing 1
7 - Margins - Left 1.5"
Right 1.5"
8 - Tab Set Rel; -1", every 0.5"
9 - Widow/Orphan Protection No

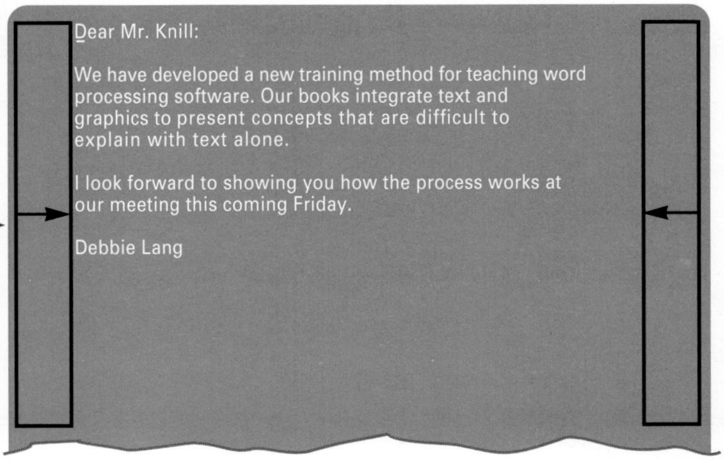
Dear Mr. Knill:
We have developed a new training method for teaching word processing software. Our books integrate text and graphics to present concepts that are difficult to explain with text alone.
I look forward to showing you how the process works at our meeting this coming Friday.
Debbie Lang

4 Press M (for **M**argins).

5 Type a new left margin in inches (example: **1.5**). Then press Enter.

6 Type a new right margin in inches (example: **1.5**). Then press Enter.

7 To return to the document, press F7.

■ The new margins are displayed.

TO REFRESH THE SCREEN

Press PgDn.

SET MARGINS

CHANGE LINE SPACING

Shift F8 Set Top and Bottom Margins

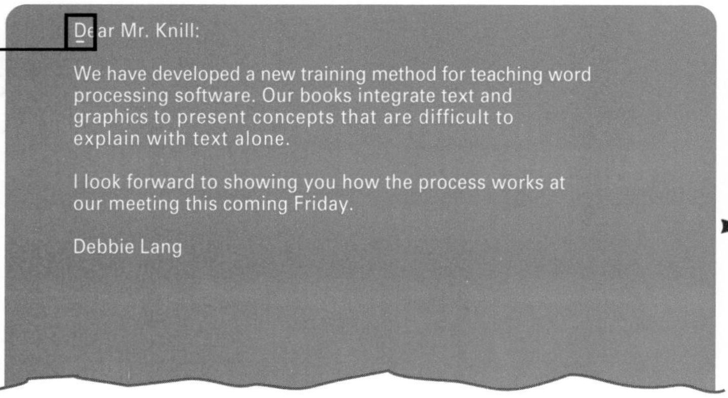

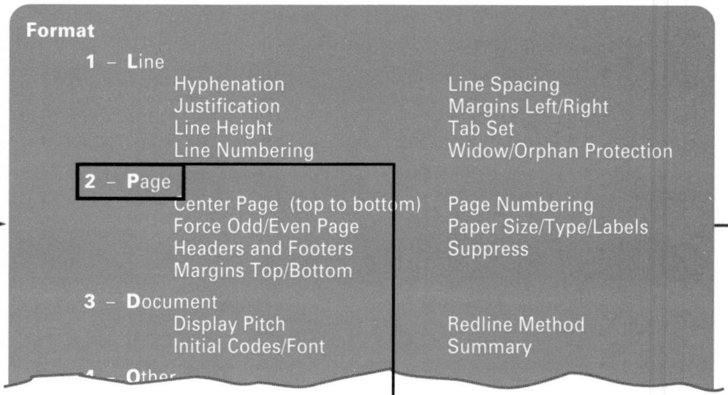

1 Position the cursor at the top of the page where you want the new margins to begin.

2 Press Shift - F8 and the **Format** screen appears.

3 Press P (for **P**age).

Shift F8 Change Line Spacing

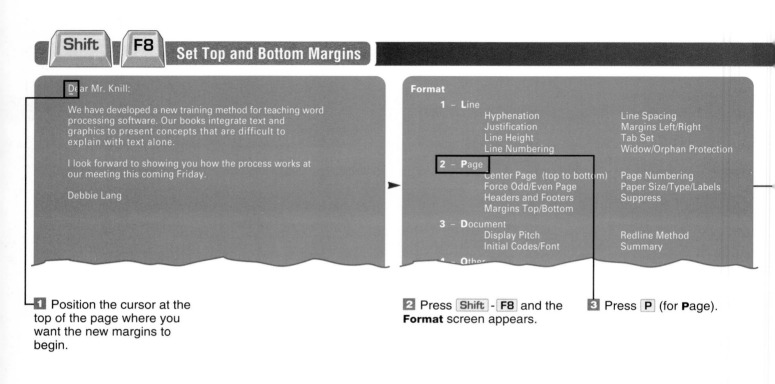

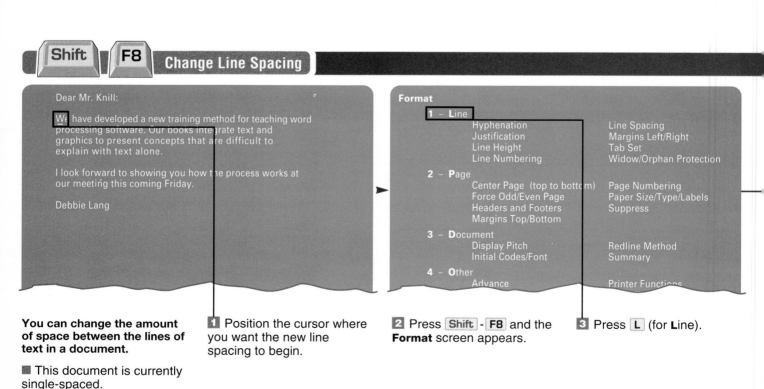

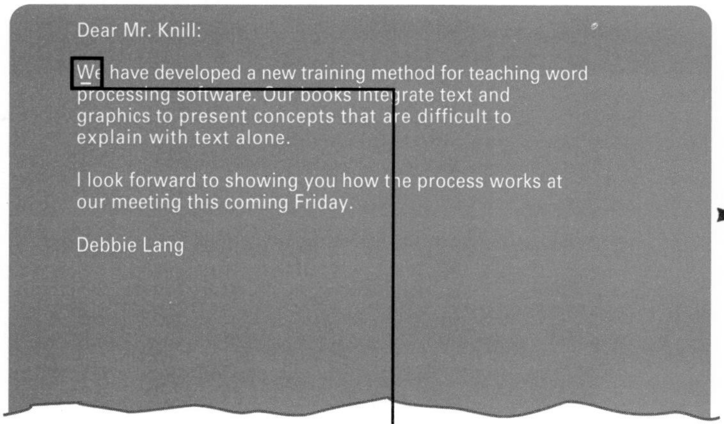

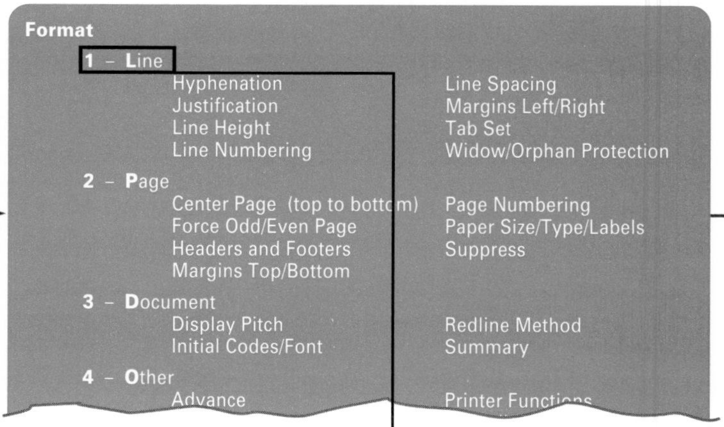

You can change the amount of space between the lines of text in a document.

■ This document is currently single-spaced.

1 Position the cursor where you want the new line spacing to begin.

2 Press Shift - F8 and the **Format** screen appears.

3 Press L (for **L**ine).

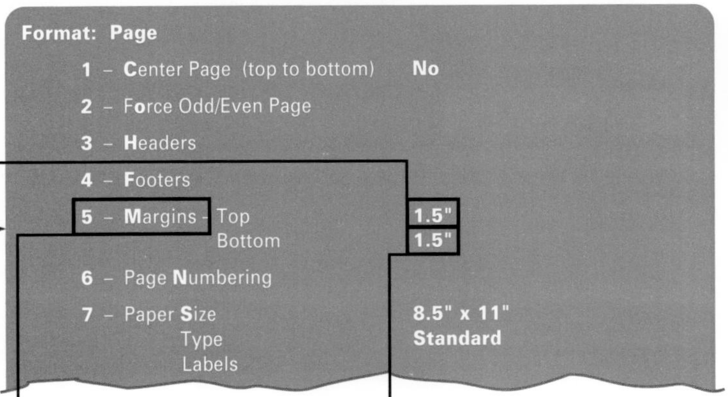

Note: The new top and bottom margins are not displayed on the screen.

To view the new margins before printing the document, refer to page 56.

4 Press M (for **M**argins).

5 Type a new top margin in inches (example: **1.5**). Then press Enter.

6 Type a new bottom margin in inches (example: **1.5**). Then press Enter.

7 To return to the document, press F7.

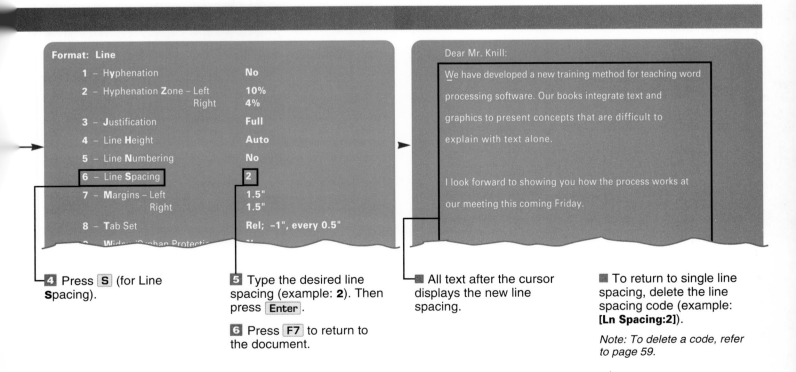

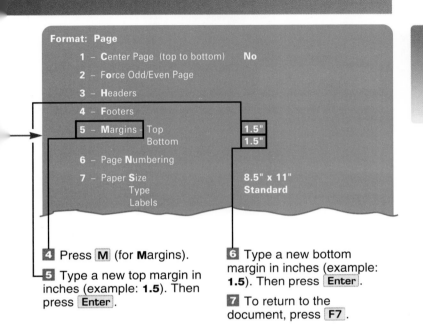

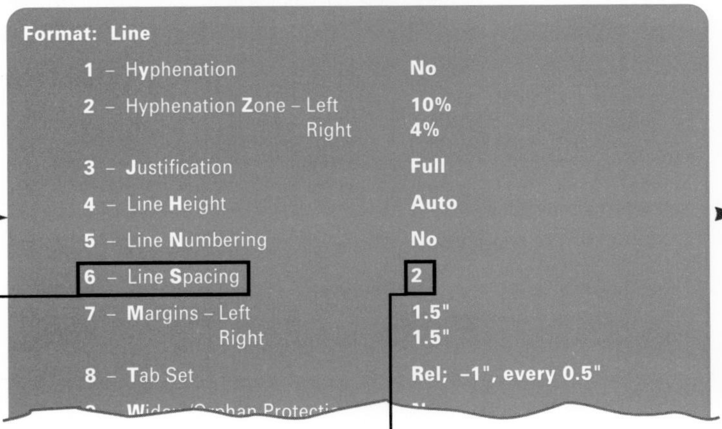

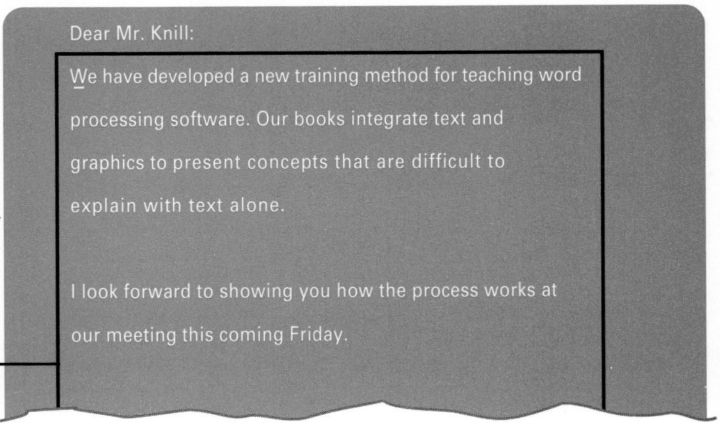

4 Press S (for Line **S**pacing).

5 Type the desired line spacing (example: **2**). Then press Enter.

6 Press F7 to return to the document.

■ All text after the cursor displays the new line spacing.

■ To return to single line spacing, delete the line spacing code (example: **[Ln Spacing:2]**).

Note: To delete a code, refer to page 59.

SET TABS

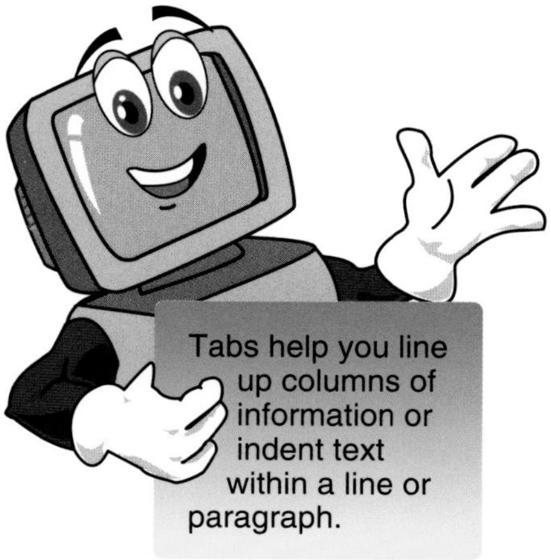

Tabs help you line up columns of information or indent text within a line or paragraph.

Tab Types

WordPerfect offers four types of tabs:

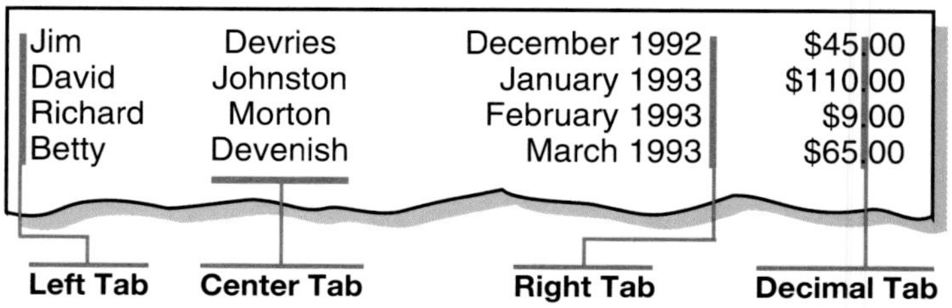

Shift F8 Display the Tab Line

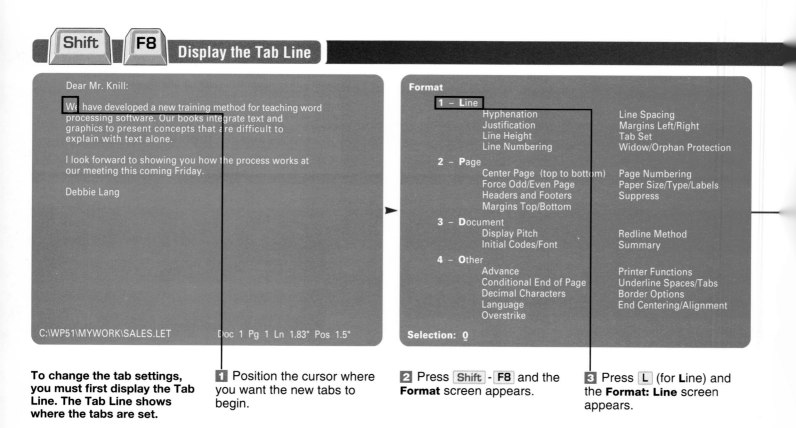

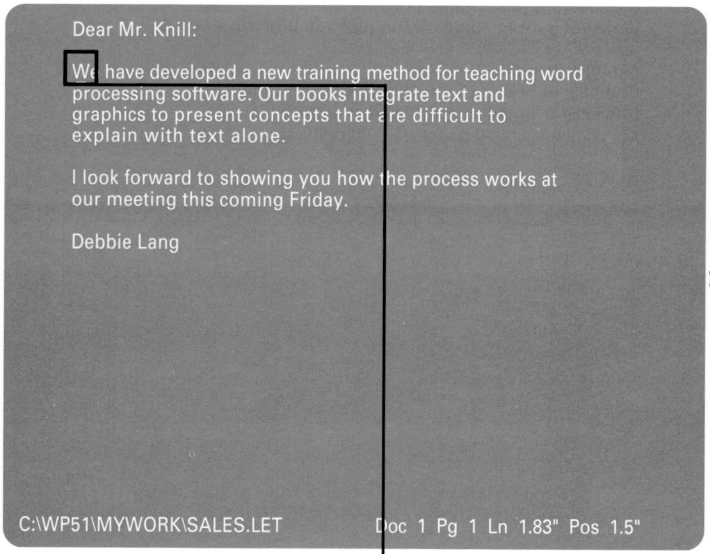

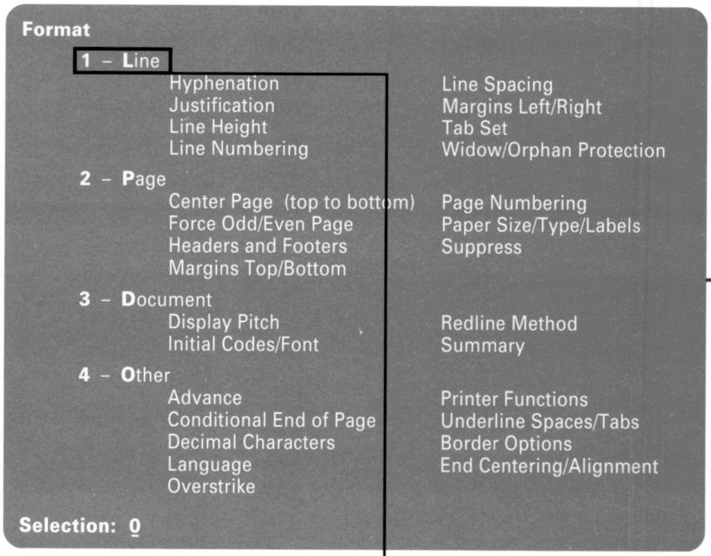

To change the tab settings, you must first display the Tab Line. The Tab Line shows where the tabs are set.

1 Position the cursor where you want the new tabs to begin.

2 Press Shift - F8 and the **Format** screen appears.

3 Press L (for **L**ine) and the **Format: Line** screen appears.

By changing a regular tab into a dot leader tab, dots will appear in front of the text. You can use dot leader tabs when creating a Table of Contents or an Index.

Jim...............Devries ....December 1992 ....$45.00
David..........Johnston................January 1993 ....$110.00
Richard ....Morton................February 1993 ....$9.00
Betty...........Devenish ....March 1993 ....$65.00

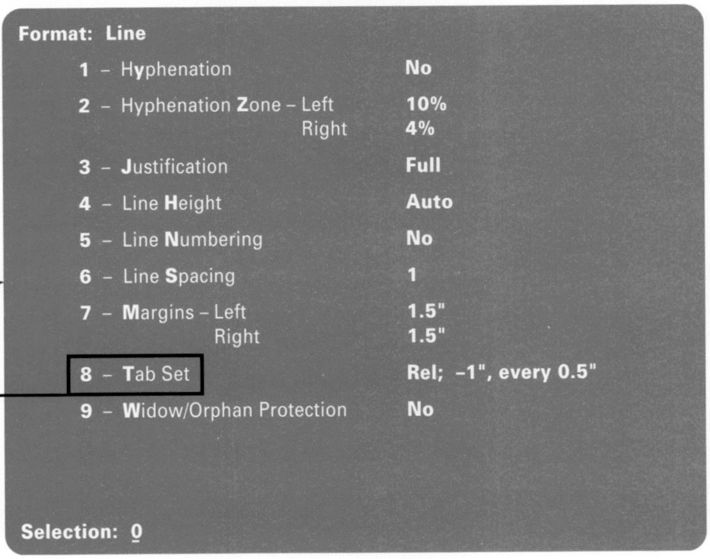

4 Press T (for **T**ab Set).

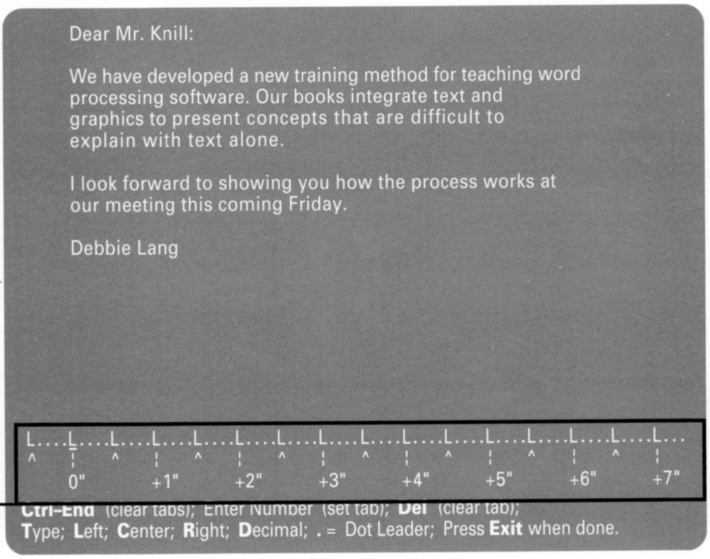

■ The Tab Line appears.

SET TABS

UNDERSTANDING THE TAB LINE

WordPerfect initially sets a left tab at every half inch. The letter **L** on the Tab Line represents a **L**eft tab setting.

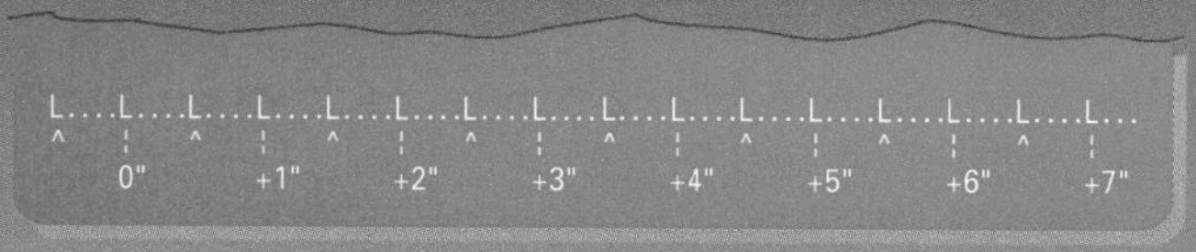

L....L....L....L....L....L....L....L....L....L....L....L....L....L....L....L...
0" +1" +2" +3" +4" +5" +6" +7"

You add or delete tabs using the Tab Line.

L represents a **L**eft tab setting.
C represents a **C**enter tab setting.
R represents a **R**ight tab setting.
D represents a **D**ecimal tab setting.

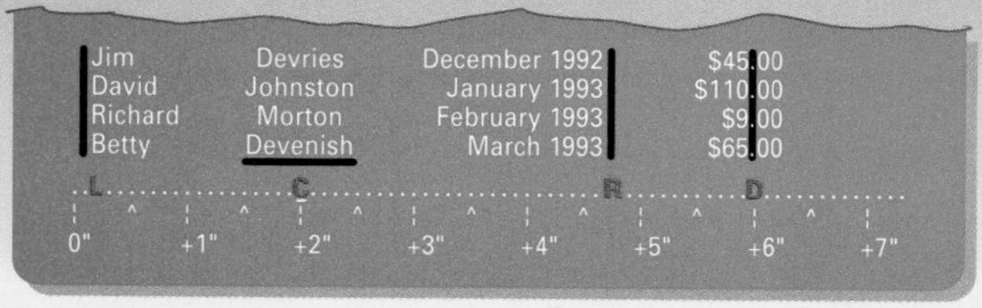

Jim Devries December 1992 $45.00
David Johnston January 1993 $110.00
Richard Morton February 1993 $9.00
Betty Devenish March 1993 $65.00
L C R D
0" +1" +2" +3" +4" +5" +6" +7"

Delete Tabs

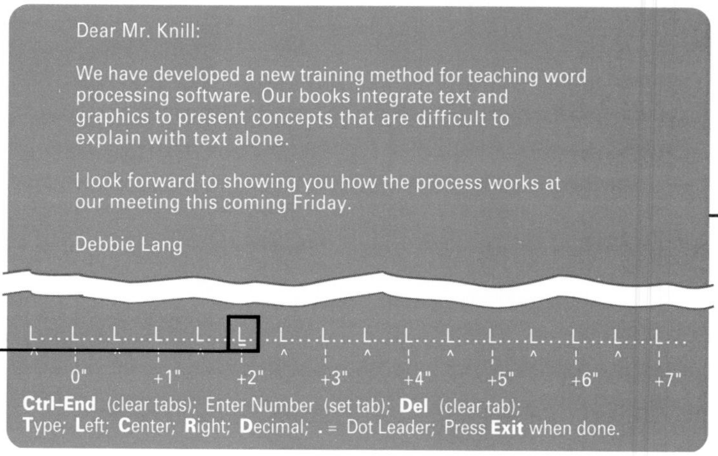

Dear Mr. Knill:
We have developed a new training method for teaching word processing software. Our books integrate text and graphics to present concepts that are difficult to explain with text alone.
I look forward to showing you how the process works at our meeting this coming Friday.
Debbie Lang
0" +1" +2" +3" +4" +5" +6" +7"
Ctrl-End (clear tabs); Enter Number (set tab); Del (clear tab);
Type; Left; Center; Right; Decimal; . = Dot Leader; Press Exit when done.

1 Press → or ← until the cursor is under the tab you want to delete.

Note: To display the Tab Line, refer to page 48.

Add a Tab

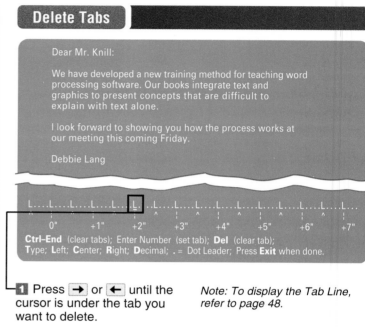

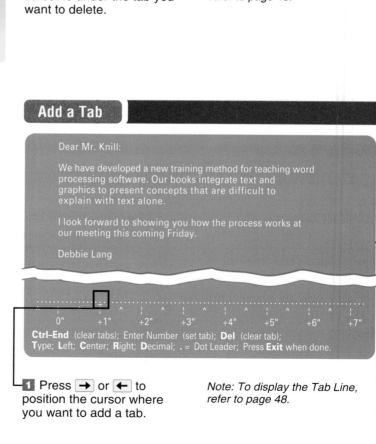

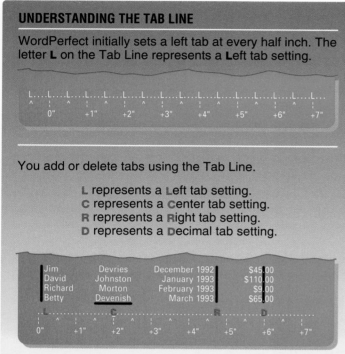

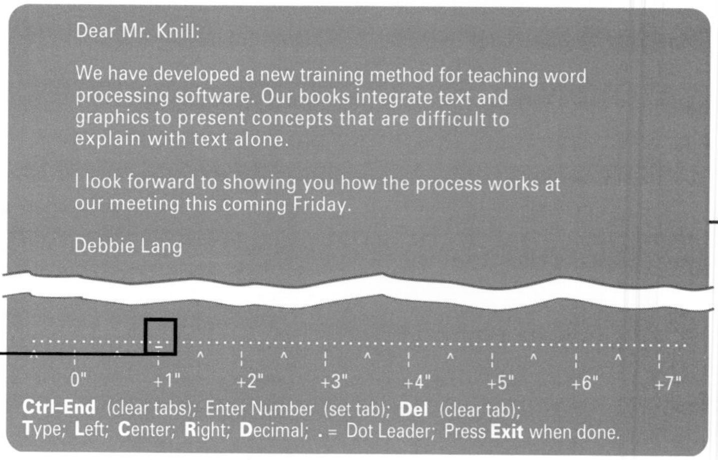

Dear Mr. Knill:
We have developed a new training method for teaching word processing software. Our books integrate text and graphics to present concepts that are difficult to explain with text alone.
I look forward to showing you how the process works at our meeting this coming Friday.
Debbie Lang
0" +1" +2" +3" +4" +5" +6" +7"
Ctrl-End (clear tabs); Enter Number (set tab); Del (clear tab);
Type; Left; Center; Right; Decimal; . = Dot Leader; Press Exit when done.

1 Press → or ← to position the cursor where you want to add a tab.

Note: To display the Tab Line, refer to page 48.

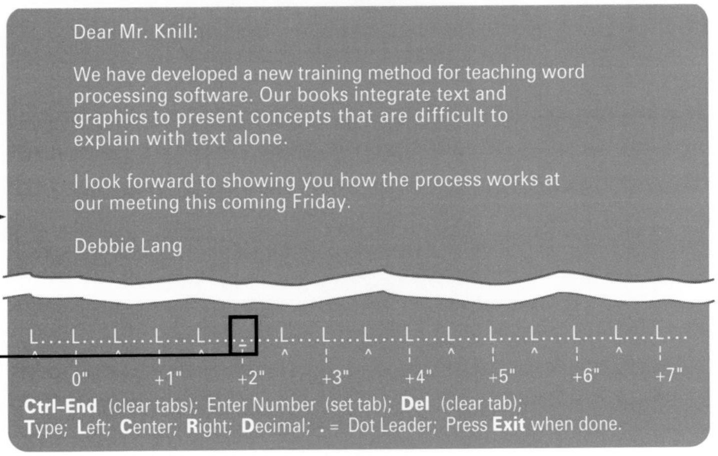
Dear Mr. Knill:
We have developed a new training method for teaching word processing software. Our books integrate text and graphics to present concepts that are difficult to explain with text alone.
I look forward to showing you how the process works at our meeting this coming Friday.
Debbie Lang
0" +1" +2" +3" +4" +5" +6" +7"
Ctrl-End (clear tabs); Enter Number (set tab); Del (clear tab);
Type; Left; Center; Right; Decimal; . = Dot Leader; Press Exit when done.

2 Press Delete to remove the tab.

TO CLEAR ALL TABS

Position the cursor under the far left tab and press Ctrl-End.

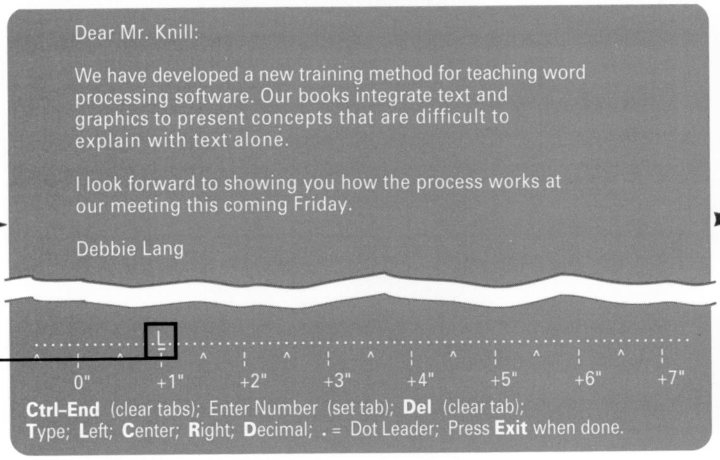
Dear Mr. Knill:
We have developed a new training method for teaching word processing software. Our books integrate text and graphics to present concepts that are difficult to explain with text alone.
I look forward to showing you how the process works at our meeting this coming Friday.
Debbie Lang
0" +1" +2" +3" +4" +5" +6" +7"
Ctrl-End (clear tabs); Enter Number (set tab); Del (clear tab);
Type; Left; Center; Right; Decimal; . = Dot Leader; Press Exit when done.

2 To add a tab, press one of the following:

- **L** for **L**eft tab
- **C** for **C**enter tab
- **R** for **R**ight tab
- **D** for **D**ecimal tab

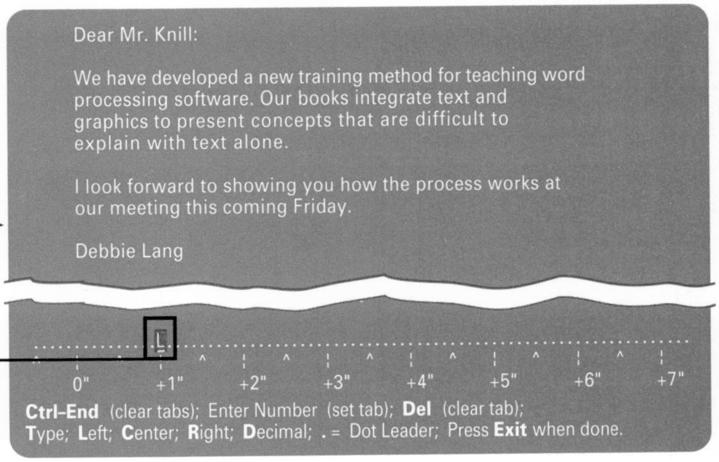
Dear Mr. Knill:
We have developed a new training method for teaching word processing software. Our books integrate text and graphics to present concepts that are difficult to explain with text alone.
I look forward to showing you how the process works at our meeting this coming Friday.
Debbie Lang
0" +1" +2" +3" +4" +5" +6" +7"
Ctrl-End (clear tabs); Enter Number (set tab); Del (clear tab);
Type; Left; Center; Right; Decimal; . = Dot Leader; Press Exit when done.

3 To turn the tab into a dot leader tab, press . (period). The tab setting is now highlighted.

4 To return to the document, press F7 twice.

INDENT TEXT

F4 Indent Left Edge of Paragraph

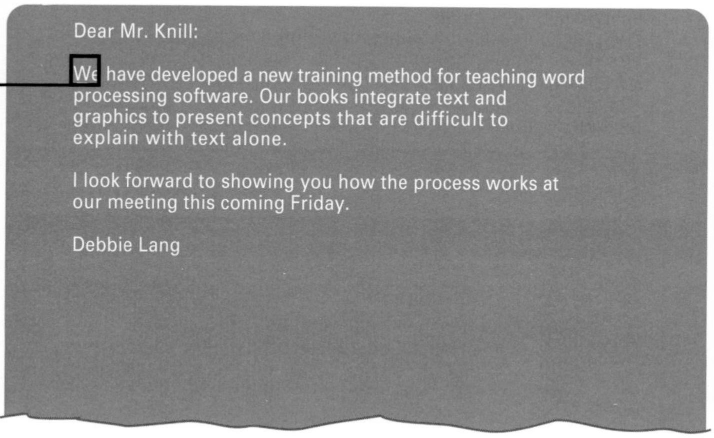
Dear Mr. Knill:
We have developed a new training method for teaching word processing software. Our books integrate text and graphics to present concepts that are difficult to explain with text alone.
I look forward to showing you how the process works at our meeting this coming Friday.
Debbie Lang

1 Position the cursor at the beginning of the paragraph you want to indent.

Note: Indents are dependent upon tab settings.

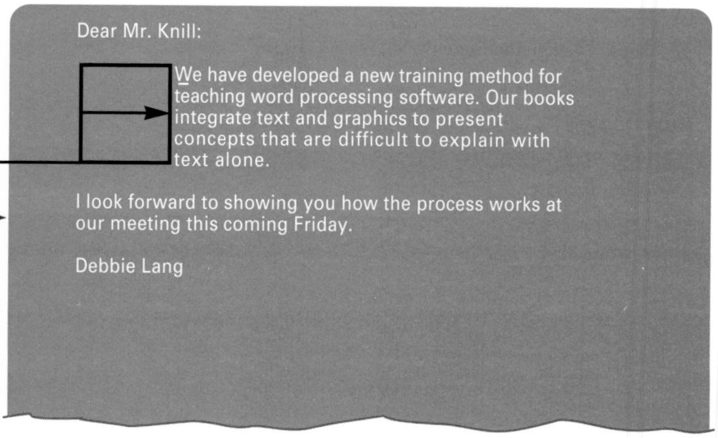
Dear Mr. Knill:
We have developed a new training method for teaching word processing software. Our books integrate text and graphics to present concepts that are difficult to explain with text alone.
I look forward to showing you how the process works at our meeting this coming Friday.
Debbie Lang

2 Press F4 to indent the entire left edge of the paragraph.

TO REMOVE THE INDENT

Press ←Backspace.

Shift F4 Indent Both Edges of Paragraph

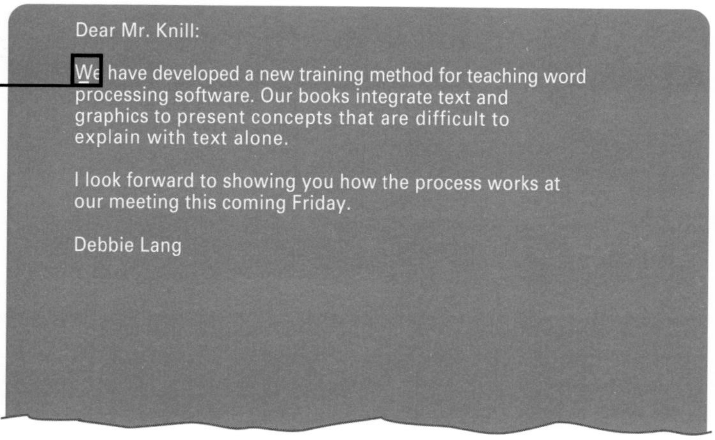
Dear Mr. Knill:
We have developed a new training method for teaching word processing software. Our books integrate text and graphics to present concepts that are difficult to explain with text alone.
I look forward to showing you how the process works at our meeting this coming Friday.
Debbie Lang

1 Position the cursor at the beginning of the paragraph you want to indent.

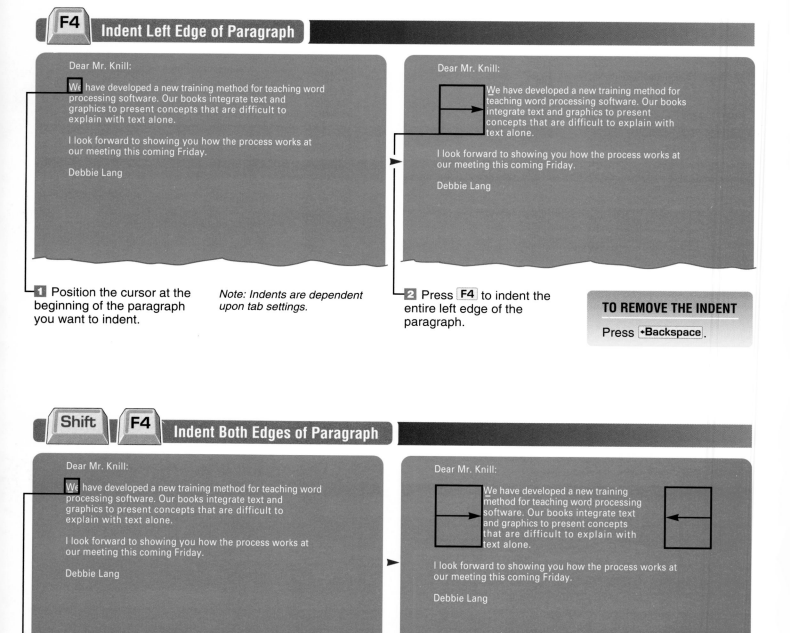

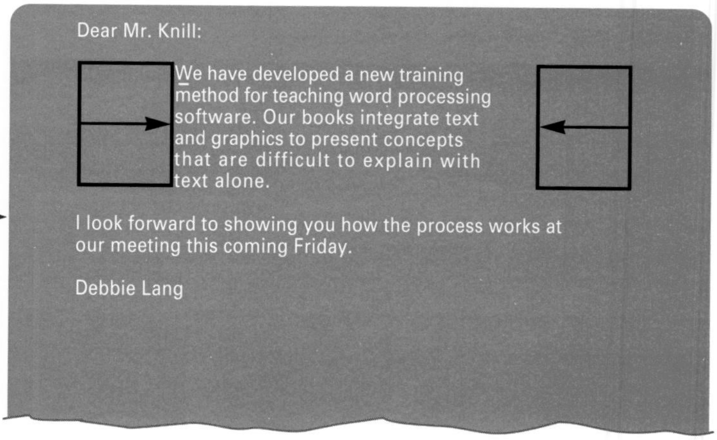
Dear Mr. Knill:
We have developed a new training method for teaching word processing software. Our books integrate text and graphics to present concepts that are difficult to explain with text alone.
I look forward to showing you how the process works at our meeting this coming Friday.
Debbie Lang

2 Press Shift - F4 to indent both edges of the paragraph.

TO REMOVE THE INDENT

Press ←Backspace.

INDENT NEW TEXT

Indent Left Edge of Paragraph

1. Position the cursor where you want the text to appear.
2. Press F4, then type the text.
3. Press Enter to turn off the indent.

Indent Both Edges of Paragraph

1. Position the cursor where you want the text to appear.
2. Press Shift - F4, then type the text.
3. Press Enter to turn off the indent.

Hanging Indents

1. Position the cursor where you want the text to appear.
2. Press F4.
3. Press Shift - Tab, then type the text.
4. Press Enter to turn off the indent.

Shift Tab Hanging Indents

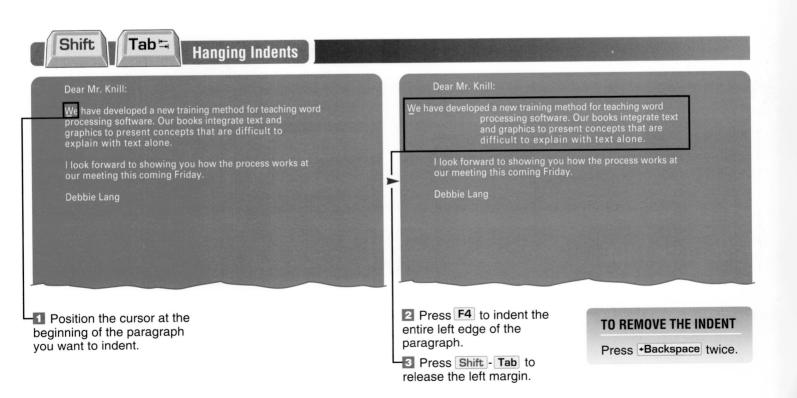

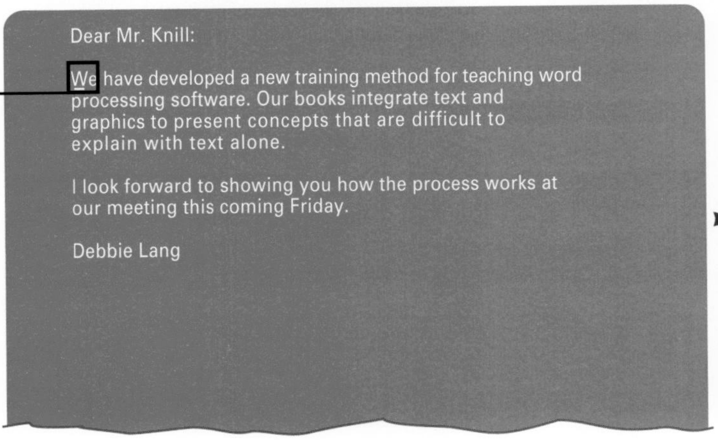
Dear Mr. Knill:
We have developed a new training method for teaching word processing software. Our books integrate text and graphics to present concepts that are difficult to explain with text alone.
I look forward to showing you how the process works at our meeting this coming Friday.
Debbie Lang

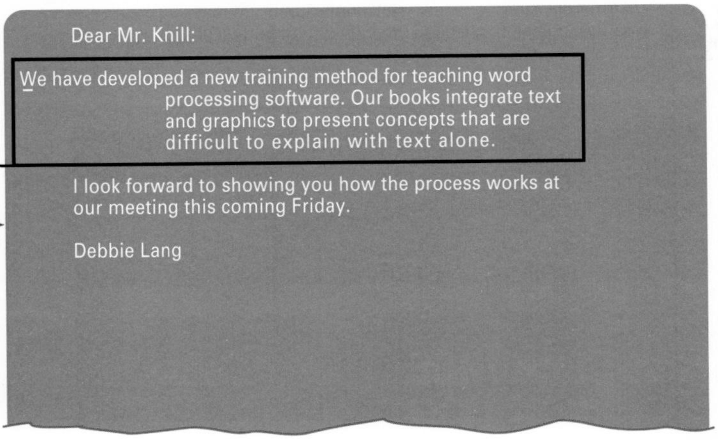
Dear Mr. Knill:
We have developed a new training method for teaching word processing software. Our books integrate text and graphics to present concepts that are difficult to explain with text alone.
I look forward to showing you how the process works at our meeting this coming Friday.
Debbie Lang

1. Position the cursor at the beginning of the paragraph you want to indent.
2. Press F4 to indent the entire left edge of the paragraph.
3. Press Shift - Tab to release the left margin.

TO REMOVE THE INDENT

Press ←Backspace twice.

JUSTIFY TEXT

WordPerfect prints your text fully justified unless you change the setting. WordPerfect cannot display fully justified text on the screen, so it appears left justified.

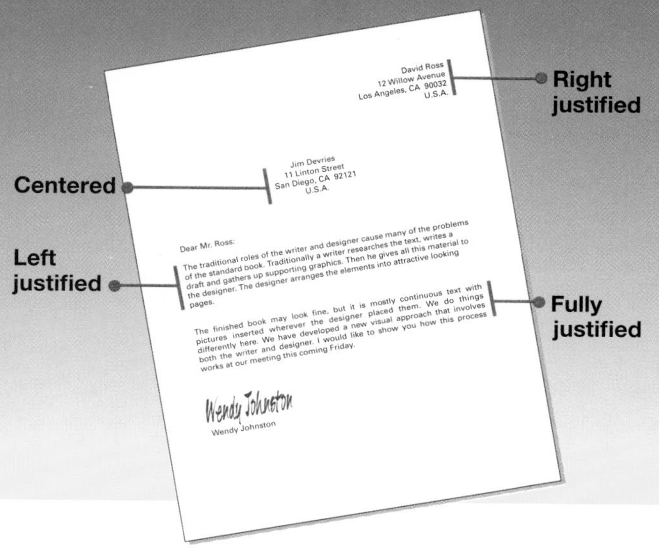

Shift F8 Left or Fully Justify Text

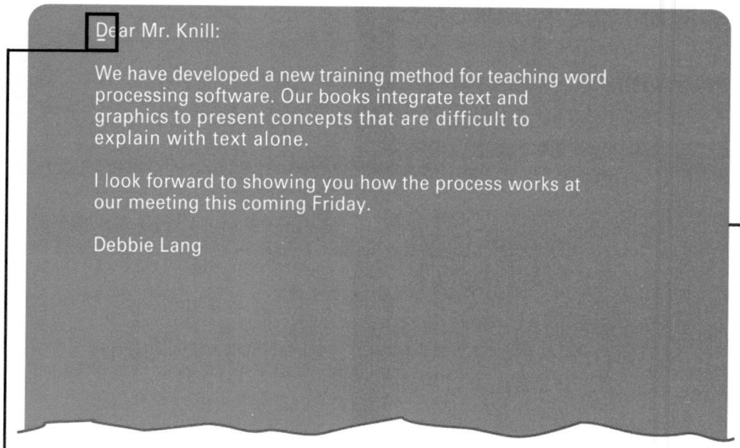

Dear Mr. Knill:

We have developed a new training method for teaching word processing software. Our books integrate text and graphics to present concepts that are difficult to explain with text alone.

I look forward to showing you how the process works at our meeting this coming Friday.

Debbie Lang

1 Position the cursor where you want the new justification to begin.

Shift F6 Center Text

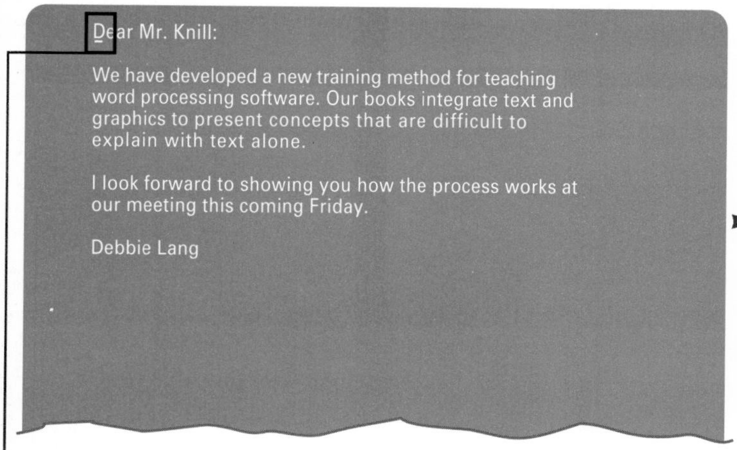

Dear Mr. Knill:

We have developed a new training method for teaching word processing software. Our books integrate text and graphics to present concepts that are difficult to explain with text alone.

I look forward to showing you how the process works at our meeting this coming Friday.

Debbie Lang

1 Position the cursor at the beginning of the line you want to center.

Dear Mr. Knill:

We have developed a new training method for teaching word processing software. Our books integrate text and graphics to present concepts that are difficult to explain with text alone.

I look forward to showing you how the process works at our meeting this coming Friday.

Debbie Lang

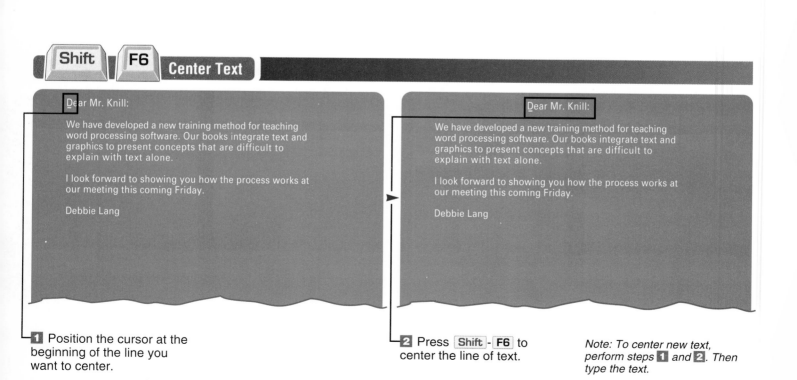

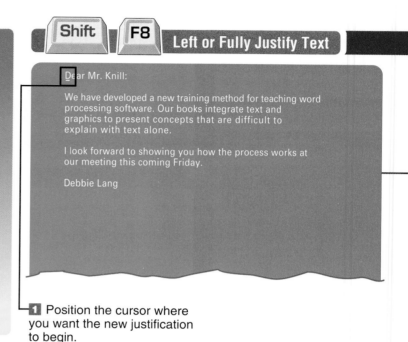

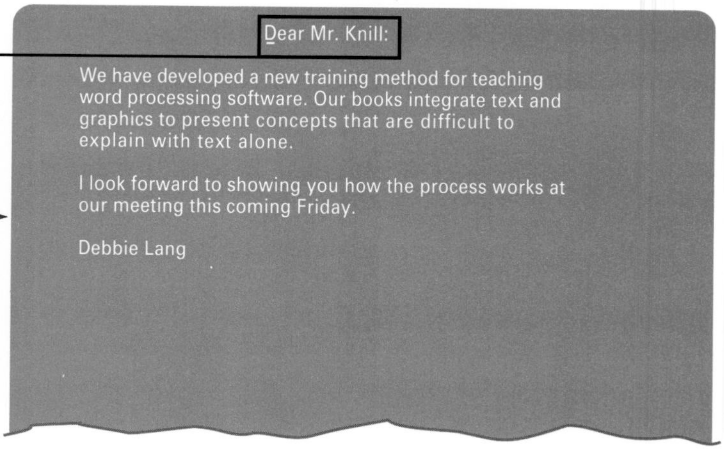

2 Press Shift - F6 to center the line of text.

Note: To center new text, perform steps 1 and 2. Then type the text.

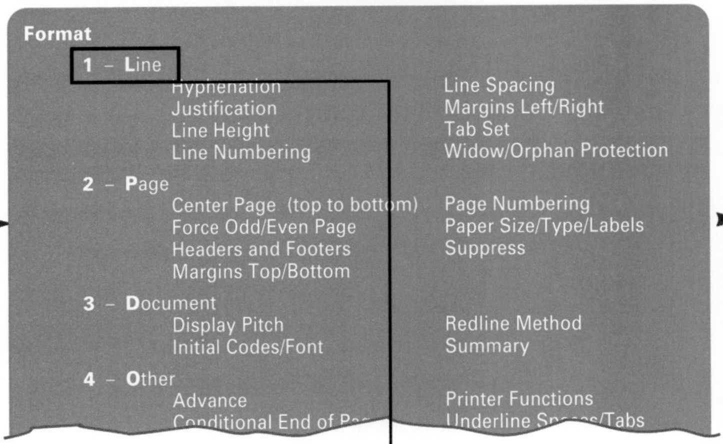

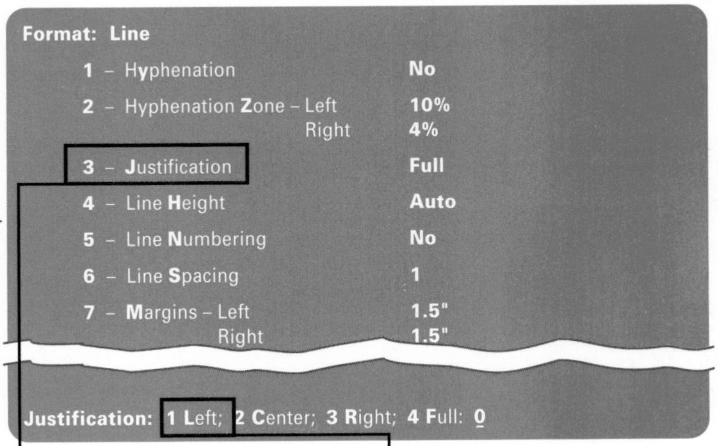

2 Press Shift - F8 and the **Format** screen appears.

3 Press L (for **L**ine).

4 Press J (for **J**ustification).

5 To left justify the text, press L (for **L**eft).

*Note: To fully justify the text, press F (for **F**ull).*

6 Press F7 to return to the document.

Alt F6 Right Justify Text

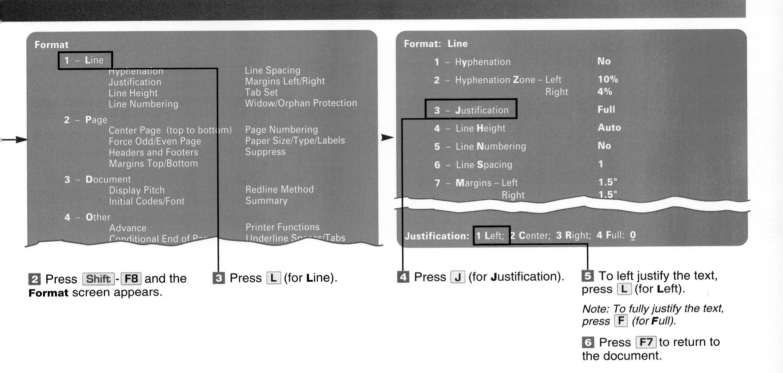

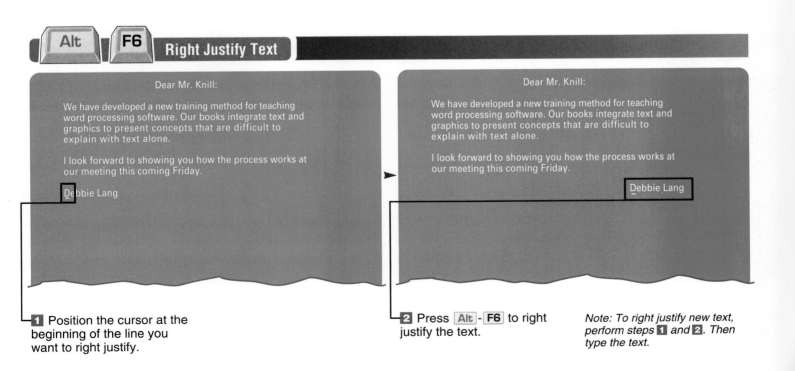

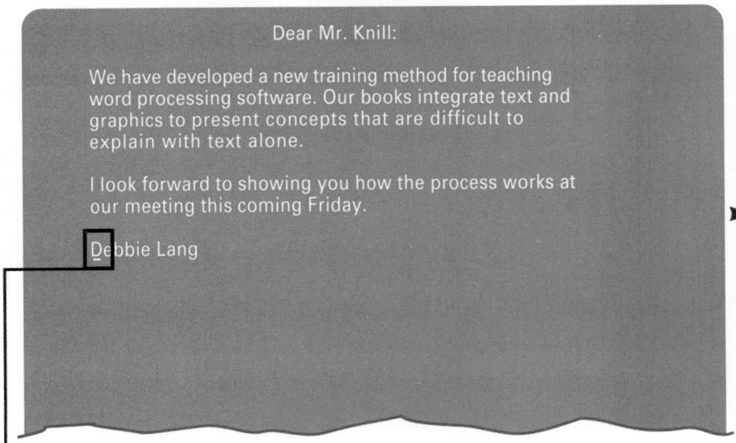

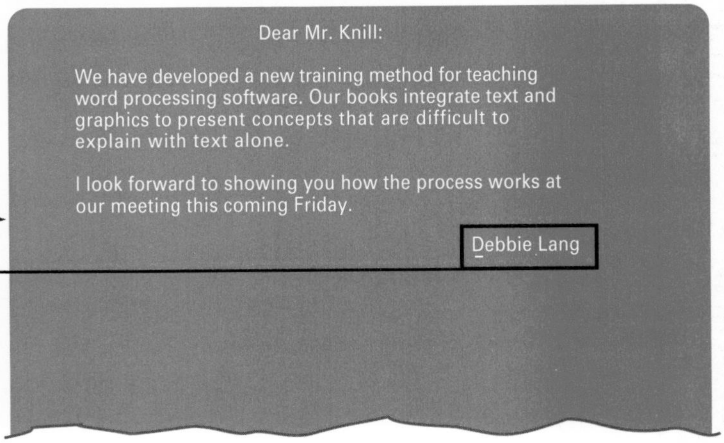

1 Position the cursor at the beginning of the line you want to right justify.

2 Press Alt - F6 to right justify the text.

*Note: To right justify new text, perform steps **1** and **2**. Then type the text.*

Ctrl F8 Change the Base Font

You can change the font of the text in your document. Here are some examples:

Avant Garde

Bookman

Courier

Helvetica

Times Roman

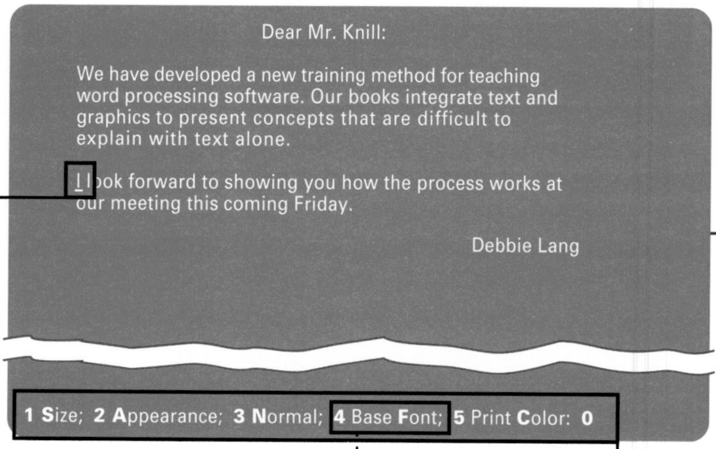
Dear Mr. Knill:
We have developed a new training method for teaching word processing software. Our books integrate text and graphics to present concepts that are difficult to explain with text alone.
I look forward to showing you how the process works at our meeting this coming Friday.
Debbie Lang
1 Size; 2 Appearance; 3 Normal; 4 Base Font; 5 Print Color: 0

1 Position the cursor where you want the new font to begin.

2 Press Ctrl - F8 and this message appears.

3 Press F (for Base **F**ont).

Shift F7 View a Document

It is possible to see how a document will appear on a printed page. This is very useful for viewing features that you do not see on the screen, but will appear on the printed document.

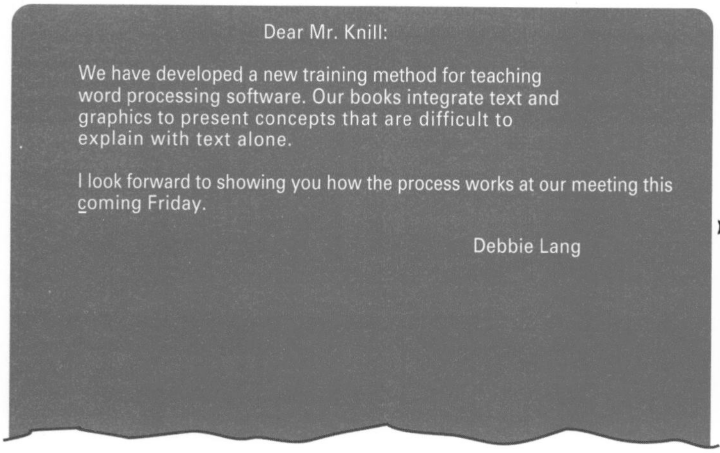
Dear Mr. Knill:
We have developed a new training method for teaching word processing software. Our books integrate text and graphics to present concepts that are difficult to explain with text alone.
I look forward to showing you how the process works at our meeting this coming Friday.
Debbie Lang

1 Press Shift - F7 and the **Print** menu appears.

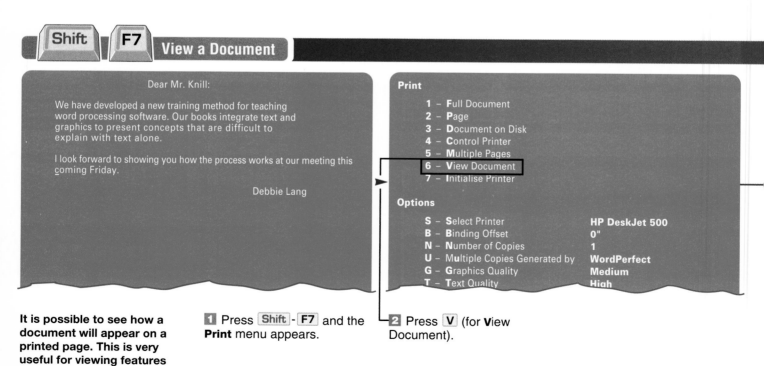

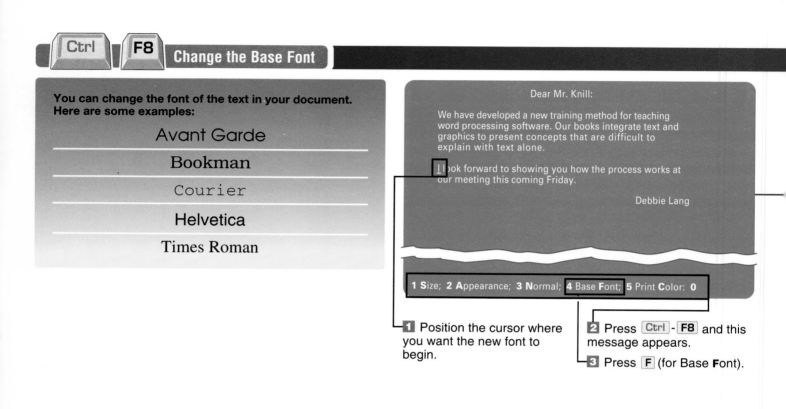

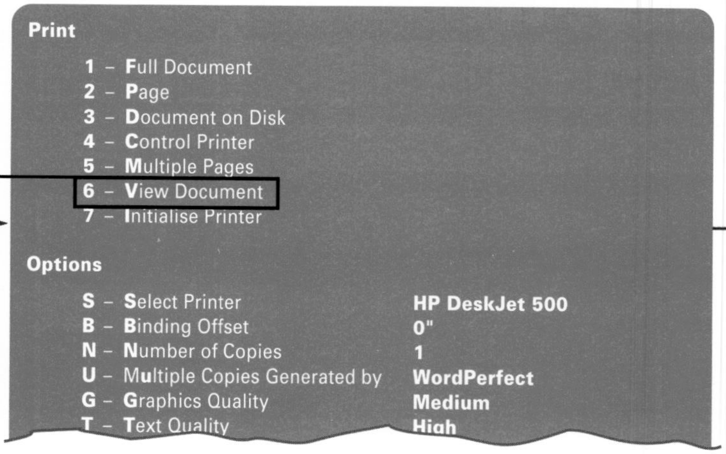
Print
1 - Full Document
2 - Page
3 - Document on Disk
4 - Control Printer
5 - Multiple Pages
6 - View Document
7 - Initialise Printer
Options
S - Select Printer
HP DeskJet 500
B - Binding Offset
0"
N - Number of Copies
1
U - Multiple Copies Generated by
WordPerfect
G - Graphics Quality
Medium
T - Text Quality
High

2 Press V (for **V**iew Document).

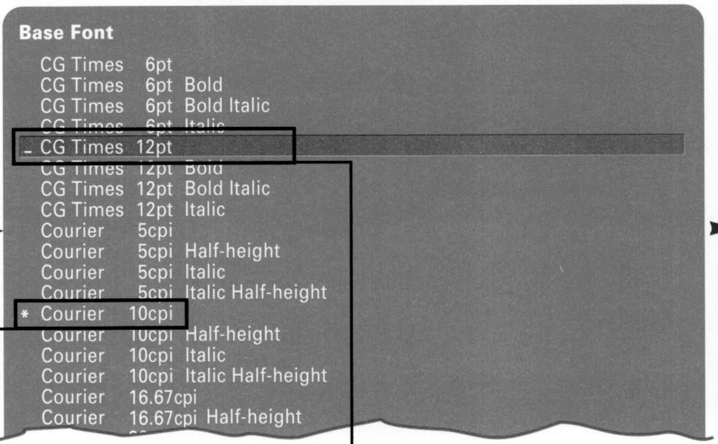
Base Font
CG Times 6pt
CG Times 6pt Bold
CG Times 6pt Bold Italic
CG Times 12pt
CG Times 12pt Bold Italic
CG Times 12pt Italic
Courier 5cpi
Courier 5cpi Half-height
Courier 5cpi Italic
Courier 5cpi Italic Half-height
* Courier 10cpi
Courier 10cpi Half-height
Courier 10cpi Italic
Courier 10cpi Italic Half-height
Courier 16.67cpi
Courier 16.67cpi Half-height

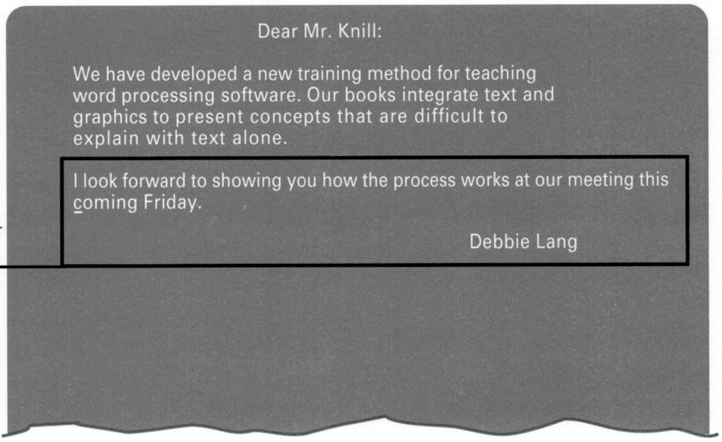
Dear Mr. Knill:
We have developed a new training method for teaching word processing software. Our books integrate text and graphics to present concepts that are difficult to explain with text alone.
I look forward to showing you how the process works at our meeting this coming Friday.
Debbie Lang

■ A list of available fonts for your printer appears.

■ The current font displays an ✱ (asterisk) beside its name.

4 Press ↑ or ↓ until you highlight the desired font (example: **CG Times 12pt**). Then press Enter.

*Note: **pt** stands for **point**. There are 72 points in an inch.*

■ All text after the cursor changes to the new font.

Note: WordPerfect cannot display the new font. To view the new font, refer to "View a Document" below.

5 Press ↓ to refresh the screen.

Note: Your text may wrap differently than shown above.

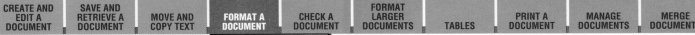

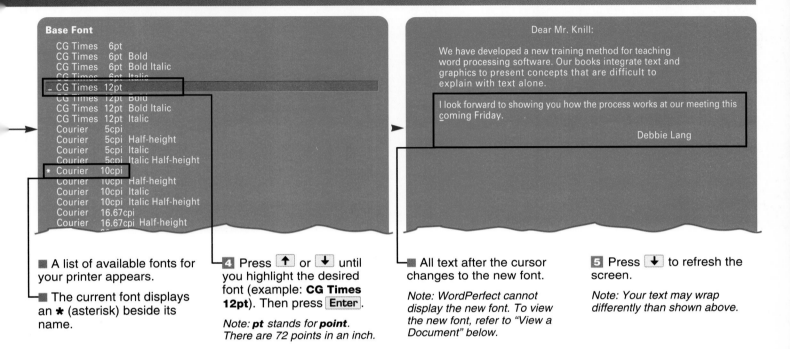

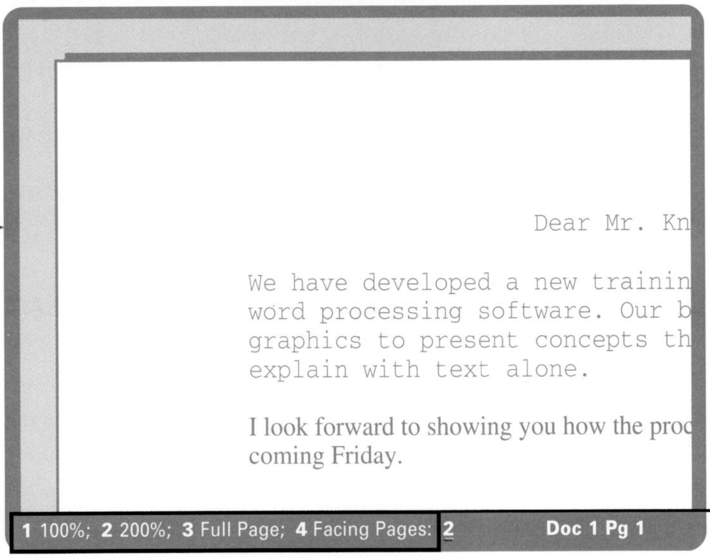
Dear Mr. Kn
We have developed a new trainin
word processing software. Our b
graphics to present concepts th
explain with text alone.
I look forward to showing you how the proc
coming Friday.
1 100%; 2 200%; 3 Full Page; 4 Facing Pages: 2
Doc 1 Pg 1

■ WordPerfect displays the document as it will look when printed.

3 Press F7 to return to the document.

VIEWING OPTIONS

Press 1 to view the document at 100%.

Press 2 to view the document at 200%.

Press 3 to view the entire page.

Press 4 to view facing pages.

BOLD OR UNDERLINE TEXT

F6 Bold Existing Text

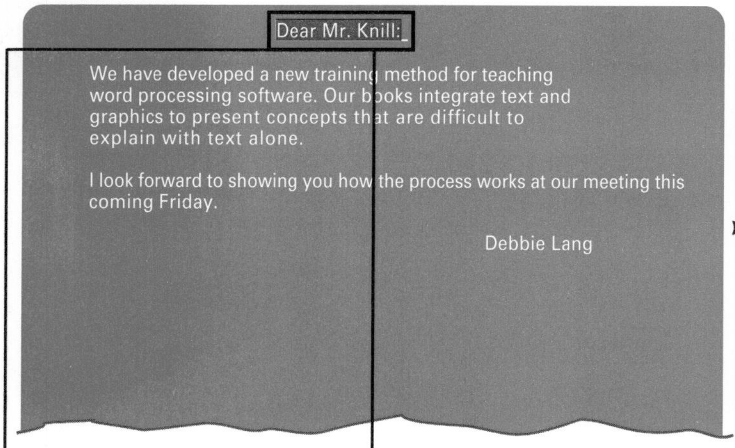
Dear Mr. Knill:_

We have developed a new training method for teaching word processing software. Our books integrate text and graphics to present concepts that are difficult to explain with text alone.

I look forward to showing you how the process works at our meeting this coming Friday.

Debbie Lang

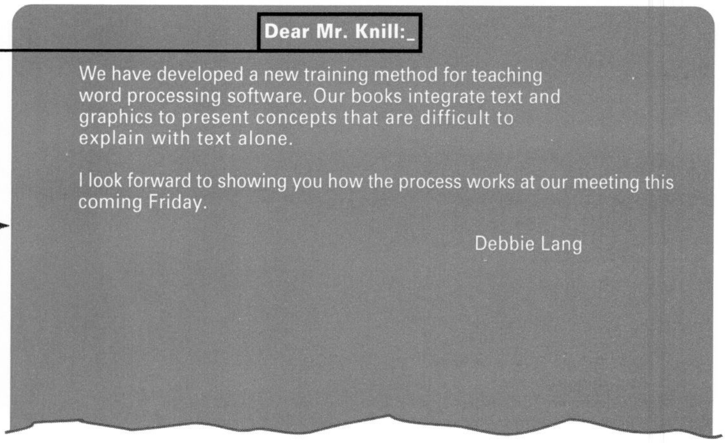
Dear Mr. Knill:_

We have developed a new training method for teaching word processing software. Our books integrate text and graphics to present concepts that are difficult to explain with text alone.

I look forward to showing you how the process works at our meeting this coming Friday.

Debbie Lang

1 Position the cursor at the beginning of the text you want to bold.

2 Press F12 or Alt-F4.

3 Press →, ↓, ← or ↑ until you highlight the text you want to bold.

4 Press F6 to bold the text.

F8 Underline Existing Text

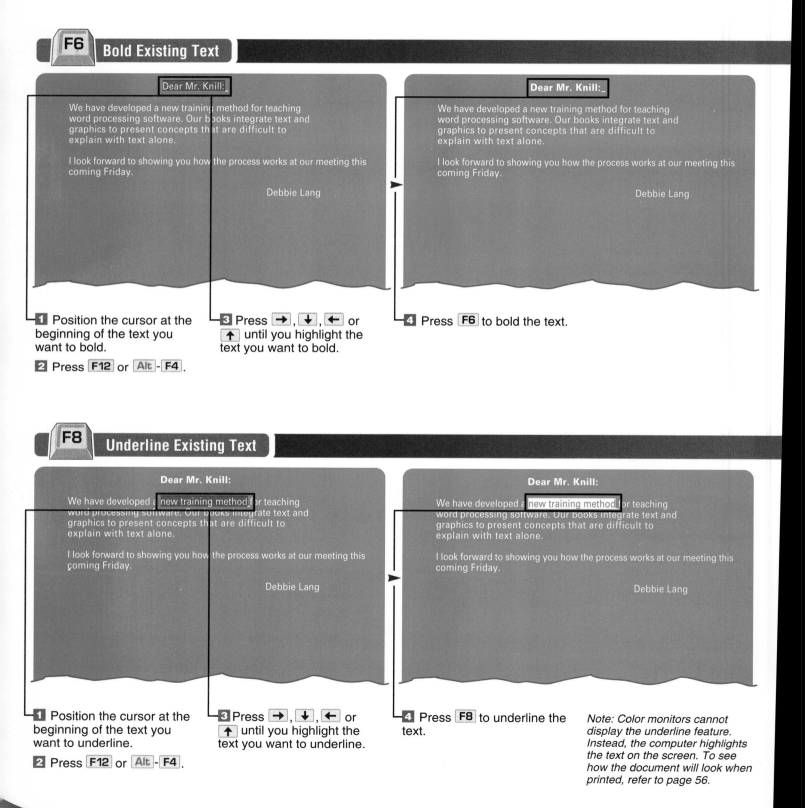

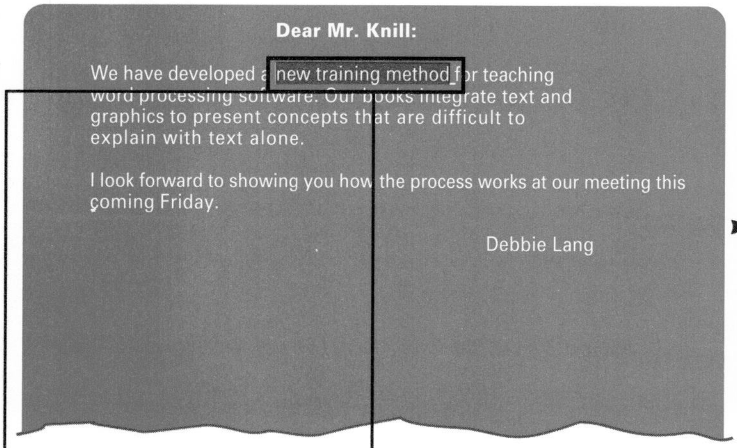
Dear Mr. Knill:

We have developed a new training method for teaching word processing software. Our books integrate text and graphics to present concepts that are difficult to explain with text alone.

I look forward to showing you how the process works at our meeting this coming Friday.

Debbie Lang

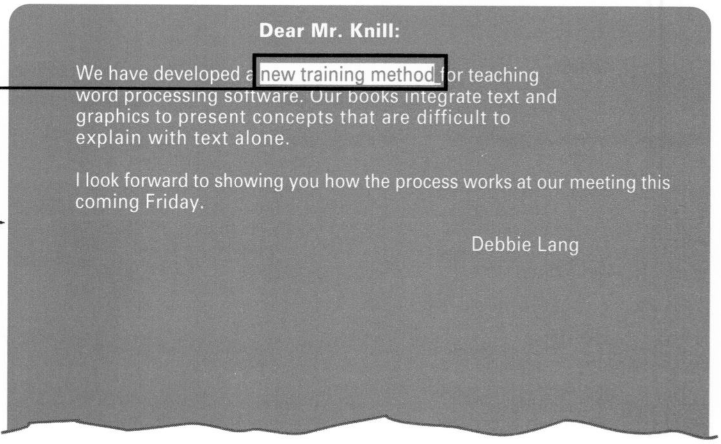
Dear Mr. Knill:

We have developed a new training method for teaching word processing software. Our books integrate text and graphics to present concepts that are difficult to explain with text alone.

I look forward to showing you how the process works at our meeting this coming Friday.

Debbie Lang

1 Position the cursor at the beginning of the text you want to underline.

2 Press F12 or Alt-F4.

3 Press →, ↓, ← or ↑ until you highlight the text you want to underline.

4 Press F8 to underline the text.

Note: Color monitors cannot display the underline feature. Instead, the computer highlights the text on the screen. To see how the document will look when printed, refer to page 56.

F11 Reveal Codes

BOLD NEW TEXT

1. Position the cursor where you want the text to appear.
2. Press F6.
3. Type the text.
4. To turn off bold, press F6 again.

UNDERLINE NEW TEXT

1. Position the cursor where you want the text to appear.
2. Press F8.
3. Type the text.
4. To turn off underline, press F8 again.

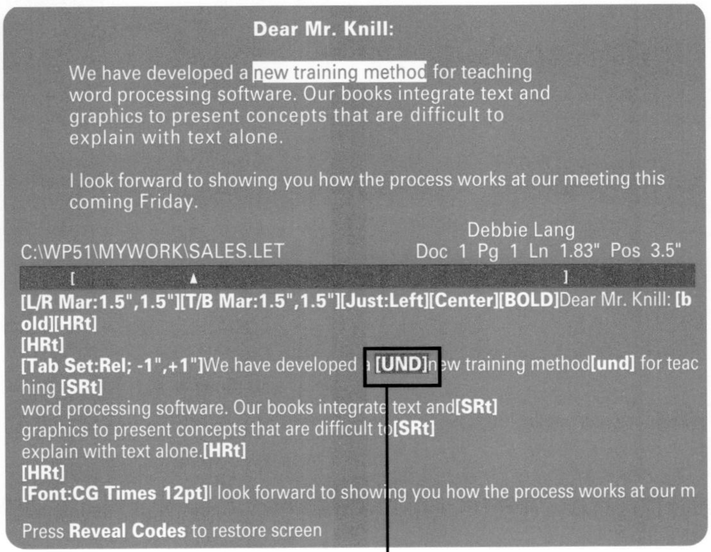
Dear Mr. Knill:
We have developed a new training method for teaching word processing software. Our books integrate text and graphics to present concepts that are difficult to explain with text alone.
I look forward to showing you how the process works at our meeting this coming Friday.
Debbie Lang
C:\WP51\MYWORK\SALES.LET
Doc 1 Pg 1 Ln 1.83" Pos 3.5"
[L/R Mar:1.5",1.5"][T/B Mar:1.5",1.5"][Just:Left][Center][BOLD]Dear Mr. Knill: [bold][HRt]
[HRt]
[Tab Set:Rel; -1",+1"]We have developed a [UND]new training method[und] for teaching [SRt]
word processing software. Our books integrate text and[SRt]
graphics to present concepts that are difficult to[SRt]
explain with text alone.[HRt]
[HRt]
[Font:CG Times 12pt]I look forward to showing you how the process works at our m
Press Reveal Codes to restore screen

1. To display the WordPerfect codes, press F11 or Alt-F3.
2. To remove a text format (example: remove an underline), position the cursor on the code you want to remove (example: **[UND]**).
3. Press Delete.

Note: To hide the Reveal Codes screen, press F11 again.

This screen displays the following format codes:

[BOLD] [bold]
The text between these two codes prints in a bold format.

[Center]
The text following this code is centered on the line.

[Font:CG Times 12pt]
The text after this code will print in the CG Times 12 point font.

[Just:Left]
The text on this line is left justified.

[L/R Mar:1.5",1.5"]
The text after this code has 1.5 inch left and right margins.

[T/B Mar:1.5",1.5"]
The text after this code has 1.5 inch top and bottom margins.

[Tab Set:Rel; -1",+1"]
The text after this code has a tab set at 1 inch.

[UND] [und]
The text between these two codes prints with an underline.

CHANGE TEXT APPEARANCE

Ctrl F8 Change Text Appearance

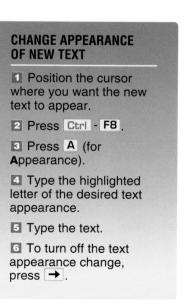

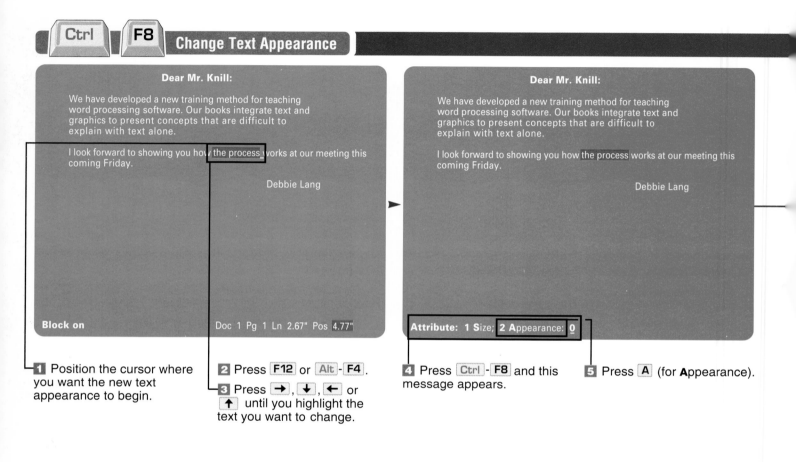

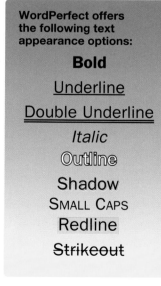

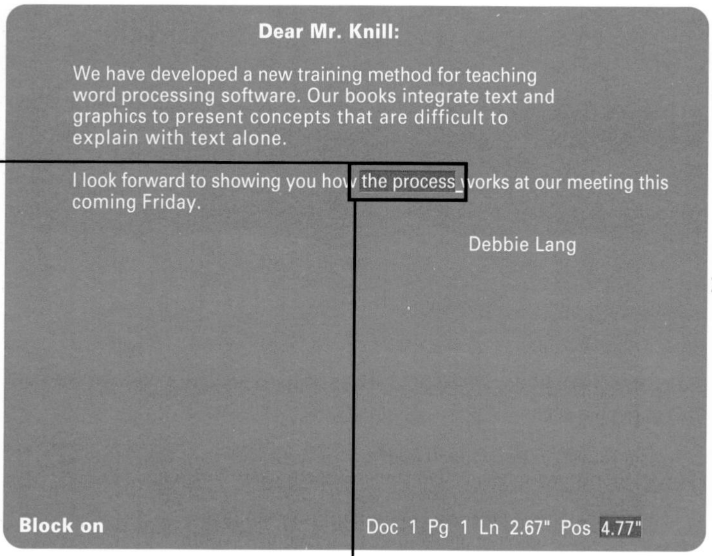
Dear Mr. Knill:
We have developed a new training method for teaching word processing software. Our books integrate text and graphics to present concepts that are difficult to explain with text alone.
I look forward to showing you how the process works at our meeting this coming Friday.
Debbie Lang
Block on
Doc 1 Pg 1 Ln 2.67" Pos 4.77"

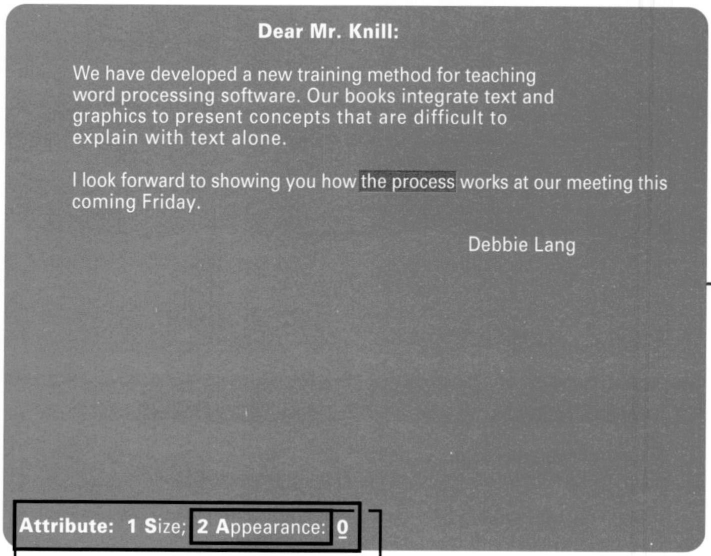
Dear Mr. Knill:
We have developed a new training method for teaching word processing software. Our books integrate text and graphics to present concepts that are difficult to explain with text alone.
I look forward to showing you how the process works at our meeting this coming Friday.
Debbie Lang
Attribute: 1 Size; 2 Appearance: 0

1 Position the cursor where you want the new text appearance to begin.

2 Press F12 or Alt - F4.

3 Press →, ↓, ← or ↑ until you highlight the text you want to change.

4 Press Ctrl - F8 and this message appears.

5 Press A (for **A**ppearance).

WordPerfect offers the following text appearance options:

Bold

Underline

Double Underline

Italic

Outline

Shadow

Small Caps

Redline

~~Strikeout~~

CHANGE APPEARANCE OF NEW TEXT

1 Position the cursor where you want the new text to appear.

2 Press Ctrl - F8.

3 Press A (for **A**ppearance).

4 Type the highlighted letter of the desired text appearance.

5 Type the text.

6 To turn off the text appearance change, press →.

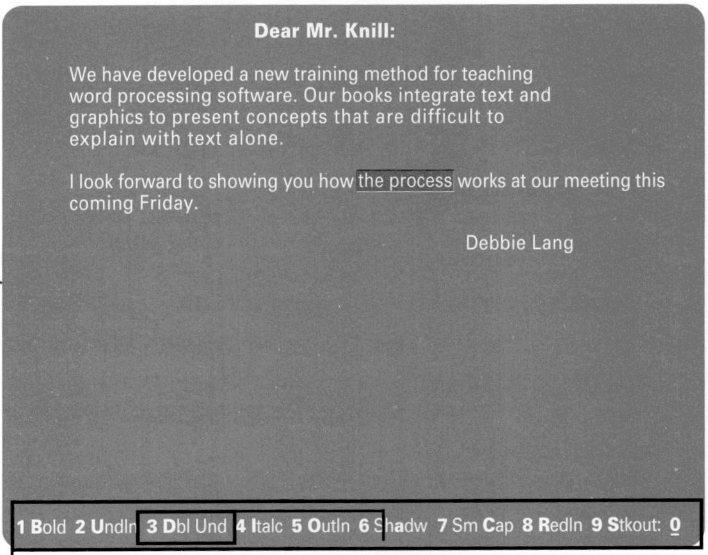
Dear Mr. Knill:
We have developed a new training method for teaching word processing software. Our books integrate text and graphics to present concepts that are difficult to explain with text alone.
I look forward to showing you how the process works at our meeting this coming Friday.
Debbie Lang
1 Bold 2 Undln 3 Dbl Und 4 Italc 5 Outln 6 Shadw 7 Sm Cap 8 Redln 9 Stkout: 0

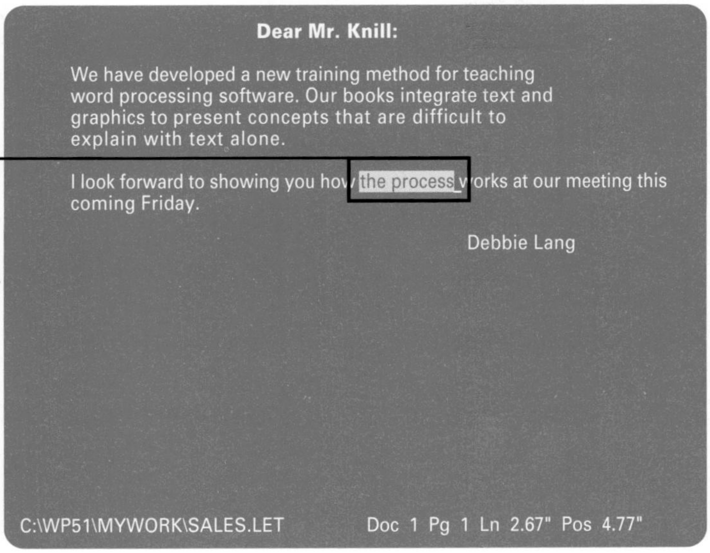
Dear Mr. Knill:
We have developed a new training method for teaching word processing software. Our books integrate text and graphics to present concepts that are difficult to explain with text alone.
I look forward to showing you how the process works at our meeting this coming Friday.
Debbie Lang
C:\WP51\MYWORK\SALES.LET
Doc 1 Pg 1 Ln 2.67" Pos 4.77"

■ The appearance options appear.

6 Type the highlighted letter of the desired text appearance (example: D for **D**bl Und).

■ All blocked text changes to the new text appearance.

■ WordPerfect cannot display the new text appearance on the screen. Instead, WordPerfect highlights the text to indicate the change. When you print the document, the text appearance change will print.

Note: To view the new text appearance before printing, refer to page 56.

Some printers cannot print all of the appearance options. Retrieve and print the file entitled **\WP51\PRINTER.TST** to see the capabilities of your printer.

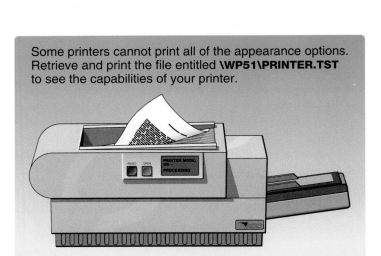

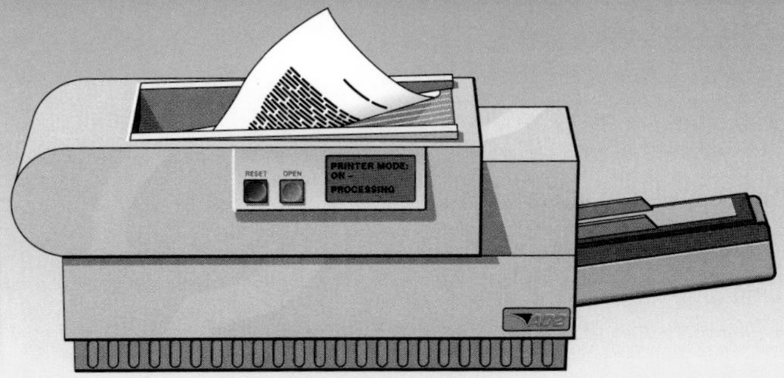
RESET
OPEN
PRINTER MODE: ON - PROCESSING

CHANGE TEXT SIZE

Ctrl F8 Change Text Size

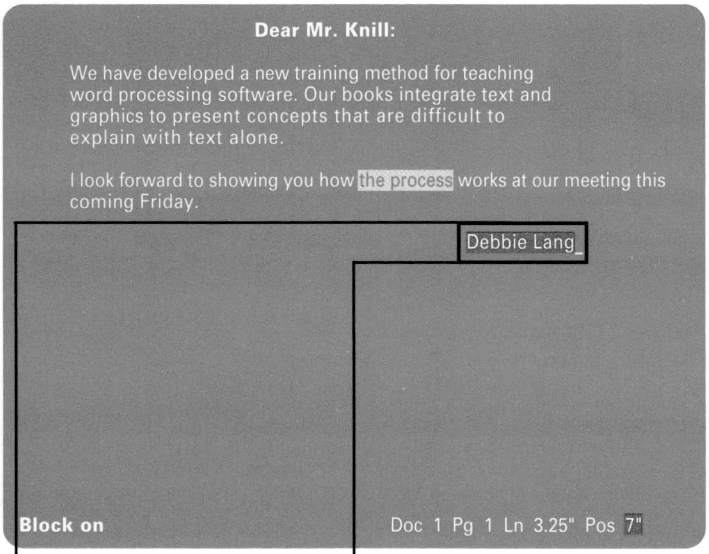

Dear Mr. Knill:
We have developed a new training method for teaching word processing software. Our books integrate text and graphics to present concepts that are difficult to explain with text alone.
I look forward to showing you how the process works at our meeting this coming Friday.
Debbie Lang_
Block on
Doc 1 Pg 1 Ln 3.25" Pos 7"

1 Position the cursor where you want the new text size to begin.

2 Press F12 or Alt - F4.

3 Press →, ↓, ← or ↑ until you highlight the text you want to change.

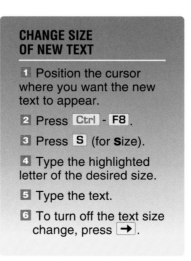

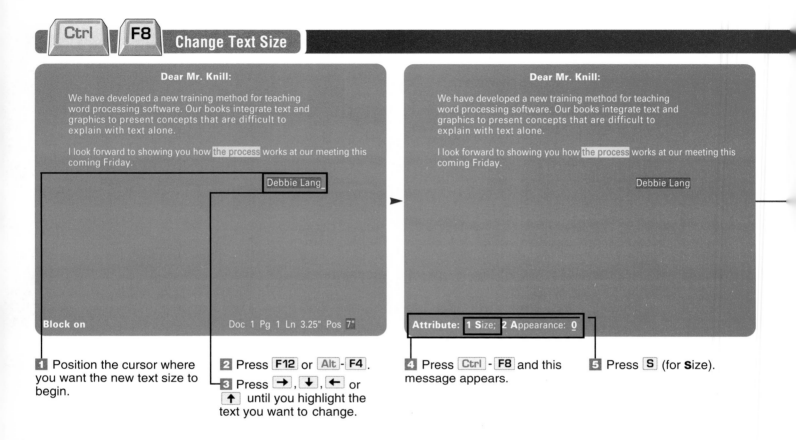

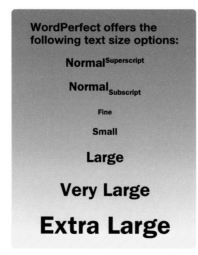

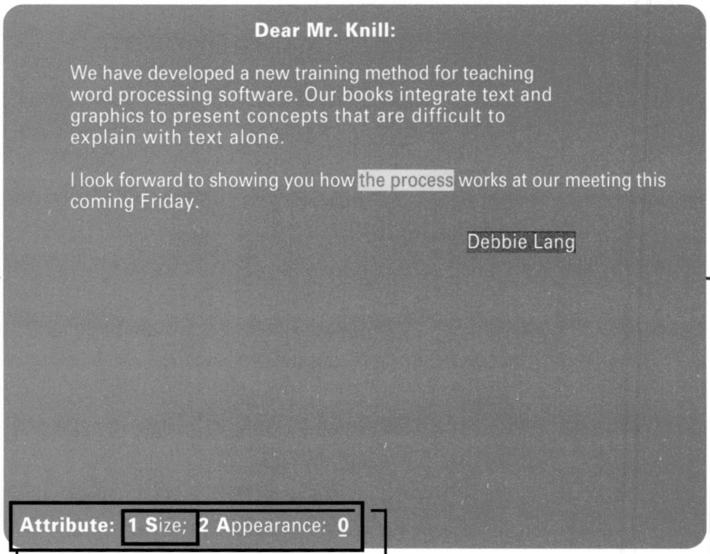

4 Press Ctrl - F8 and this message appears.

5 Press S (for **S**ize).

WordPerfect offers the following text size options:

NormalSuperscript

NormalSubscript

Fine

Small

Large

Very Large

Extra Large

CHANGE SIZE OF NEW TEXT

1 Position the cursor where you want the new text to appear.

2 Press Ctrl - F8.

3 Press S (for **S**ize).

4 Type the highlighted letter of the desired size.

5 Type the text.

6 To turn off the text size change, press →.

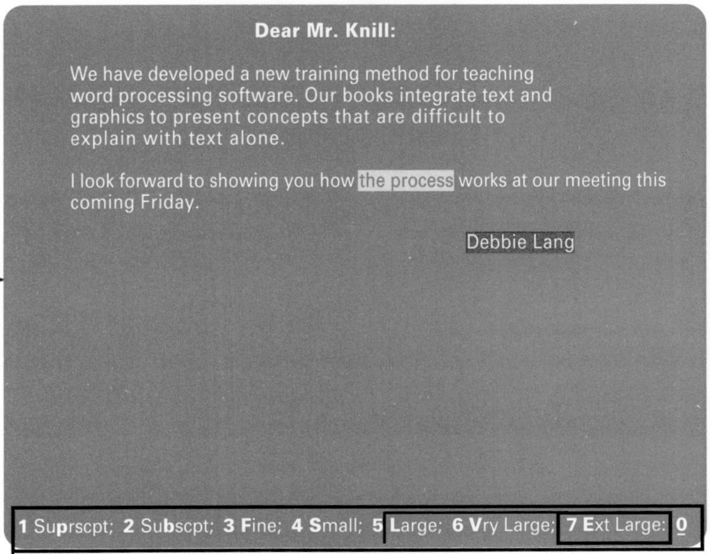
Dear Mr. Knill:
We have developed a new training method for teaching word processing software. Our books integrate text and graphics to present concepts that are difficult to explain with text alone.
I look forward to showing you how the process works at our meeting this coming Friday.
Debbie Lang
1 Suprscpt; 2 Subscpt; 3 Fine; 4 Small; 5 Large; 6 Vry Large; 7 Ext Large: 0

- The size options appear.

6 Type the highlighted letter of the desired size (example: **E** for **E**xt Large).

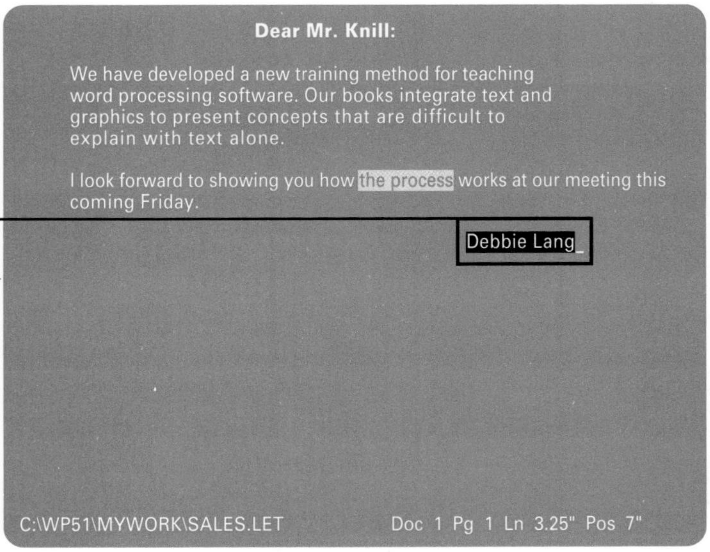
Dear Mr. Knill:
We have developed a new training method for teaching word processing software. Our books integrate text and graphics to present concepts that are difficult to explain with text alone.
I look forward to showing you how the process works at our meeting this coming Friday.
Debbie Lang
C:\WP51\MYWORK\SALES.LET
Doc 1 Pg 1 Ln 3.25" Pos 7"

- All blocked text changes to the new text size.

- WordPerfect cannot display the new text size on the screen. Instead, WordPerfect highlights the text to indicate the change. When you print the document, the text size change will print.

Note: To view the new text size before printing, refer to page 56.

Some printers cannot print all of the text size options. Retrieve and print the file entitled **\WP51\PRINTER.TST** to see the capabilities of your printer.

SPELL CHECKER

Ctrl F2 Spell Check a Document, Page or Word

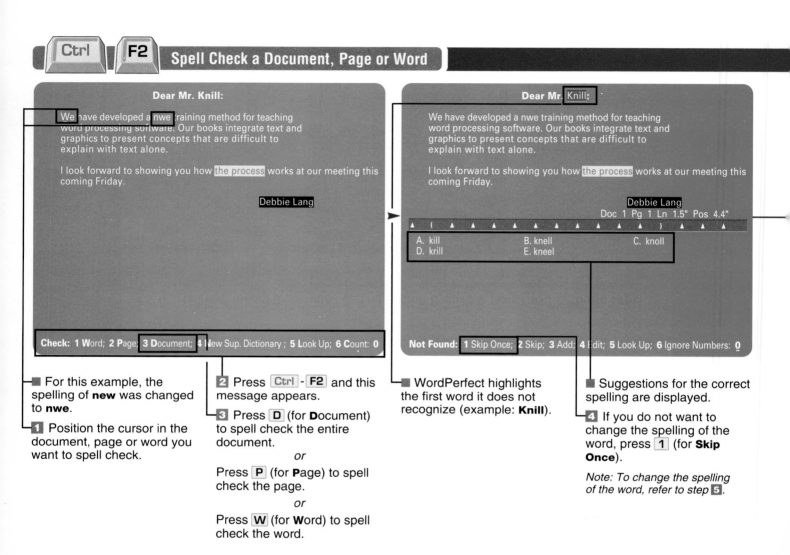

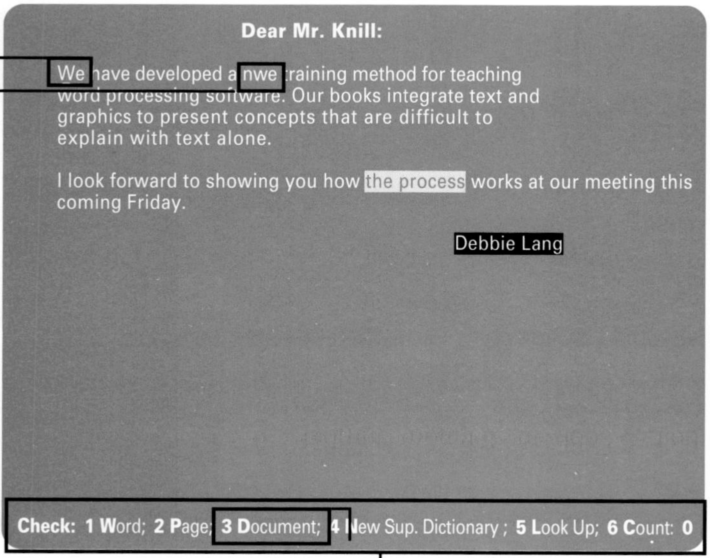

Dear Mr. Knill:
We have developed a nwe training method for teaching word processing software. Our books integrate text and graphics to present concepts that are difficult to explain with text alone.
I look forward to showing you how the process works at our meeting this coming Friday.
Debbie Lang
Check: 1 Word; 2 Page; 3 Document; 4 New Sup. Dictionary ; 5 Look Up; 6 Count: 0

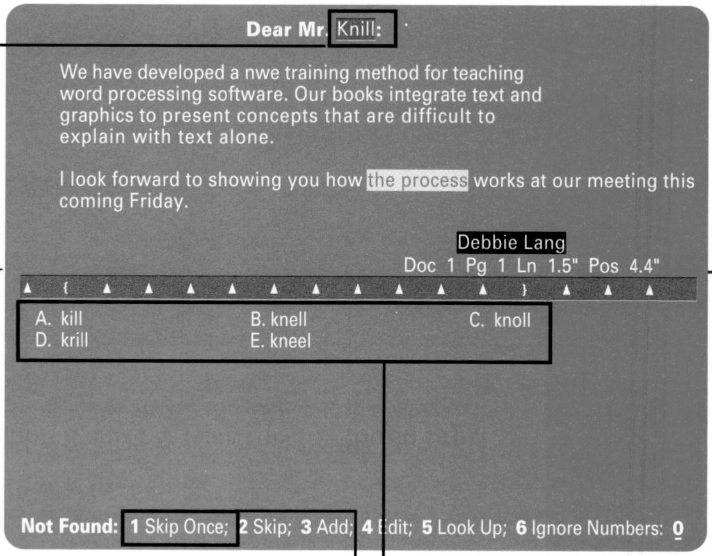

Dear Mr. Knill:
We have developed a nwe training method for teaching word processing software. Our books integrate text and graphics to present concepts that are difficult to explain with text alone.
I look forward to showing you how the process works at our meeting this coming Friday.
Debbie Lang
Doc 1 Pg 1 Ln 1.5" Pos 4.4"
A. kill
B. knell
C. knoll
D. krill
E. kneel
Not Found: 1 Skip Once; 2 Skip; 3 Add; 4 Edit; 5 Look Up; 6 Ignore Numbers: 0

■ For this example, the spelling of **new** was changed to **nwe**.

1 Position the cursor in the document, page or word you want to spell check.

2 Press Ctrl - F2 and this message appears.

3 Press D (for **D**ocument) to spell check the entire document.

or

Press P (for **P**age) to spell check the page.

or

Press W (for **W**ord) to spell check the word.

■ WordPerfect highlights the first word it does not recognize (example: **Knill**).

■ Suggestions for the correct spelling are displayed.

4 If you do not want to change the spelling of the word, press 1 (for **Skip Once**).

Note: To change the spelling of the word, refer to step **5**.

The Spell Checker finds the following errors:

■ Misspelled words
(example: The boy is ten **yearss** old).

■ Words that appear twice
(example: The boy is **ten ten** years old).

■ Capitalization errors
(example: **THe** boy is ten years old).

TO CANCEL SPELL CHECK

Press F1.

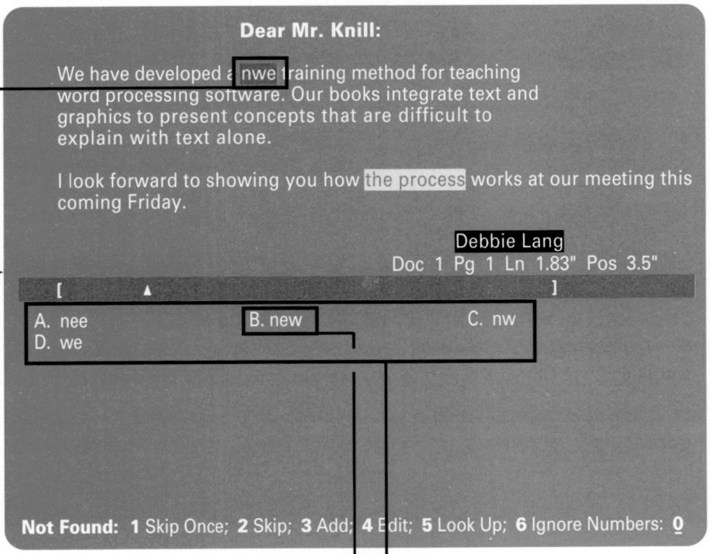
Dear Mr. Knill:
We have developed a nwe training method for teaching word processing software. Our books integrate text and graphics to present concepts that are difficult to explain with text alone.
I look forward to showing you how the process works at our meeting this coming Friday.
Debbie Lang
Doc 1 Pg 1 Ln 1.83" Pos 3.5"
A. nee
B. new
C. nw
D. we
Not Found: 1 Skip Once; 2 Skip; 3 Add; 4 Edit; 5 Look Up; 6 Ignore Numbers: 0

■ WordPerfect highlights the next word it does not recognize (example: **nwe**).

■ Suggestions for the correct spelling are displayed.

5 To replace the misspelled word with a word from the list, type the letter beside the correct spelling (example: **B**).

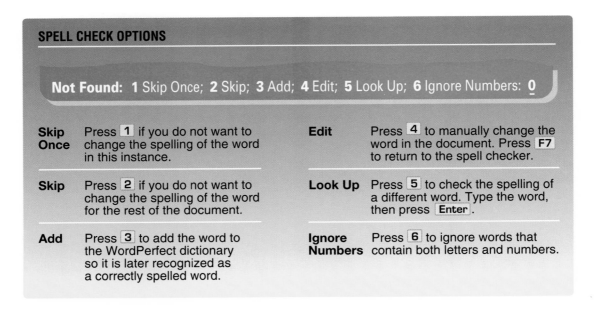

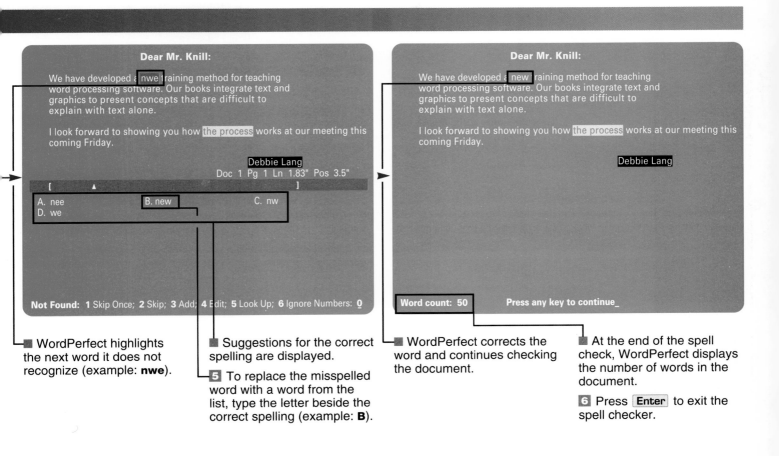

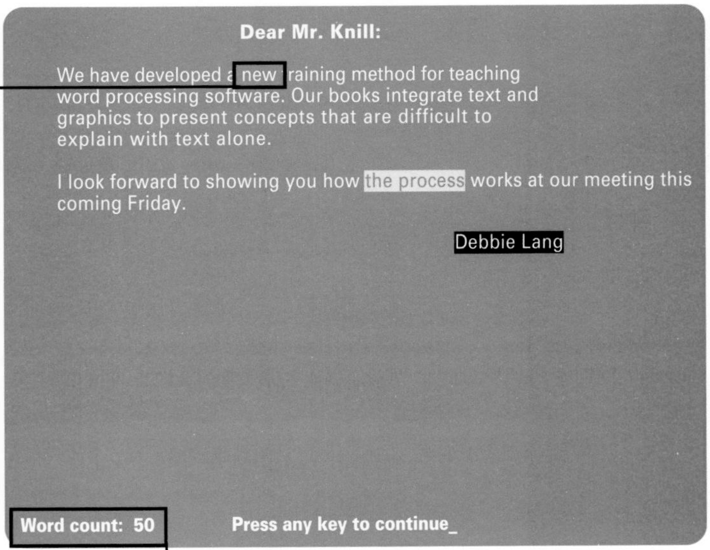
Dear Mr. Knill:
We have developed a new training method for teaching word processing software. Our books integrate text and graphics to present concepts that are difficult to explain with text alone.
I look forward to showing you how the process works at our meeting this coming Friday.
Debbie Lang
Word count: 50
Press any key to continue_

■ WordPerfect corrects the word and continues checking the document.

■ At the end of the spell check, WordPerfect displays the number of words in the document.

6 Press **Enter** to exit the spell checker.

SPELL CHECK OPTIONS

Not Found: 1 Skip Once; **2** Skip; **3** Add; **4** Edit; **5** Look Up; **6** Ignore Numbers: 0

Skip Once Press **1** if you do not want to change the spelling of the word in this instance.

Skip Press **2** if you do not want to change the spelling of the word for the rest of the document.

Add Press **3** to add the word to the WordPerfect dictionary so it is later recognized as a correctly spelled word.

Edit Press **4** to manually change the word in the document. Press **F7** to return to the spell checker.

Look Up Press **5** to check the spelling of a different word. Type the word, then press **Enter**.

Ignore Numbers Press **6** to ignore words that contain both letters and numbers.

Ctrl F2 Word Count

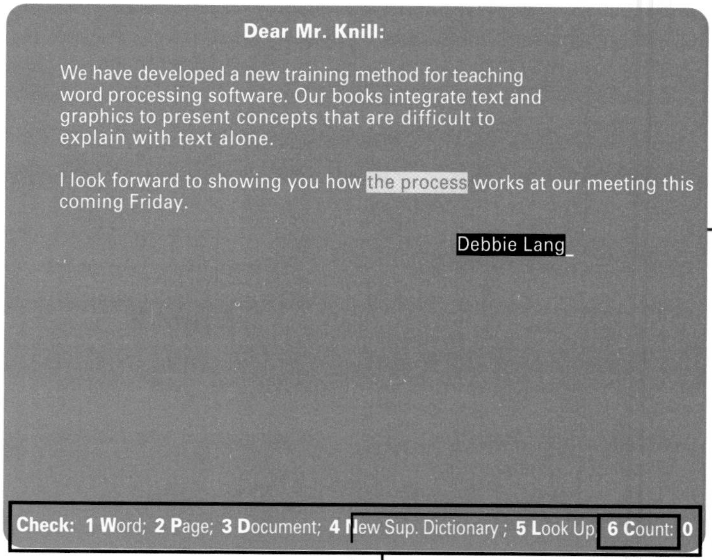
Dear Mr. Knill:
We have developed a new training method for teaching word processing software. Our books integrate text and graphics to present concepts that are difficult to explain with text alone.
I look forward to showing you how the process works at our meeting this coming Friday.
Debbie Lang
Check: 1 Word; 2 Page; 3 Document; 4 New Sup. Dictionary; 5 Look Up; 6 Count: 0

WordPerfect can count the number of words in a document without performing a spell check.

1 Press Ctrl - F2 and this message appears.

2 Press C (for **C**ount).

F2 Search for Text

SEARCH GUIDELINES

- If you search for the word **place** in lowercase letters, WordPerfect will find **place**, **Place** or **PLACE**.
- If you search for the word **place**, WordPerfect will also find common**place**, **place**ment, **place**s, etc.
- If you search for the word **PLACE** in uppercase letters, WordPerfect will only find **PLACE**.

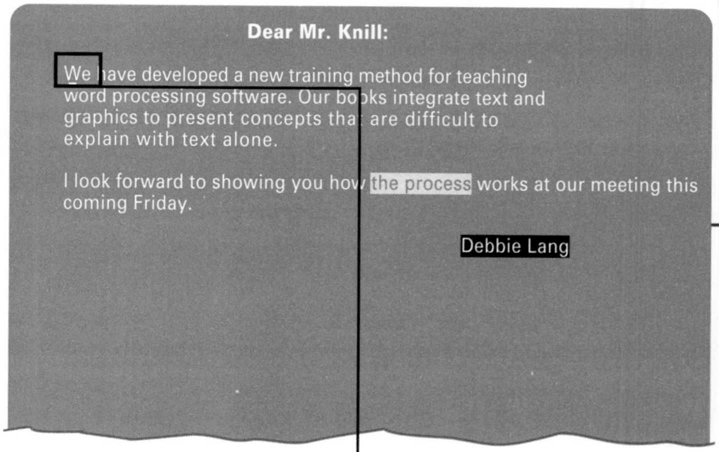
Dear Mr. Knill:
We have developed a new training method for teaching word processing software. Our books integrate text and graphics to present concepts that are difficult to explain with text alone.
I look forward to showing you how the process works at our meeting this coming Friday.
Debbie Lang

The Search feature helps you find a word or phrase in a document.

1 Position the cursor where you want the search to begin.

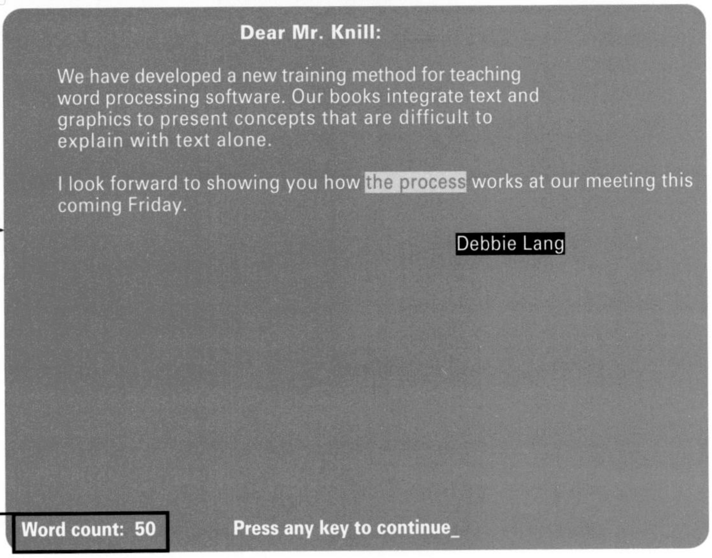
Dear Mr. Knill:
We have developed a new training method for teaching word processing software. Our books integrate text and graphics to present concepts that are difficult to explain with text alone.
I look forward to showing you how the process works at our meeting this coming Friday.
Debbie Lang
Word count: 50
Press any key to continue_

■ WordPerfect displays the number of words in the document.

3 Press Enter to exit the spell checker.

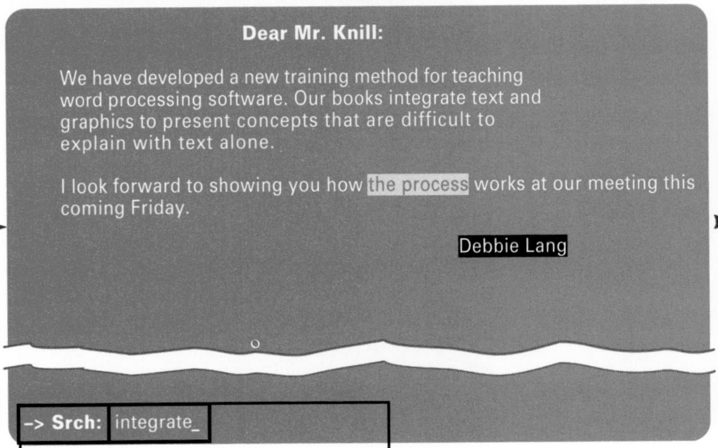
Dear Mr. Knill:
We have developed a new training method for teaching word processing software. Our books integrate text and graphics to present concepts that are difficult to explain with text alone.
I look forward to showing you how the process works at our meeting this coming Friday.
Debbie Lang
-> Srch: integrate_

2 Press F2 and this message appears.

3 Type the text you want to find (example: **integrate**).

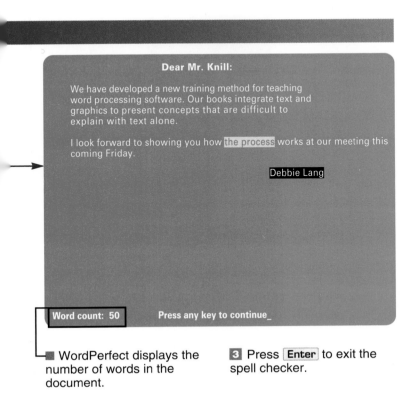

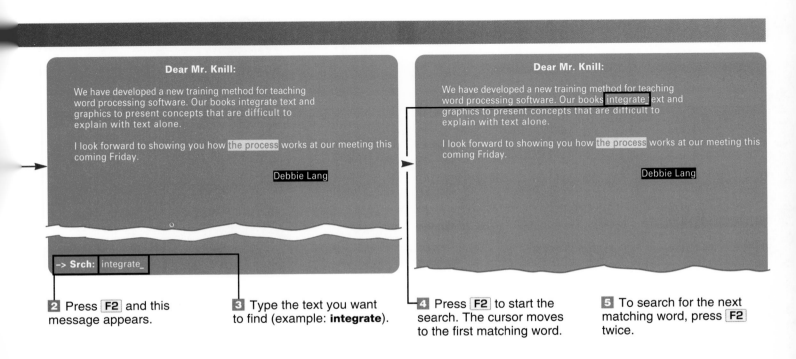

Dear Mr. Knill:
We have developed a new training method for teaching word processing software. Our books integrate_ext and graphics to present concepts that are difficult to explain with text alone.
I look forward to showing you how the process works at our meeting this coming Friday.
Debbie Lang

4 Press F2 to start the search. The cursor moves to the first matching word.

5 To search for the next matching word, press F2 twice.

REPLACE TEXT

Alt F2 Replace Text

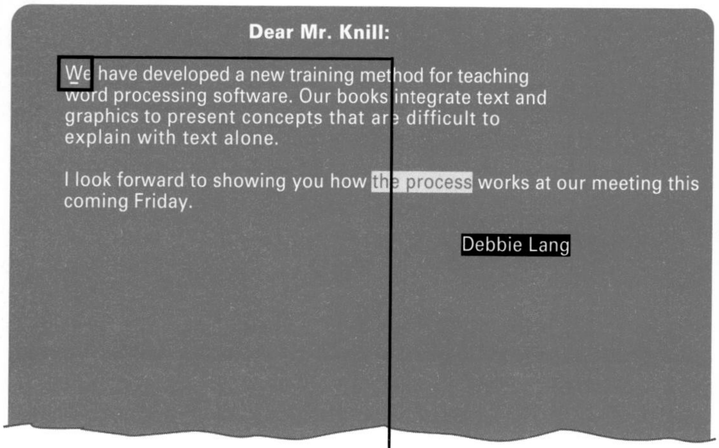

Dear Mr. Knill:
We have developed a new training method for teaching word processing software. Our books integrate text and graphics to present concepts that are difficult to explain with text alone.
I look forward to showing you how the process works at our meeting this coming Friday.
Debbie Lang

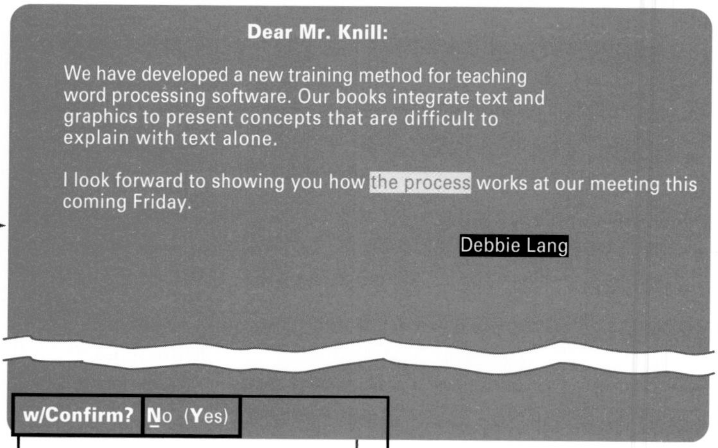

Dear Mr. Knill:
We have developed a new training method for teaching word processing software. Our books integrate text and graphics to present concepts that are difficult to explain with text alone.
I look forward to showing you how the process works at our meeting this coming Friday.
Debbie Lang
w/Confirm? No (Yes)

The Replace feature helps you find a word in a document and replace it with another word.

1 Position the cursor where you want the Replace feature to begin.

2 Press Alt - F2 and this message appears.

3 Press Y (for **Y**es) to stop at each matching word that WordPerfect finds. This way, you can decide which words you want to replace.

*Note: Press N (for **N**o) to replace all matching words at the same time.*

TIP Let's say after finishing a long document you realize a client's name was spelled incorrectly throughout (example: Cathy instead of Kathy). The Replace feature will search through the document and replace all occurrences of the wrong word with the correct one.

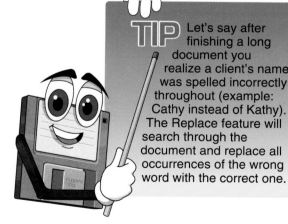

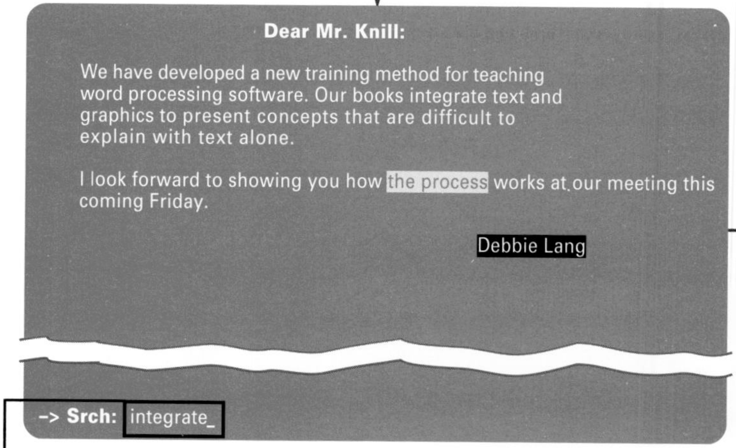

Dear Mr. Knill:
We have developed a new training method for teaching word processing software. Our books integrate text and graphics to present concepts that are difficult to explain with text alone.
I look forward to showing you how the process works at our meeting this coming Friday.
Debbie Lang
-> Srch: integrate_

4 Type the text you want to find (example: **integrate**).

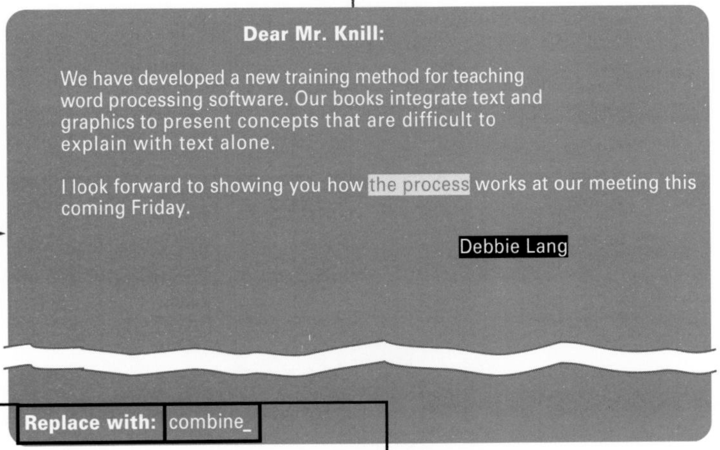
Dear Mr. Knill:
We have developed a new training method for teaching word processing software. Our books integrate text and graphics to present concepts that are difficult to explain with text alone.
I look forward to showing you how the process works at our meeting this coming Friday.
Debbie Lang
Replace with: combine_

5 Press **F2** and this message appears.

6 Type the text you want to replace the searched term (example: **combine**).

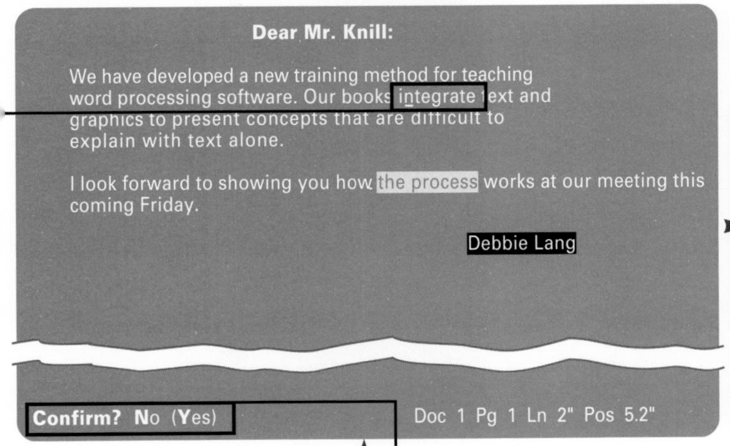
Dear Mr. Knill:
We have developed a new training method for teaching word processing software. Our books integrate text and graphics to present concepts that are difficult to explain with text alone.
I look forward to showing you how the process works at our meeting this coming Friday.
Debbie Lang
Confirm? No (Yes)
Doc 1 Pg 1 Ln 2" Pos 5.2"

7 Press **F2** and the cursor moves to the first matching word.

8 To replace the word, press **Y** (for **Y**es).

Note: If you do not want to replace the word, press **N** *(for* **N***o).*

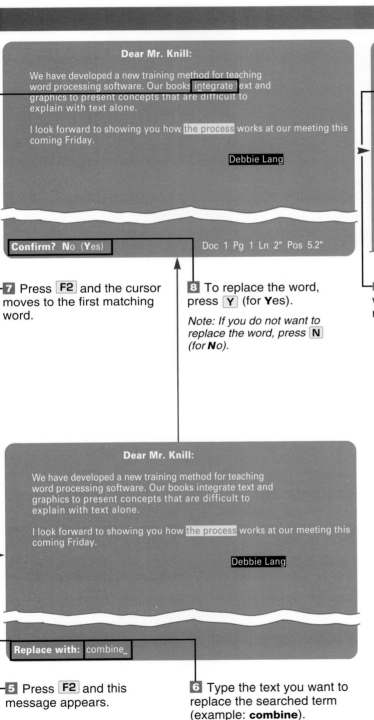

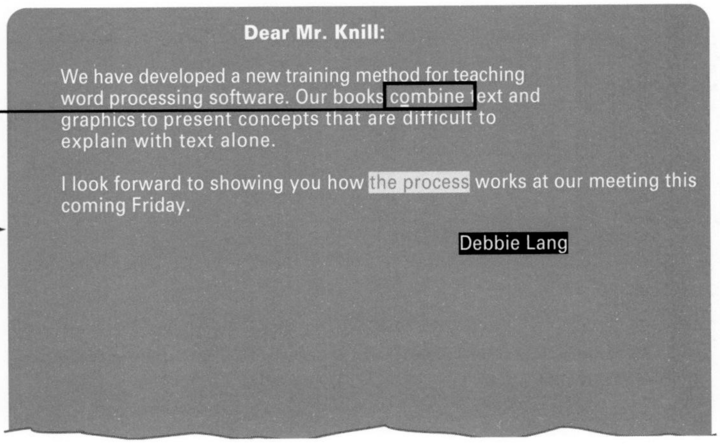
Dear Mr. Knill:
We have developed a new training method for teaching word processing software. Our books combine text and graphics to present concepts that are difficult to explain with text alone.
I look forward to showing you how the process works at our meeting this coming Friday.
Debbie Lang

■ WordPerfect replaces the word and searches for the next matching word.

TO CANCEL REPLACE

Press **F1**.

THESAURUS

Alt F1 Look Up a Word

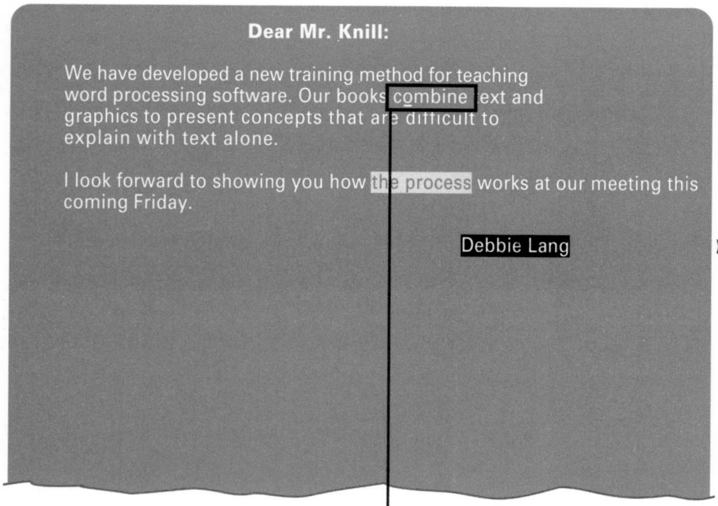

Dear Mr. Knill:
We have developed a new training method for teaching word processing software. Our books combine text and graphics to present concepts that are difficult to explain with text alone.
I look forward to showing you how the process works at our meeting this coming Friday.
Debbie Lang

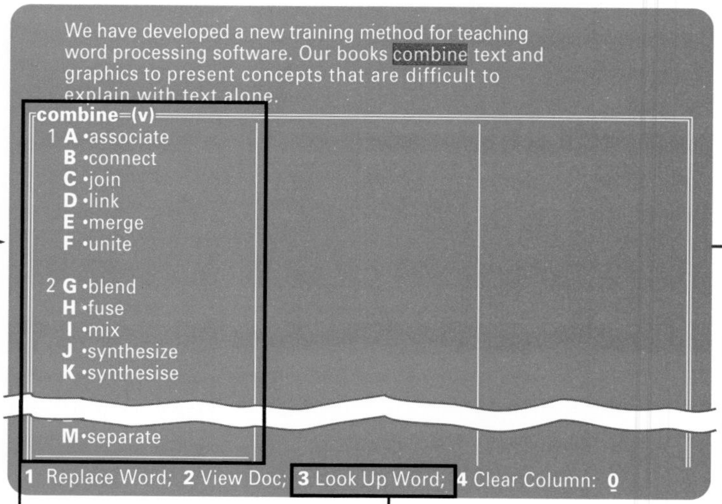

We have developed a new training method for teaching word processing software. Our books combine text and graphics to present concepts that are difficult to explain with text alone.
combine=(v)
1 A •associate
B •connect
C •join
D •link
E •merge
F •unite
2 G •blend
H •fuse
I •mix
J •synthesize
K •synthesise
M•separate
1 Replace Word; 2 View Doc; 3 Look Up Word; 4 Clear Column: 0

A thesaurus adds variety to your writing by suggesting alternative words for use in the document.

1 Position the cursor under the word you want to look up (example: **combine**).

2 Press Alt - F1 and WordPerfect displays a list of alternative words.

3 To look up another word, press 3 (for **Look Up Word**).

Replace a Word

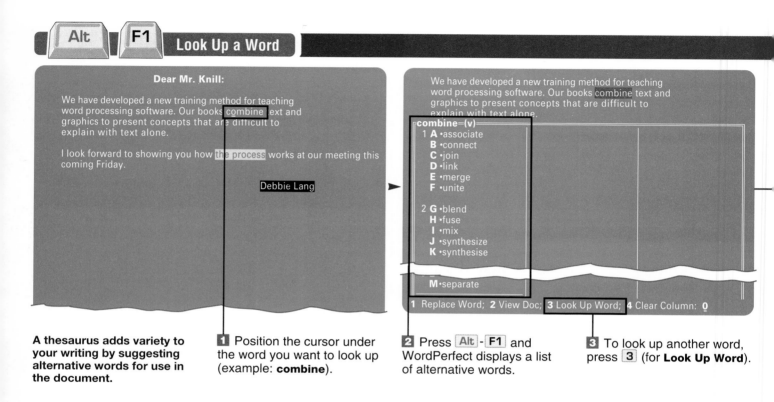

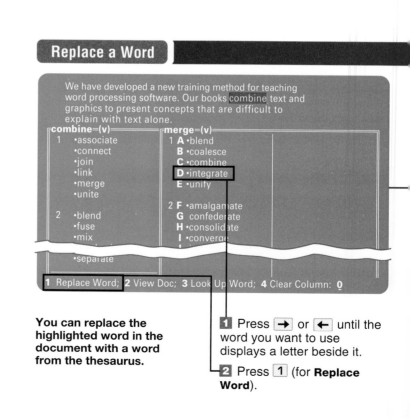

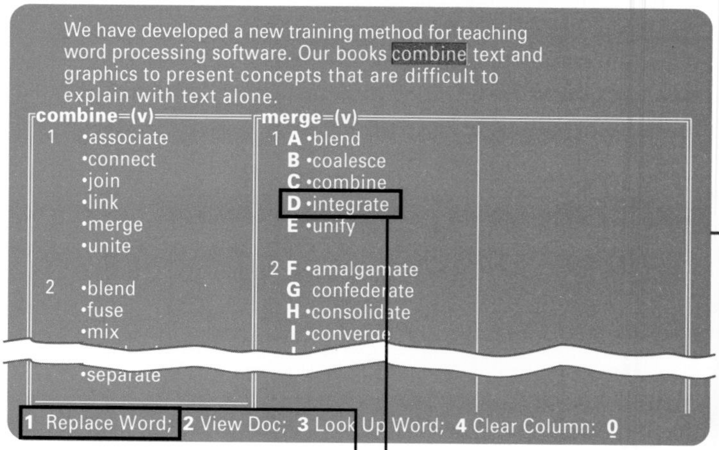

We have developed a new training method for teaching word processing software. Our books combine text and graphics to present concepts that are difficult to explain with text alone.
combine=(v)
1 •associate
•connect
•join
•link
•merge
•unite
2 •blend
•fuse
•mix
•separate
merge=(v)
1 A •blend
B •coalesce
C •combine
D •integrate
E •unify
2 F •amalgamate
G confederate
H •consolidate
I •converge
1 Replace Word; 2 View Doc; 3 Look Up Word; 4 Clear Column: 0

You can replace the highlighted word in the document with a word from the thesaurus.

1 Press → or ← until the word you want to use displays a letter beside it.

2 Press 1 (for **Replace Word**).

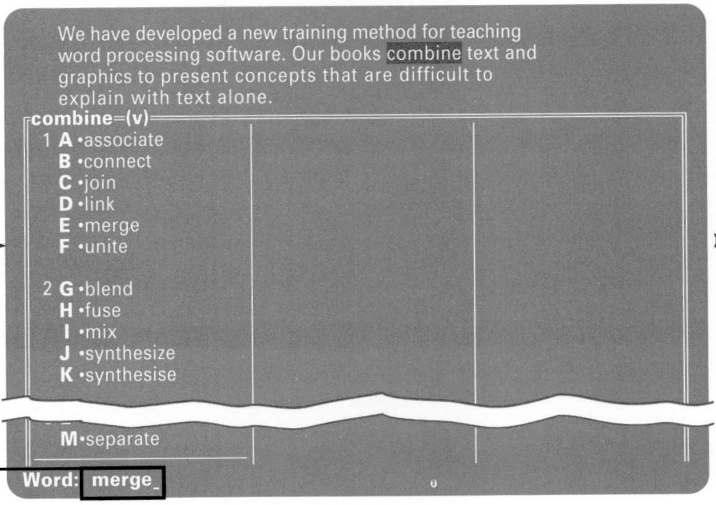
We have developed a new training method for teaching word processing software. Our books combine text and graphics to present concepts that are difficult to explain with text alone.
combine=(v)
1 A •associate
B •connect
C •join
D •link
E •merge
F •unite
2 G •blend
H •fuse
I •mix
J •synthesize
K •synthesise
M•separate
Word: merge

4 Type the word you want to look up (example: **merge**). Then press Enter.

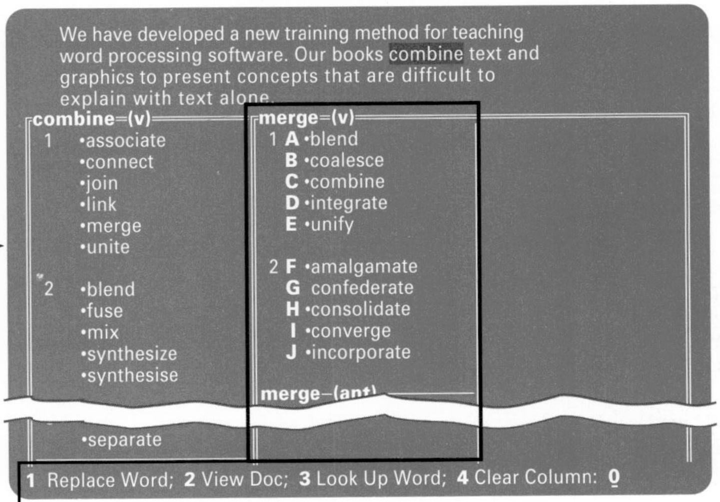
We have developed a new training method for teaching word processing software. Our books combine text and graphics to present concepts that are difficult to explain with text alone.
combine=(v)
1 •associate
•connect
•join
•link
•merge
•unite
2 •blend
•fuse
•mix
•synthesize
•synthesise
•separate
merge=(v)
1 A •blend
B •coalesce
C •combine
D •integrate
E •unify
2 F •amalgamate
G confederate
H •consolidate
I •converge
J •incorporate
1 Replace Word; 2 View Doc; 3 Look Up Word; 4 Clear Column: 0

■ WordPerfect displays a list of alternative words.

Note: To exit the thesaurus without changing the highlighted word in the document, press F7.

Note: To remove a column of information in the thesaurus, press 4 *(for* ***Clear Column****).*

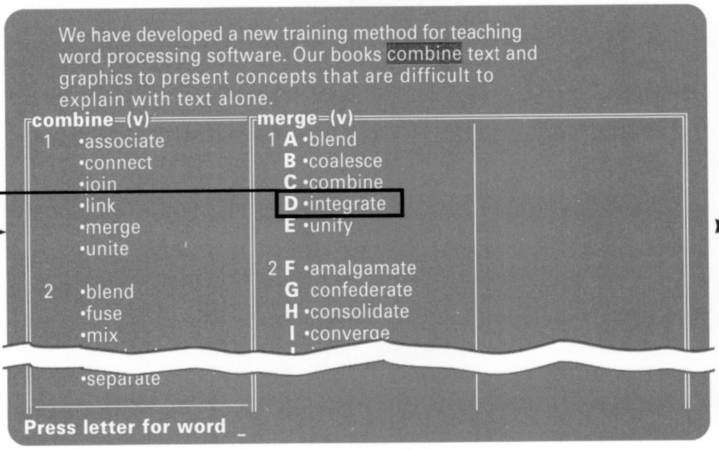
We have developed a new training method for teaching word processing software. Our books combine text and graphics to present concepts that are difficult to explain with text alone.
combine=(v)
1 •associate
•connect
•join
•link
•merge
•unite
2 •blend
•fuse
•mix
•separate
merge=(v)
1 A •blend
B •coalesce
C •combine
D •integrate
E •unify
2 F •amalgamate
G confederate
H •consolidate
I •converge
Press letter for word

3 Type the letter beside the word you want to use (example: **D**).

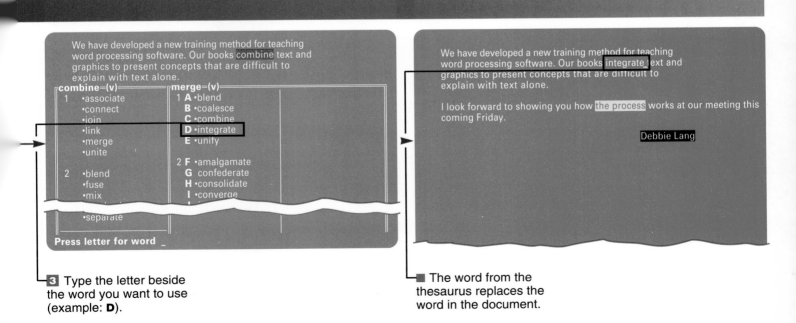

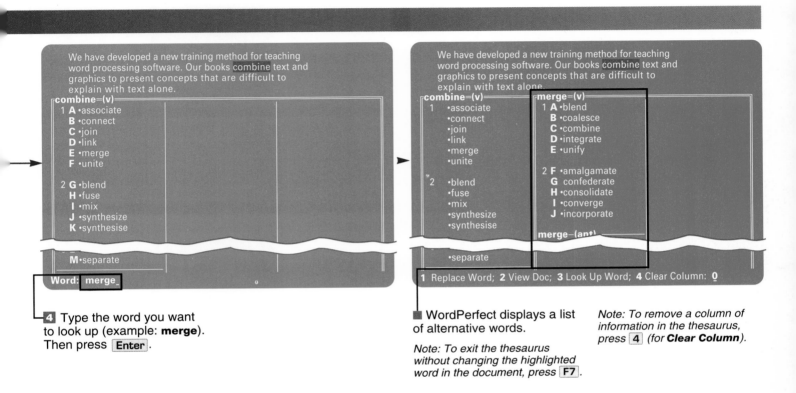

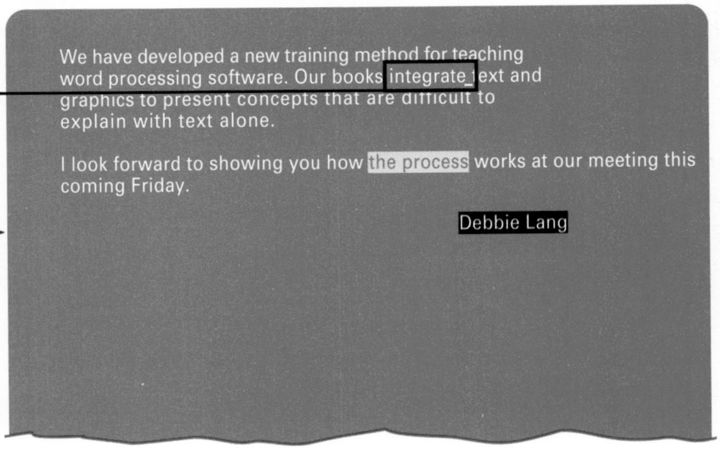
We have developed a new training method for teaching word processing software. Our books integrate text and graphics to present concepts that are difficult to explain with text alone.
I look forward to showing you how the process works at our meeting this coming Friday.
Debbie Lang

■ The word from the thesaurus replaces the word in the document.

ADD PAGE NUMBERS

Shift F8 Add Page Numbers

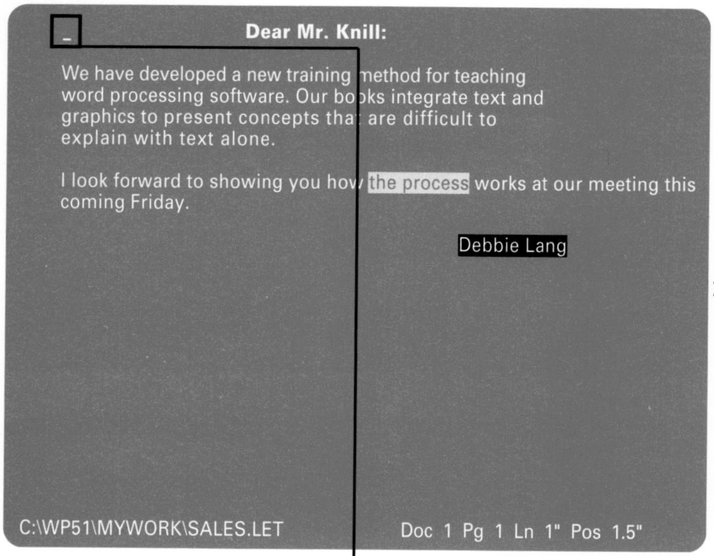

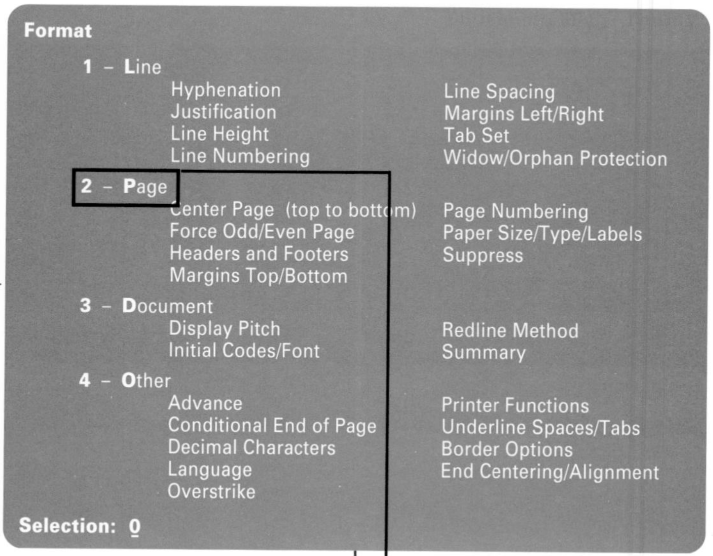

WordPerfect can automatically number the pages in a document. You can specify the position of the page numbers on each page.

1 Position the cursor at the top of the page where you want the page numbering to begin.

2 Press Shift - F8 and the **Format** screen appears.

3 Press P (for **P**age).

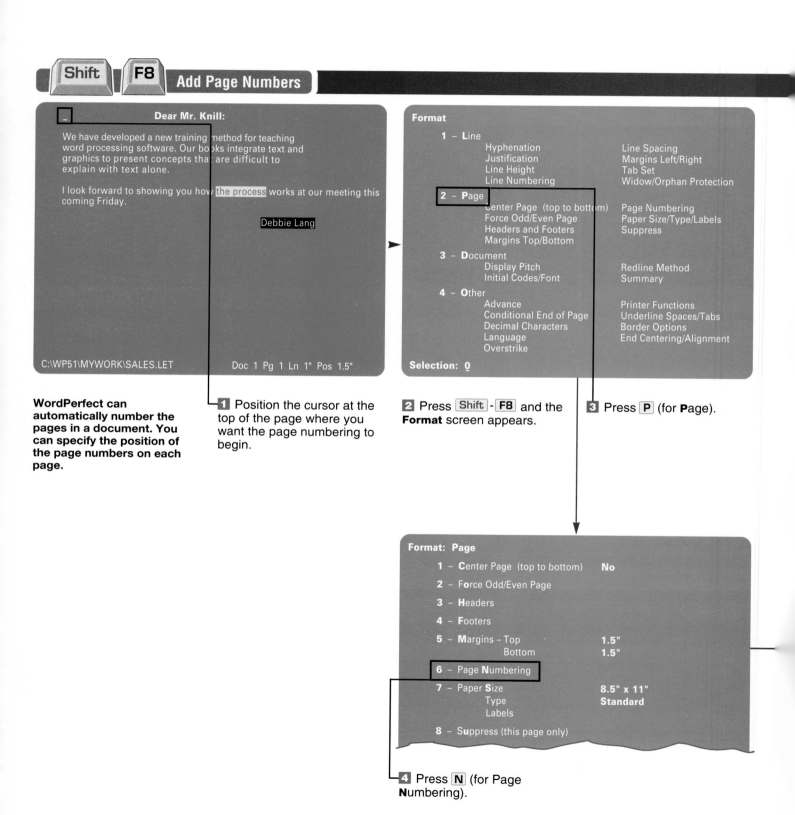

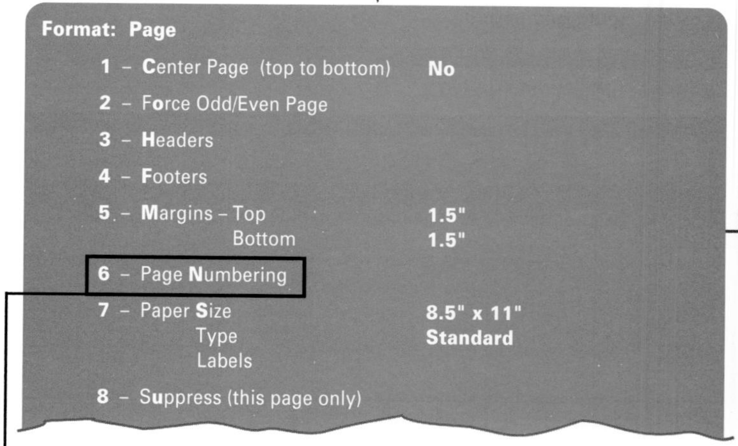

4 Press N (for Page **N**umbering).

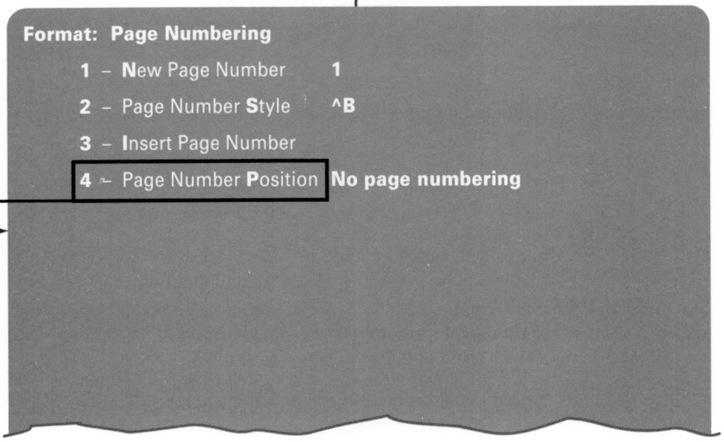

5 Press P (for Page Number **P**osition).

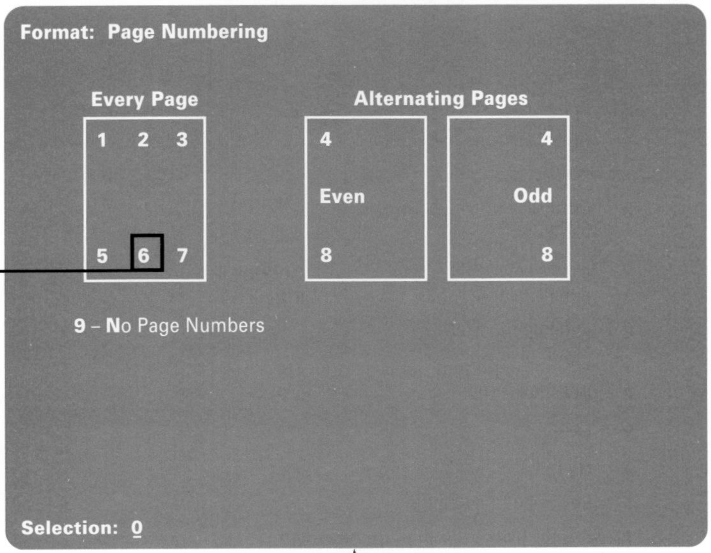

6 Type the number corresponding to the page number position you want to use (example: **6**).

7 Press F7 to return to the document.

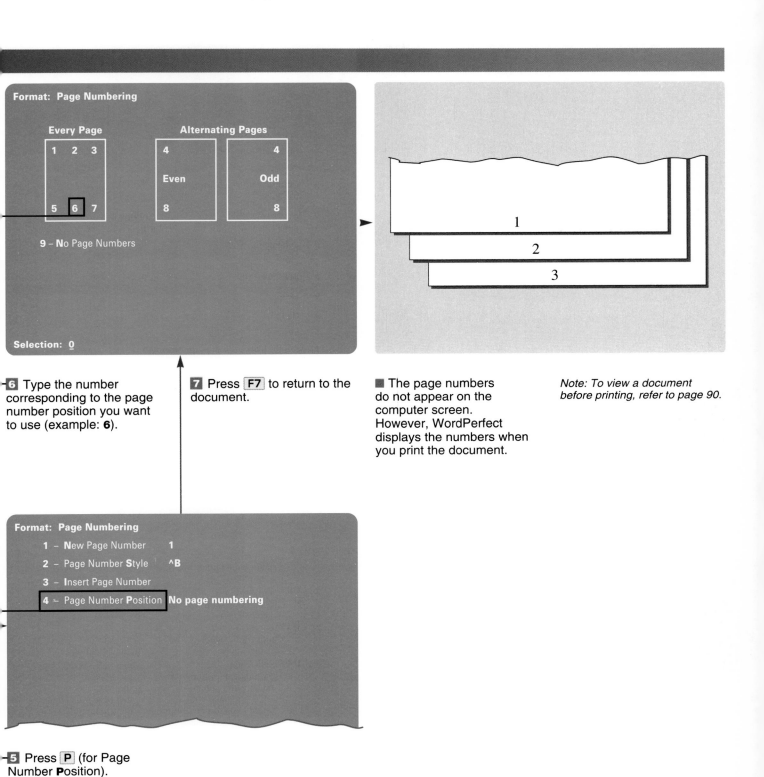

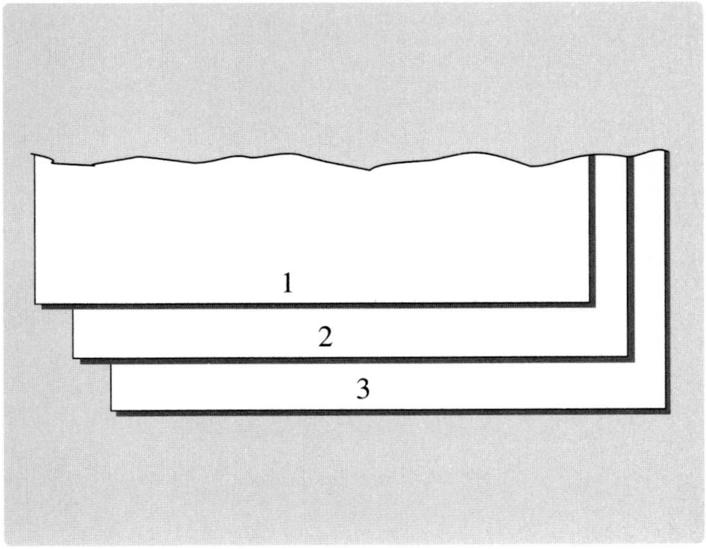

■ The page numbers do not appear on the computer screen. However, WordPerfect displays the numbers when you print the document.

Note: To view a document before printing, refer to page 90.

CREATE HEADERS AND FOOTERS

Shift F8 Create Headers and Footers

Dear Mr. Knill:

We have developed a new training method for teaching word processing software. Our books integrate text and graphics to present concepts that are difficult to explain with text alone.

I look forward to showing you how the process works at our meeting this coming Friday.

Debbie Lang

C:\WP51\MYWORK\SALES.LET   Doc 1 Pg 1 Ln 1" Pos 1"

1 Position the cursor at the top of the first page that you want to include a header or footer.

Note: To move to the top of the document before any text and codes, press Home, Home, Home, ↑.

Format

1 – **L**ine
- Hyphenation — Line Spacing
- Justification — Margins Left/Right
- Line Height — Tab Set
- Line Numbering — Widow/Orphan Protection

2 – **P**age
- Center Page (top to bottom) — Page Numbering
- Force Odd/Even Page — Paper Size/Type/Labels
- Headers and Footers — Suppress
- Margins Top/Bottom

3 – **D**ocument
- Display Pitch — Redline Method
- Initial Codes/Font — Summary

4 – **O**ther
- Advance — Printer Functions
- Conditional End of Page — Underline Spaces/Tabs
- Decimal Characters — Border Options
- Language — End Centering/Alignment
- Overstrike

Selection: 0

2 Press Shift - F8 and the **Format** screen appears.

3 Press P (for **P**age).

HEADERS AND FOOTERS

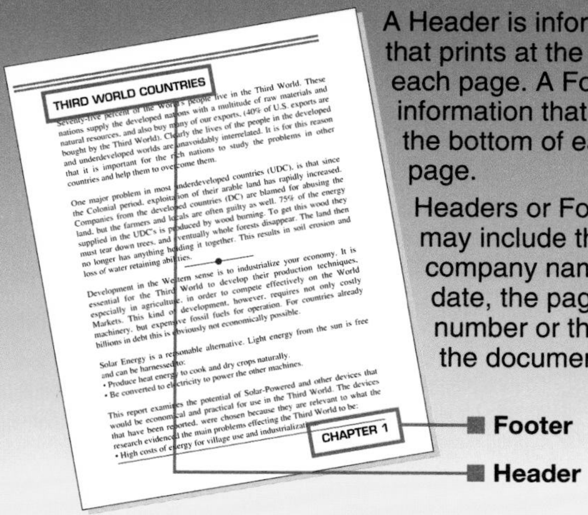

A Header is information that prints at the top of each page. A Footer is information that prints at the bottom of each page.

Headers or Footers may include the company name, the date, the page number or the title of the document.

Format: Page

1 – **C**enter Page (top to bottom)		**No**
2 – **F**orce Odd/Even Page		
3 – **H**eaders		
4 – **F**ooters		
5 – **M**argins – Top		**1"**
	Bottom	**1"**
6 – Page **N**umbering		
7 – Paper **S**ize		**8.5" x 11"**
	Type	**Standard**
	Labels	
8 – S**u**ppress (this page only)		

4 To create a header, press H (for **H**eaders).

or

To create a footer, press F (for **F**ooters).

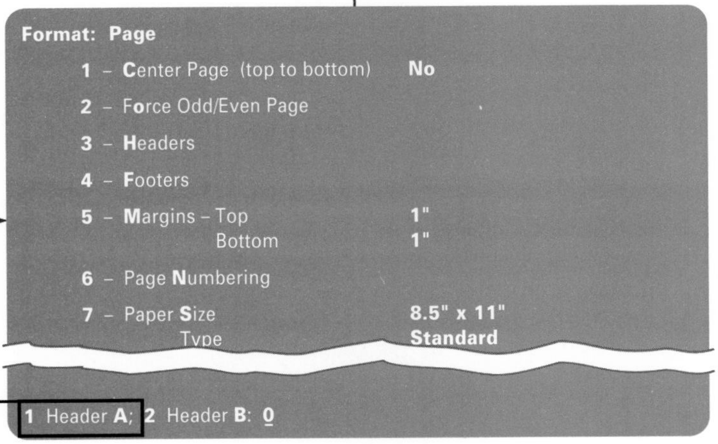

5 Press A to select Header **A** or Footer **A**.

*Note: You can create two headers and two footers for each page (**A** and **B**).*

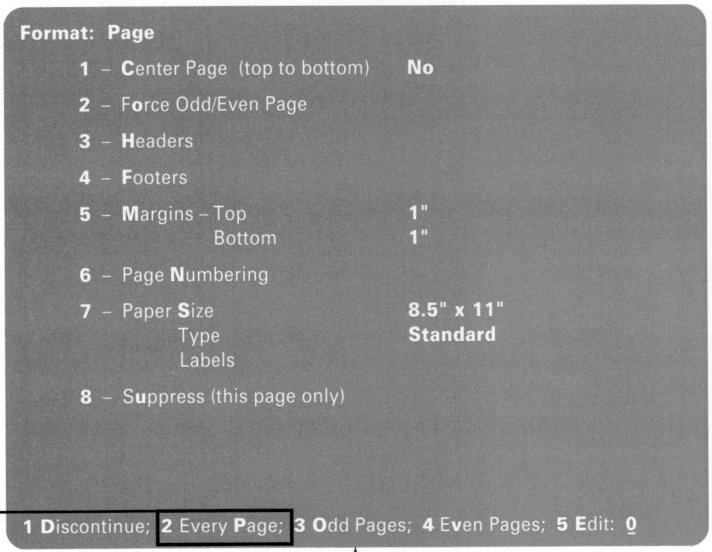

6 Type the highlighted letter of the pages you want to include a header or footer (example: P for Every **P**age). The header or footer screen appears.

7 Type the text for the header or footer.

8 Press F7 twice to return to the document.

■ Headers and footers do not appear on the computer screen. However, WordPerfect displays them when you print the document.

Note: To view the document before printing, refer to page 90.

CHANGE PAPER SIZE AND TYPE

Shift F8 Change Paper Size and Type

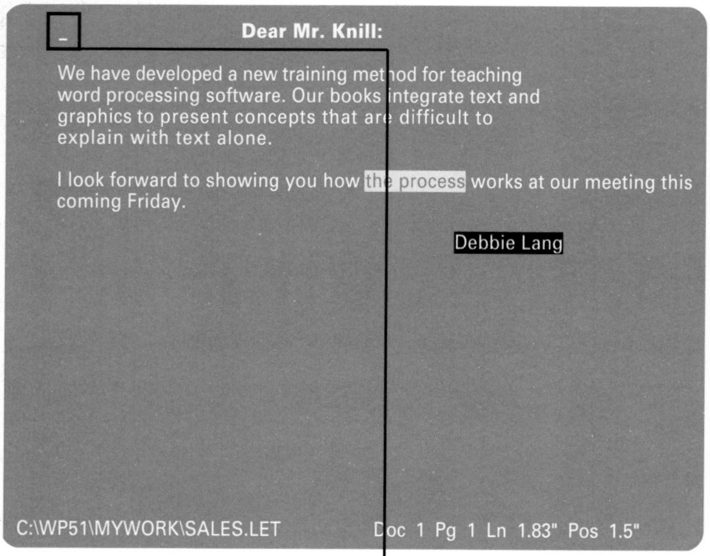

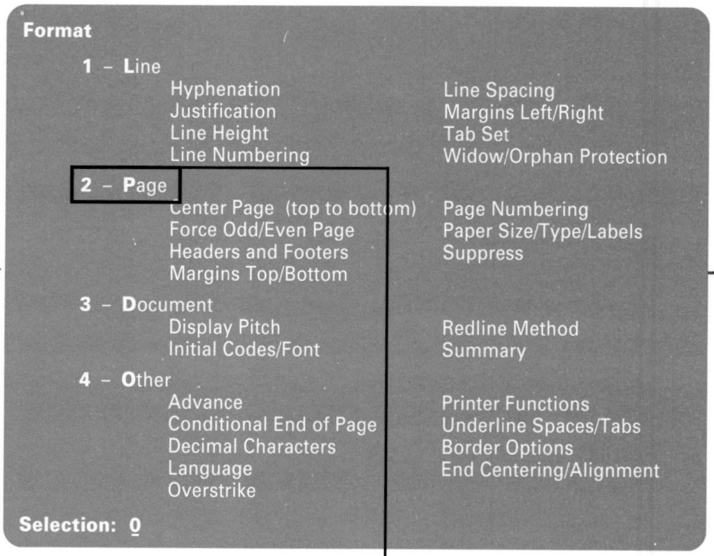

WordPerfect automatically sets each page with an 8.5 by 11 inch paper size. You can easily change this setting.

1 Position the cursor at the top of the page you want to print on the new paper.

2 Press Shift - F8 and the **Format** screen appears.

3 Press P (for **P**age).

PAPER OPTIONS

The following paper options are available in the above example:

Note: The available paper options depend on the printer you are using.

Envelope - Wide

Select this setting when you want to print an envelope.

Standard

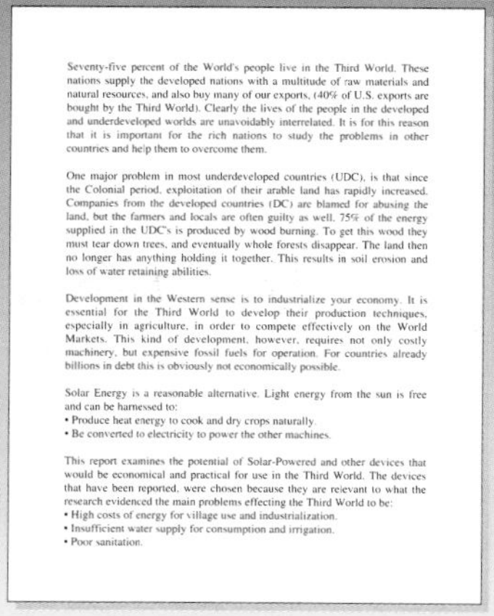

This is the default page setting.

Standard - Wide

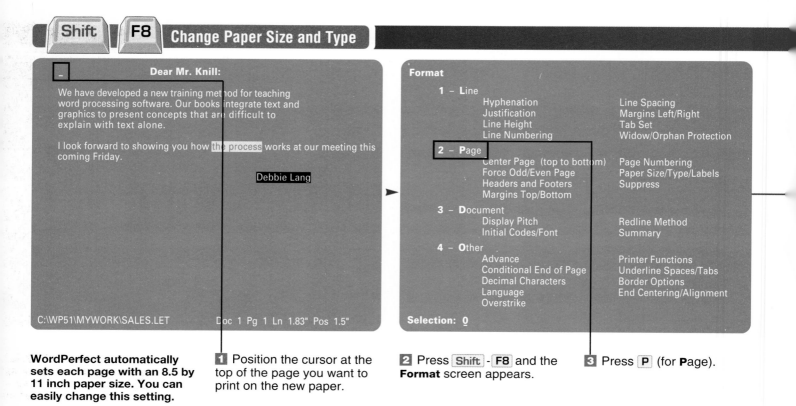

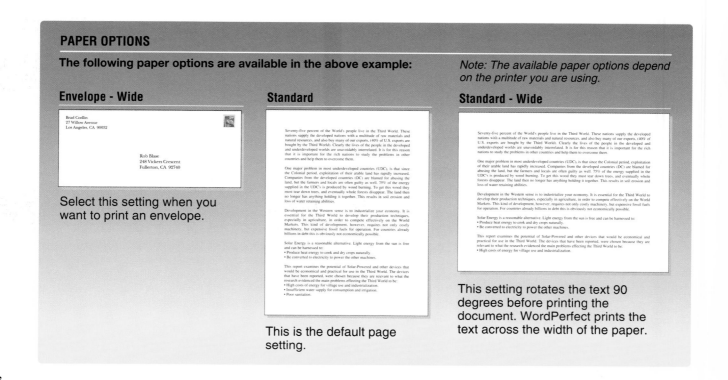

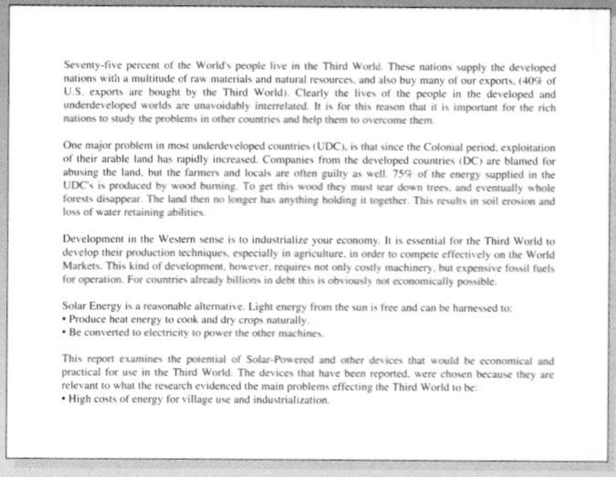

This setting rotates the text 90 degrees before printing the document. WordPerfect prints the text across the width of the paper.

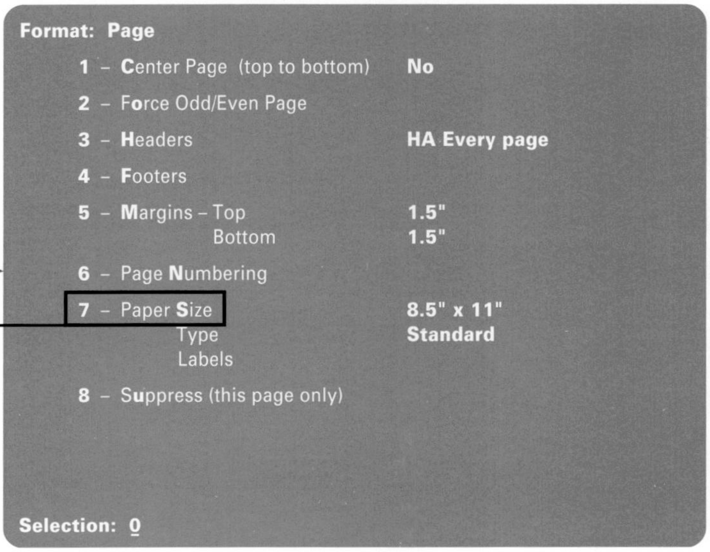

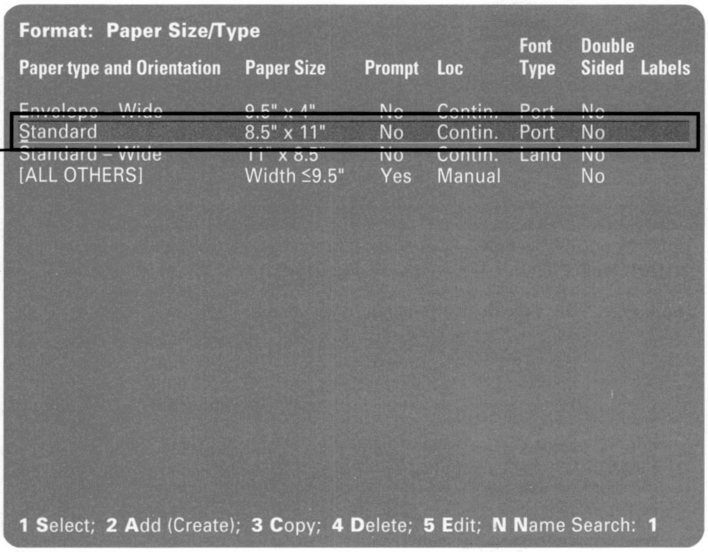

4 Press S (for Paper **S**ize).

5 Press ↑ or ↓ to highlight the desired paper type and size. Then press Enter.

6 Press F7 to return to the document.

If you need to use a paper type or size that does not appear on the screen, press A (for **A**dd) and refer to your WordPerfect documentation.

Ctrl Enter Add a Page Break

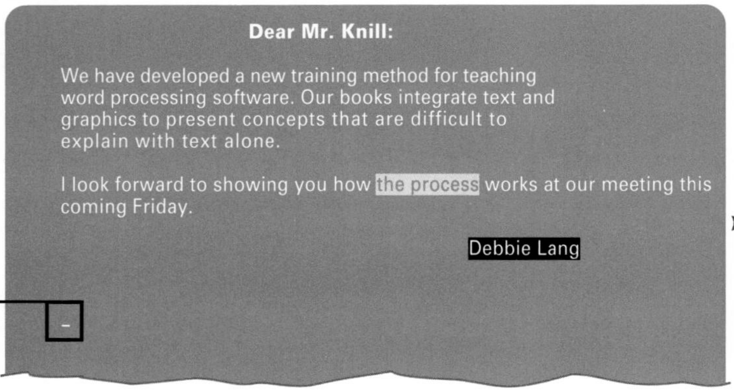
Dear Mr. Knill:
We have developed a new training method for teaching word processing software. Our books integrate text and graphics to present concepts that are difficult to explain with text alone.
I look forward to showing you how the process works at our meeting this coming Friday.
Debbie Lang

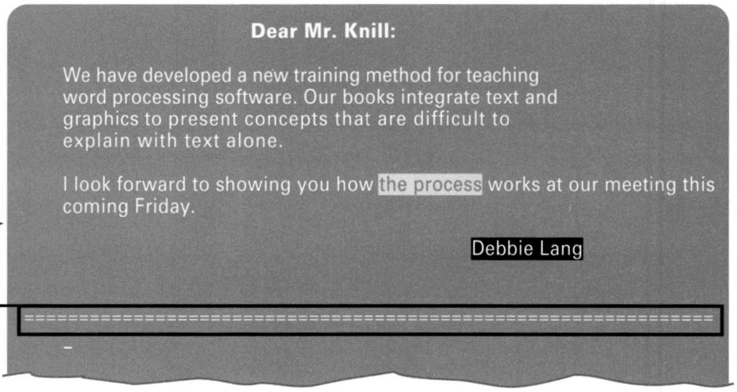
Dear Mr. Knill:
We have developed a new training method for teaching word processing software. Our books integrate text and graphics to present concepts that are difficult to explain with text alone.
I look forward to showing you how the process works at our meeting this coming Friday.
Debbie Lang

All text after a page break will print on the next page.

1 Position the cursor where you want the page break to appear.

Note: To position the cursor below existing text, you may have to press Enter *several times after the last sentence you typed.*

2 Press Ctrl - Enter and a double line appears. This represents the end of the page.

Shift F8 Center a Page

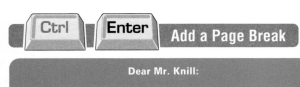

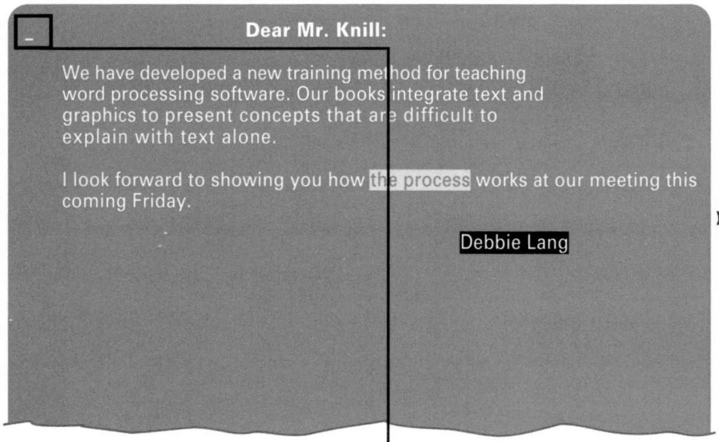
Dear Mr. Knill:
We have developed a new training method for teaching word processing software. Our books integrate text and graphics to present concepts that are difficult to explain with text alone.
I look forward to showing you how the process works at our meeting this coming Friday.
Debbie Lang

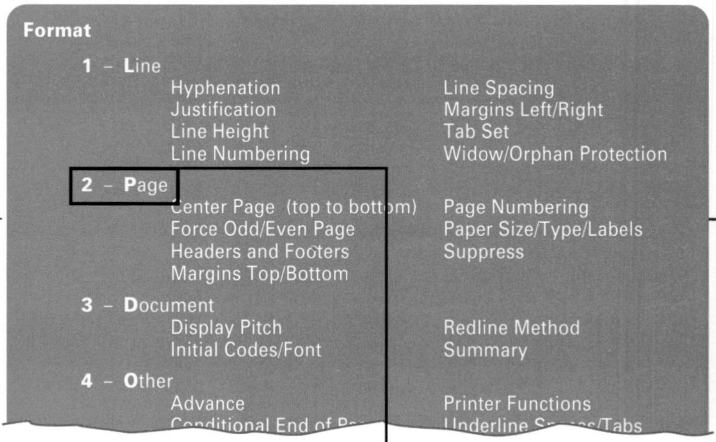
Format
1 - Line
Hyphenation
Justification
Line Height
Line Numbering
Line Spacing
Margins Left/Right
Tab Set
Widow/Orphan Protection
2 - Page
Center Page (top to bottom)
Force Odd/Even Page
Headers and Footers
Margins Top/Bottom
Page Numbering
Paper Size/Type/Labels
Suppress
3 - Document
Display Pitch
Initial Codes/Font
Redline Method
Summary
4 - Other
Advance
Printer Functions

You can vertically center text on a page. This is useful when creating title pages or short memos.

1 Position the cursor at the top of the page you want to center vertically. You must place the cursor in front of any text and codes.

Note: To move to the top of the document before any text and codes, press Home, Home, Home, ↑.

2 Press Shift - F8 and the **Format** screen appears.

3 Press P (for **P**age).

REMOVE A PAGE BREAK

1 Display the Reveal Codes screen by pressing F11 or Alt - F3.

2 Position the cursor on the page break code **[HPg]**.

3 Press Delete.

TIP

WordPerfect automatically breaks pages when a document is longer than one page of type. Page breaks that WordPerfect inserts appear as a single line.

Format: Page

1 - **C**enter Page (top to bottom) — No (Yes)
2 - F**o**rce Odd/Even Page
3 - **H**eaders
4 - **F**ooters
5 - **M**argins - Top — 1"
Bottom — 1"
6 - Page **N**umbering
7 - Paper **S**ize — 8.5" x 11"
Type — Standard
Labels
8 - S**u**ppress (this page only)

4 Press C (for **C**enter Page).

5 Press Y (for **Y**es).

6 Press F7 to return to the document.

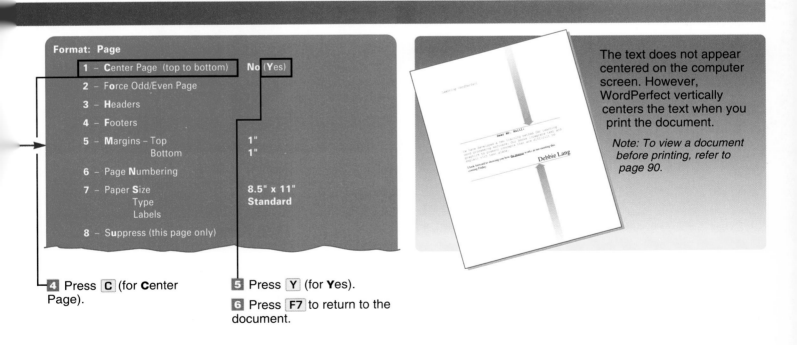

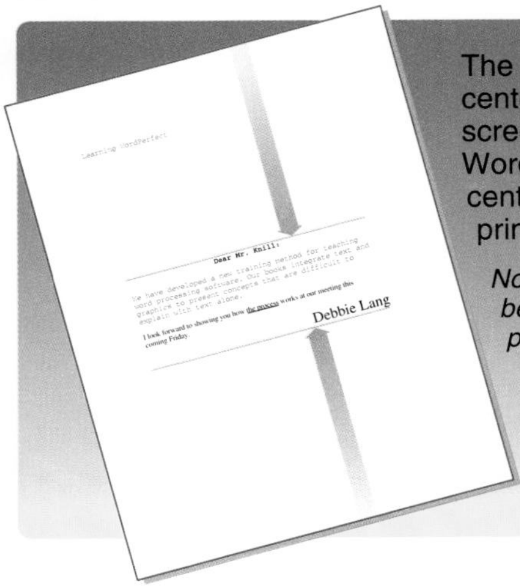

The text does not appear centered on the computer screen. However, WordPerfect vertically centers the text when you print the document.

Note: To view a document before printing, refer to page 90.

CREATE A TABLE

Alt F7 Create a Table

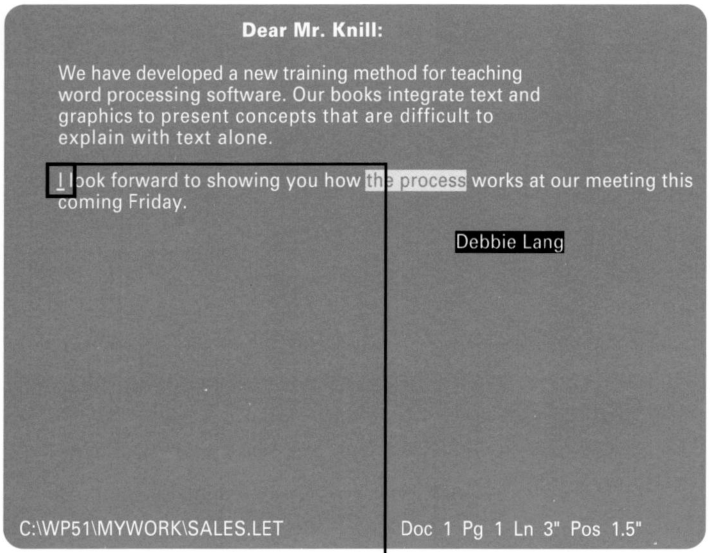
Dear Mr. Knill:
We have developed a new training method for teaching word processing software. Our books integrate text and graphics to present concepts that are difficult to explain with text alone.
I look forward to showing you how the process works at our meeting this coming Friday.
Debbie Lang
C:\WP51\MYWORK\SALES.LET
Doc 1 Pg 1 Ln 3" Pos 1.5"

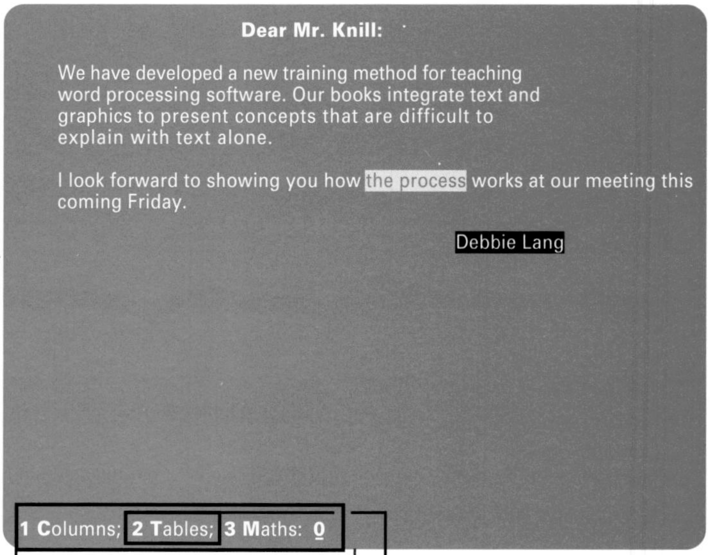
Dear Mr. Knill:
We have developed a new training method for teaching word processing software. Our books integrate text and graphics to present concepts that are difficult to explain with text alone.
I look forward to showing you how the process works at our meeting this coming Friday.
Debbie Lang
1 Columns; 2 Tables; 3 Maths: 0

Tables can help you organize information into rows and columns.

1 Position the cursor where you want the table to appear.

Note: All text after the cursor moves down to accommodate the table.

2 Press Alt - F7 and this message appears.

3 Press T (for **T**ables).

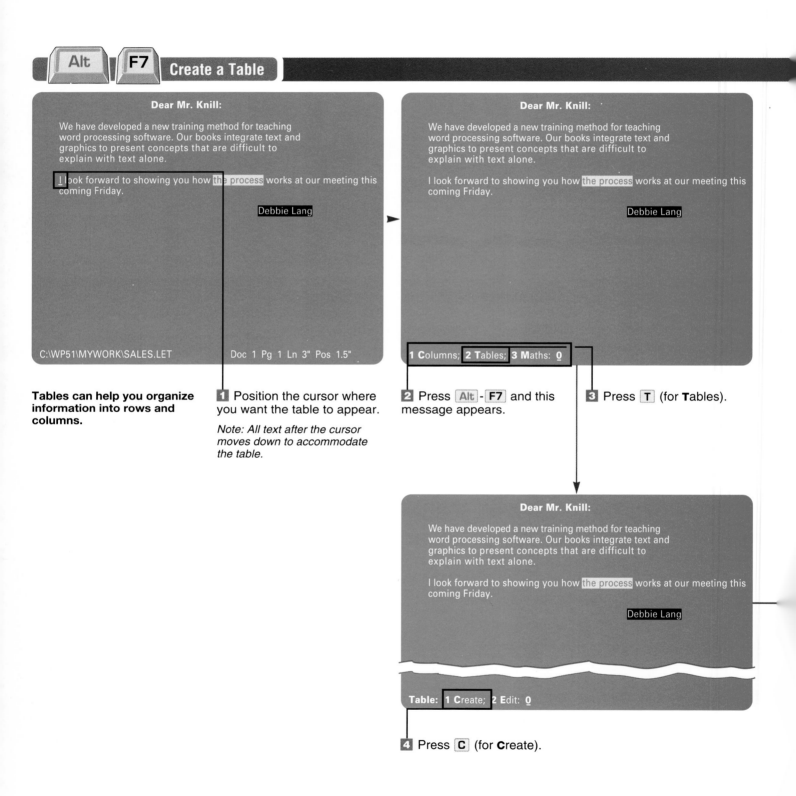

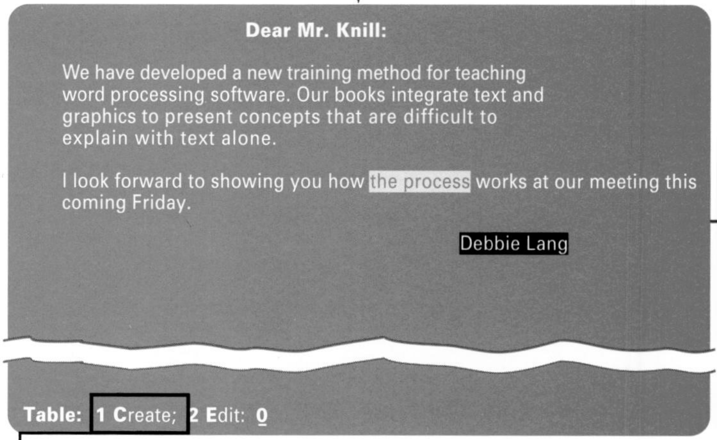
Dear Mr. Knill:
We have developed a new training method for teaching word processing software. Our books integrate text and graphics to present concepts that are difficult to explain with text alone.
I look forward to showing you how the process works at our meeting this coming Friday.
Debbie Lang
Table: 1 Create; 2 Edit: 0

4 Press C (for **C**reate).

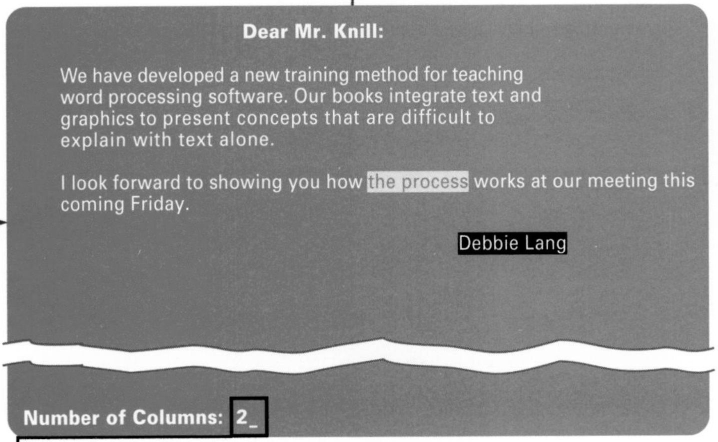
Dear Mr. Knill:
We have developed a new training method for teaching word processing software. Our books integrate text and graphics to present concepts that are difficult to explain with text alone.
I look forward to showing you how the process works at our meeting this coming Friday.
Debbie Lang
Number of Columns: 2_

5 Type the number of columns you want in the table (example: **2**). Then press **Enter**.

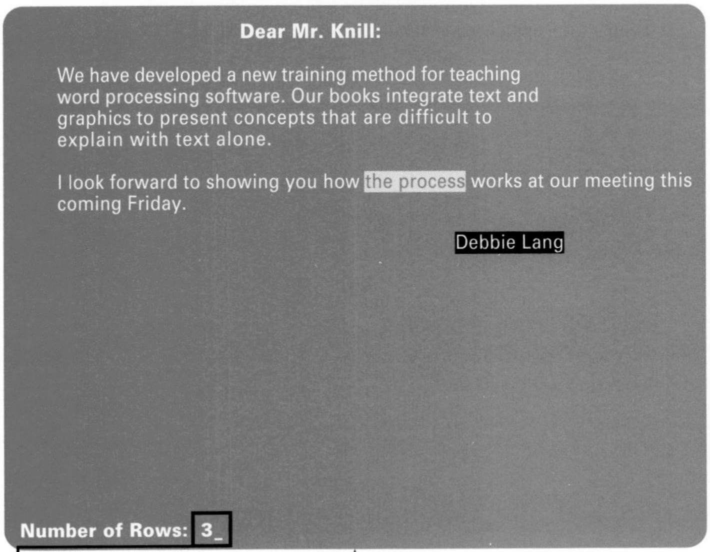
Dear Mr. Knill:
We have developed a new training method for teaching word processing software. Our books integrate text and graphics to present concepts that are difficult to explain with text alone.
I look forward to showing you how the process works at our meeting this coming Friday.
Debbie Lang
Number of Rows: 3_

6 Type the number of rows you want in the table (example: **3**). Then press **Enter**.

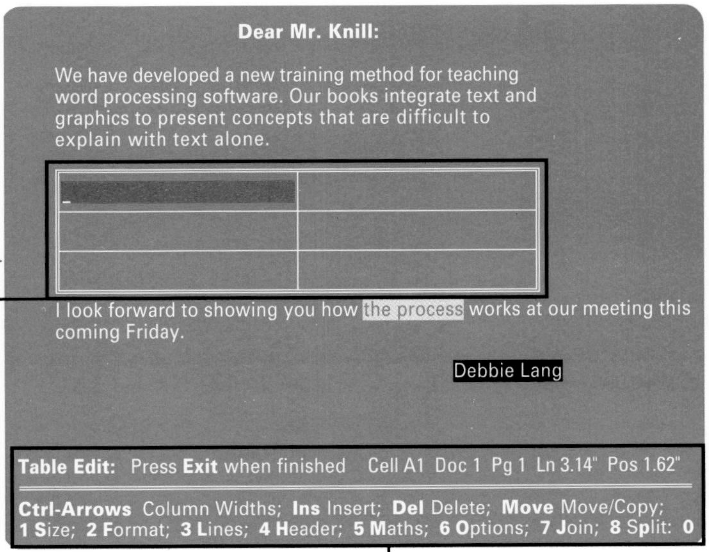
Dear Mr. Knill:
We have developed a new training method for teaching word processing software. Our books integrate text and graphics to present concepts that are difficult to explain with text alone.
I look forward to showing you how the process works at our meeting this coming Friday.
Debbie Lang
Table Edit: Press Exit when finished Cell A1 Doc 1 Pg 1 Ln 3.14" Pos 1.62"
Ctrl-Arrows Column Widths; Ins Insert; Del Delete; Move Move/Copy;
1 Size; 2 Format; 3 Lines; 4 Header; 5 Maths; 6 Options; 7 Join; 8 Split: 0

- The table appears.

7 Press **F7** to hide the **Table Edit:** menu and return to the normal editing mode.

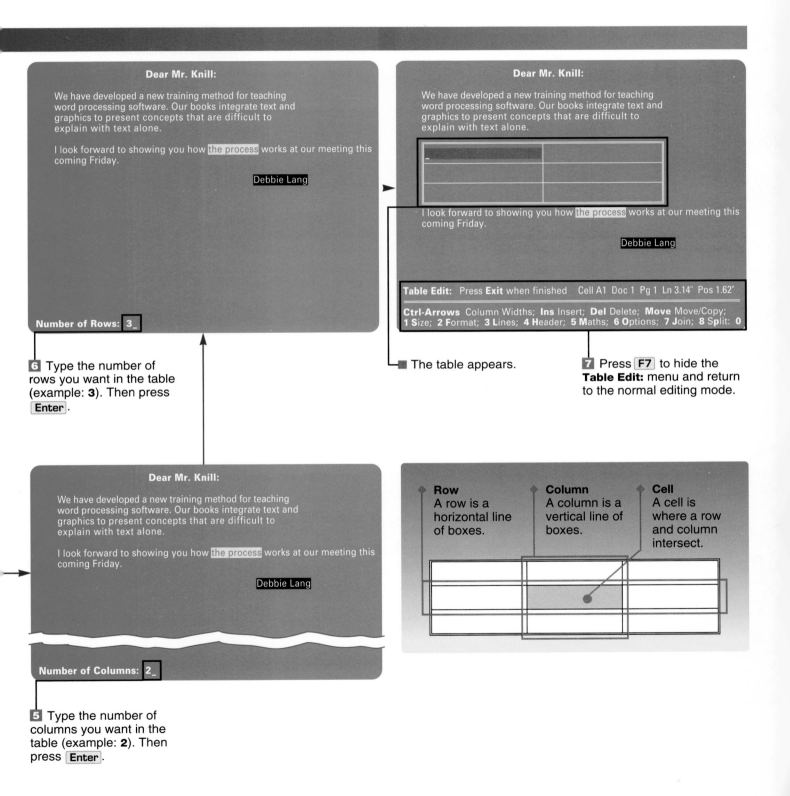

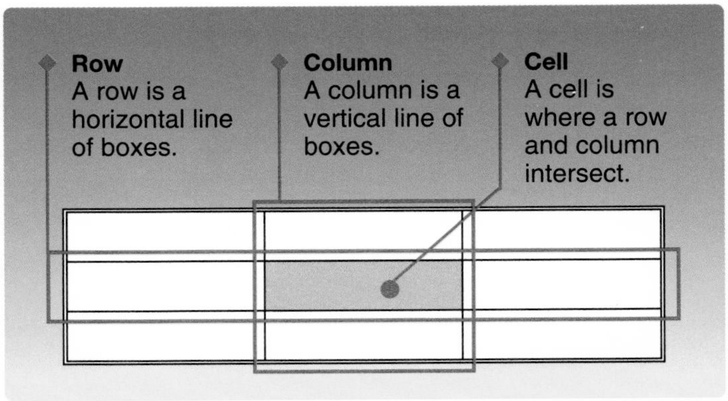
Row
A row is a horizontal line of boxes.
Column
A column is a vertical line of boxes.
Cell
A cell is where a row and column intersect.

JOIN CELLS

Alt F7 Join Cells

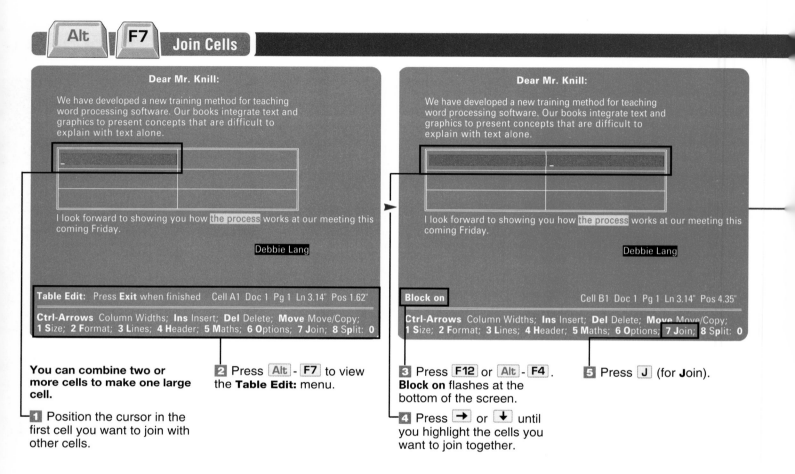

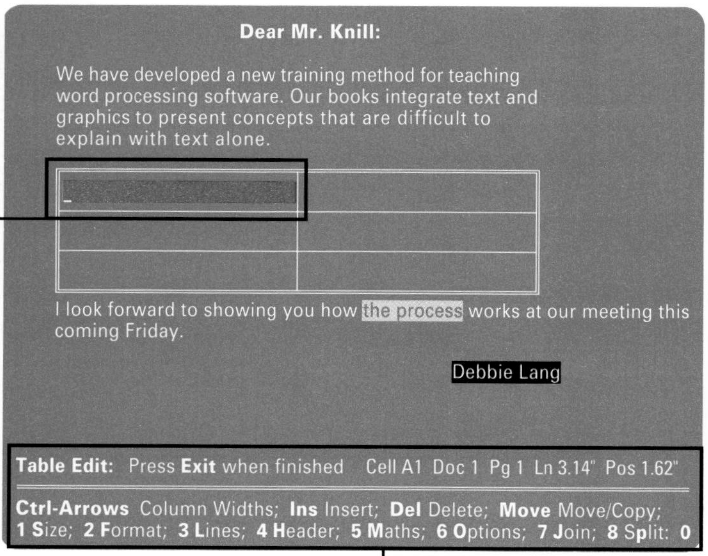
Dear Mr. Knill:
We have developed a new training method for teaching word processing software. Our books integrate text and graphics to present concepts that are difficult to explain with text alone.
I look forward to showing you how the process works at our meeting this coming Friday.
Debbie Lang
Table Edit: Press Exit when finished Cell A1 Doc 1 Pg 1 Ln 3.14" Pos 1.62"
Ctrl-Arrows Column Widths; Ins Insert; Del Delete; Move Move/Copy;
1 Size; 2 Format; 3 Lines; 4 Header; 5 Maths; 6 Options; 7 Join; 8 Split: 0

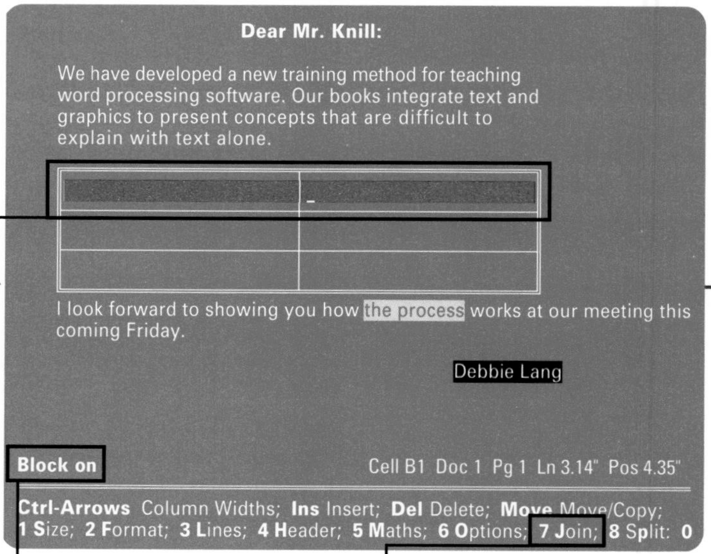
Dear Mr. Knill:
We have developed a new training method for teaching word processing software. Our books integrate text and graphics to present concepts that are difficult to explain with text alone.
I look forward to showing you how the process works at our meeting this coming Friday.
Debbie Lang
Block on
Cell B1 Doc 1 Pg 1 Ln 3.14" Pos 4.35"
Ctrl-Arrows Column Widths; Ins Insert; Del Delete; Move Move/Copy;
1 Size; 2 Format; 3 Lines; 4 Header; 5 Maths; 6 Options; 7 Join; 8 Split: 0

You can combine two or more cells to make one large cell.

1 Position the cursor in the first cell you want to join with other cells.

2 Press Alt - F7 to view the **Table Edit:** menu.

3 Press F12 or Alt - F4. **Block on** flashes at the bottom of the screen.

4 Press → or ↓ until you highlight the cells you want to join together.

5 Press J (for **J**oin).

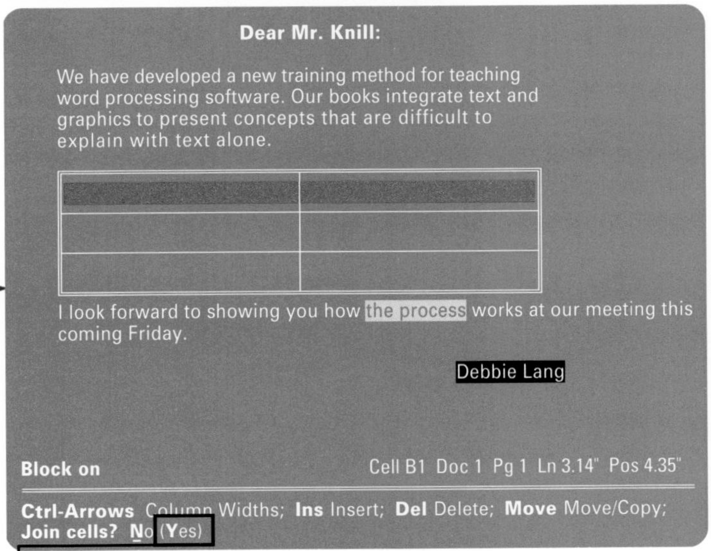
Dear Mr. Knill:
We have developed a new training method for teaching word processing software. Our books integrate text and graphics to present concepts that are difficult to explain with text alone.
I look forward to showing you how the process works at our meeting this coming Friday.
Debbie Lang
Block on
Cell B1 Doc 1 Pg 1 Ln 3.14" Pos 4.35"
Ctrl-Arrows Column Widths; Ins Insert; Del Delete; Move Move/Copy;
Join cells? No (Yes)

6 Press Y (for **Y**es) to join the cells.

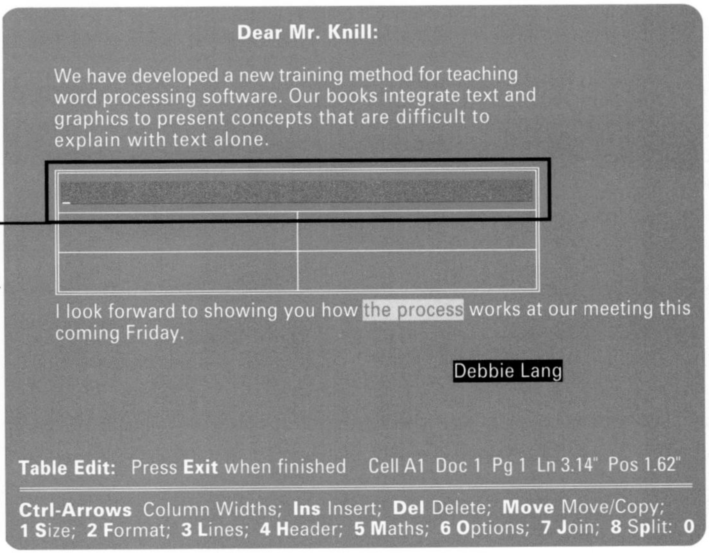
Dear Mr. Knill:
We have developed a new training method for teaching word processing software. Our books integrate text and graphics to present concepts that are difficult to explain with text alone.
I look forward to showing you how the process works at our meeting this coming Friday.
Debbie Lang
Table Edit: Press Exit when finished
Cell A1 Doc 1 Pg 1 Ln 3.14" Pos 1.62"
Ctrl-Arrows Column Widths; Ins Insert; Del Delete; Move Move/Copy;
1 Size; 2 Format; 3 Lines; 4 Header; 5 Maths; 6 Options; 7 Join; 8 Split: 0

■ The cells are joined.

7 Press F7 to return to the normal editing mode.

SPLIT CELLS

You can split one cell into two or more cells.

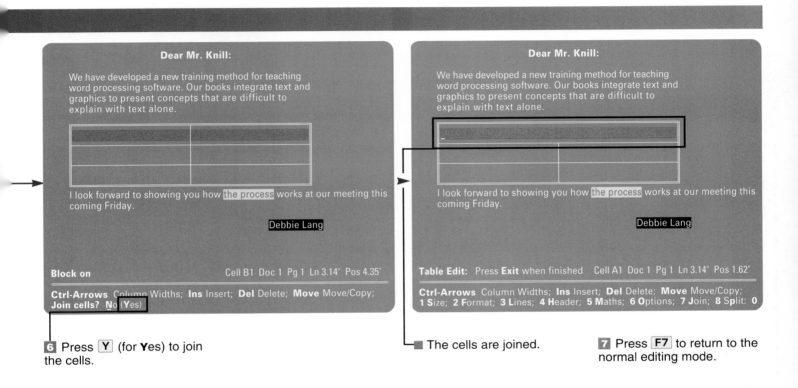

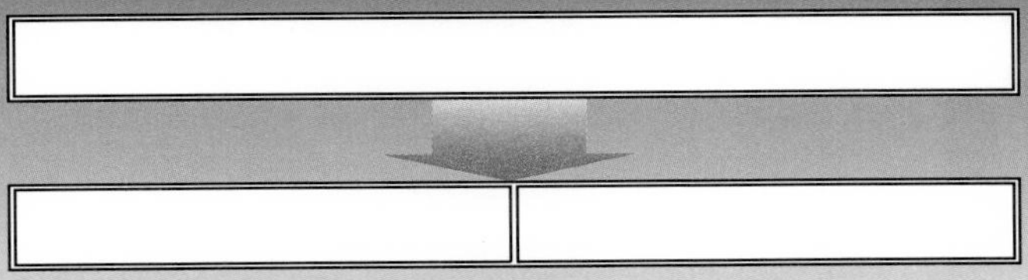

1 Position the cursor in the cell you want to split.

2 Press Alt - F7 to view the **Table Edit:** menu.

3 Press P (for S**p**lit).

4 To split a cell into two or more columns, press C (for **C**olumns).

*Note: To split a cell into two or more rows, press R (for **R**ows).*

5 Type the number of columns or rows you want to create (example: **2**). Then press Enter.

Enter Text in a Table

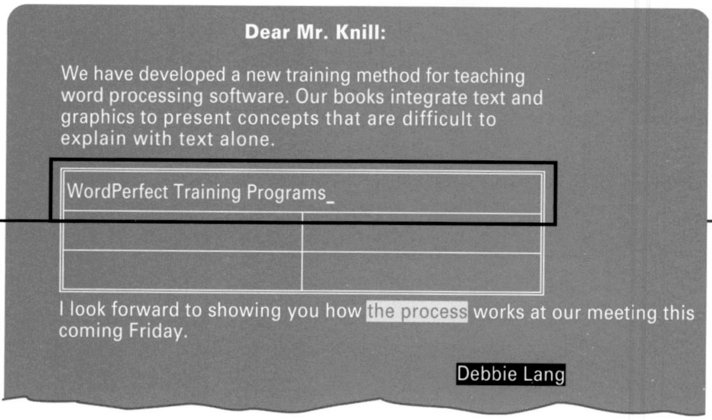

Dear Mr. Knill:
We have developed a new training method for teaching word processing software. Our books integrate text and graphics to present concepts that are difficult to explain with text alone.
WordPerfect Training Programs_
I look forward to showing you how the process works at our meeting this coming Friday.
Debbie Lang

1. Press →, ↓, ↑ or ← to move to the cell where you want to type the text.
2. Type the text.

*Note: You cannot enter text in a table when viewing the **Table Edit:** menu.*

Alt F7 Add a Row or Column

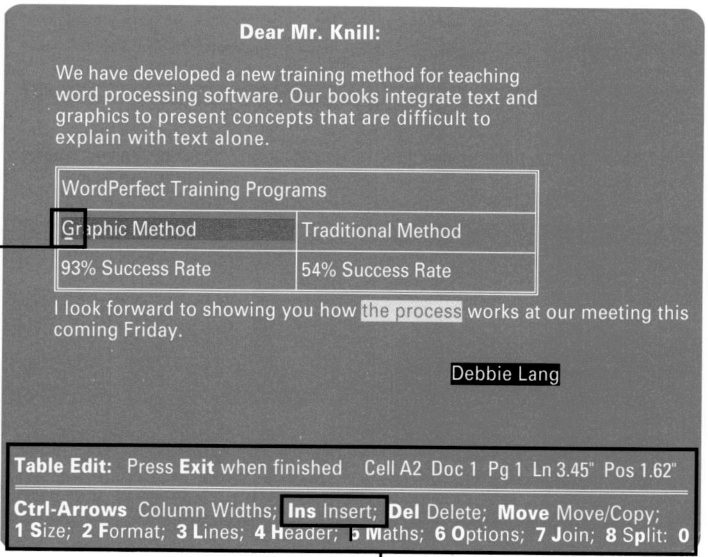

1. Position the cursor where you want to add the row or column.
2. Press Alt - F7 to view the **Table Edit:** menu.
3. Press Insert.

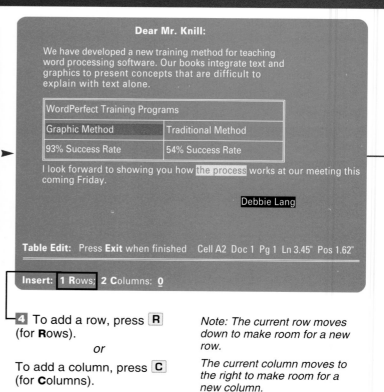

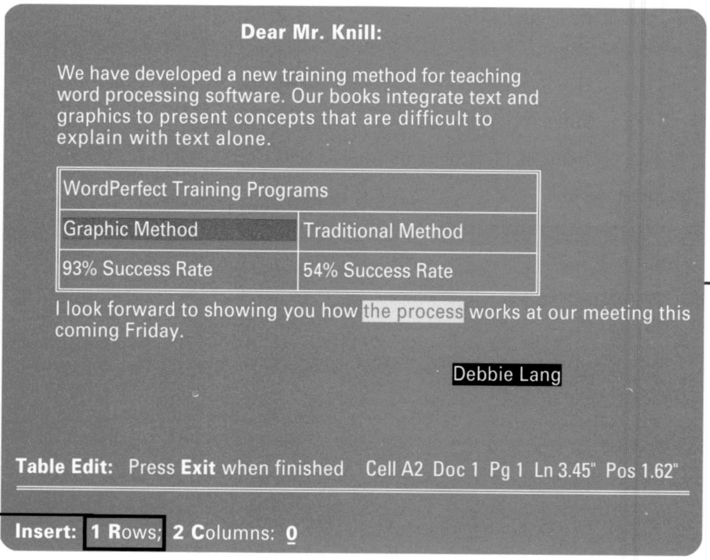

4. To add a row, press R (for **R**ows).

   or

   To add a column, press C (for **C**olumns).

Note: The current row moves down to make room for a new row.

The current column moves to the right to make room for a new column.

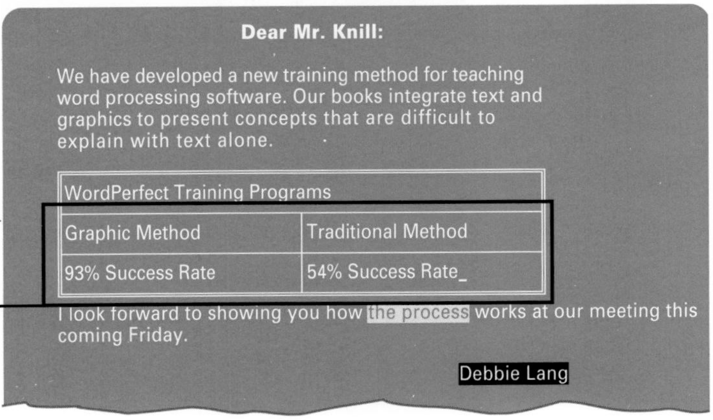
Dear Mr. Knill:
We have developed a new training method for teaching word processing software. Our books integrate text and graphics to present concepts that are difficult to explain with text alone.
WordPerfect Training Programs
Graphic Method
Traditional Method
93% Success Rate
54% Success Rate_
I look forward to showing you how the process works at our meeting this coming Friday.
Debbie Lang

3 Repeat steps 1 and 2 until you have entered all the text.

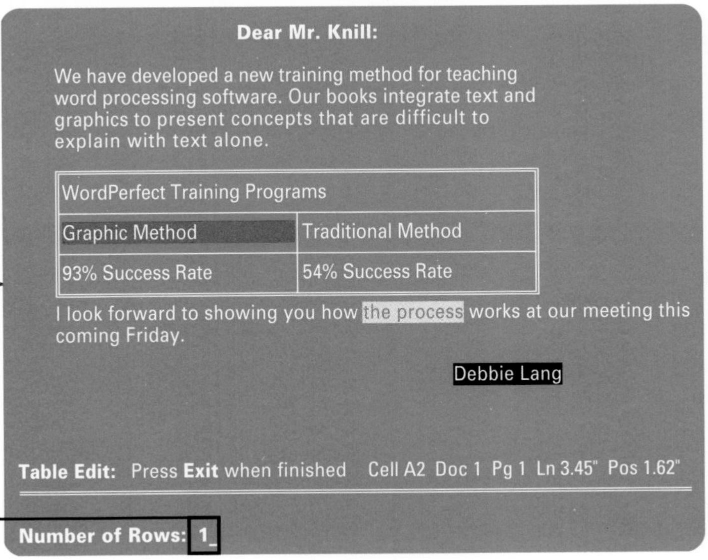
Dear Mr. Knill:
We have developed a new training method for teaching word processing software. Our books integrate text and graphics to present concepts that are difficult to explain with text alone.
WordPerfect Training Programs
Graphic Method
Traditional Method
93% Success Rate
54% Success Rate
I look forward to showing you how the process works at our meeting this coming Friday.
Debbie Lang
Table Edit: Press Exit when finished Cell A2 Doc 1 Pg 1 Ln 3.45" Pos 1.62"
Number of Rows: 1_

5 Type the number of rows (or columns) you want to add (example: **1**). Then press **Enter**.

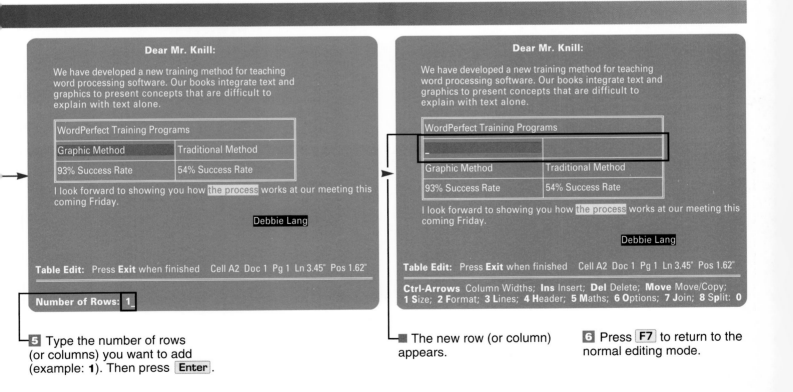

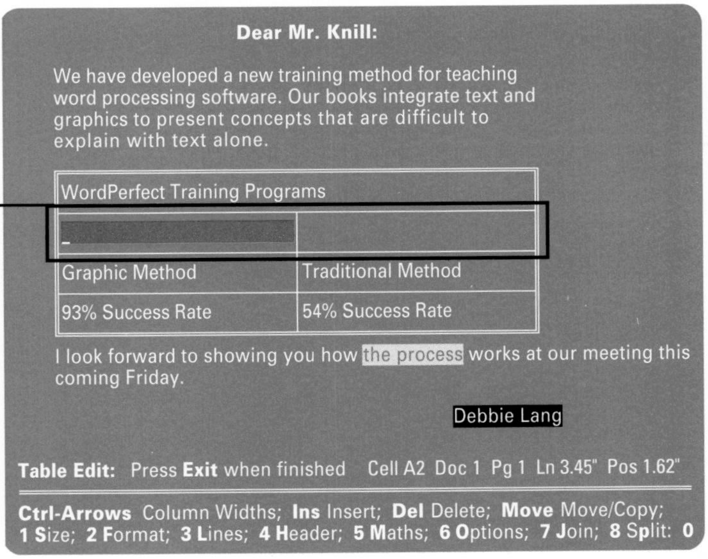
Dear Mr. Knill:
We have developed a new training method for teaching word processing software. Our books integrate text and graphics to present concepts that are difficult to explain with text alone.
WordPerfect Training Programs
Graphic Method
Traditional Method
93% Success Rate
54% Success Rate
I look forward to showing you how the process works at our meeting this coming Friday.
Debbie Lang
Table Edit: Press Exit when finished Cell A2 Doc 1 Pg 1 Ln 3.45" Pos 1.62"
Ctrl-Arrows Column Widths; Ins Insert; Del Delete; Move Move/Copy;
1 Size; 2 Format; 3 Lines; 4 Header; 5 Maths; 6 Options; 7 Join; 8 Split: 0

■ The new row (or column) appears.

6 Press **F7** to return to the normal editing mode.

DELETE A ROW OR COLUMN

CHANGE COLUMN WIDTH

Alt F7 Delete a Row or Column

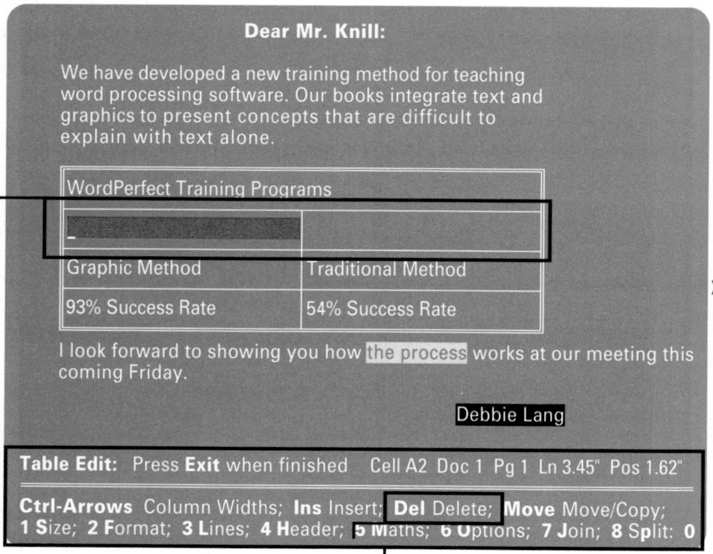

Dear Mr. Knill:
We have developed a new training method for teaching word processing software. Our books integrate text and graphics to present concepts that are difficult to explain with text alone.
WordPerfect Training Programs
Graphic Method
Traditional Method
93% Success Rate
54% Success Rate
I look forward to showing you how the process works at our meeting this coming Friday.
Debbie Lang
Table Edit: Press Exit when finished Cell A2 Doc 1 Pg 1 Ln 3.45" Pos 1.62"
Ctrl-Arrows Column Widths; Ins Insert; Del Delete; Move Move/Copy;
1 Size; 2 Format; 3 Lines; 4 Header; 5 Maths; 6 Options; 7 Join; 8 Split: 0

1 Position the cursor in the row or column you want to delete.

2 Press Alt - F7 to view the **Table Edit:** menu.

3 Press Delete.

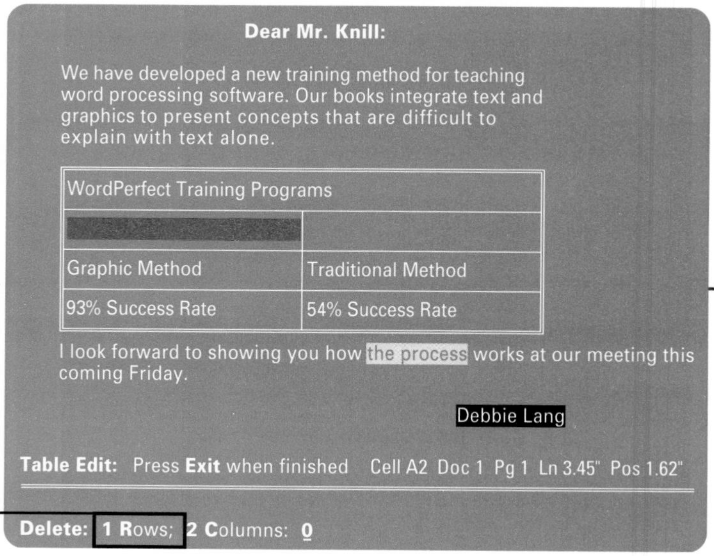

Dear Mr. Knill:
We have developed a new training method for teaching word processing software. Our books integrate text and graphics to present concepts that are difficult to explain with text alone.
WordPerfect Training Programs
Graphic Method
Traditional Method
93% Success Rate
54% Success Rate
I look forward to showing you how the process works at our meeting this coming Friday.
Debbie Lang
Table Edit: Press Exit when finished Cell A2 Doc 1 Pg 1 Ln 3.45" Pos 1.62"
Delete: 1 Rows; 2 Columns: 0

4 To delete a row, press R (for **R**ows).

or

To delete a column, press C (for **C**olumns).

Alt F7 Change Column Width

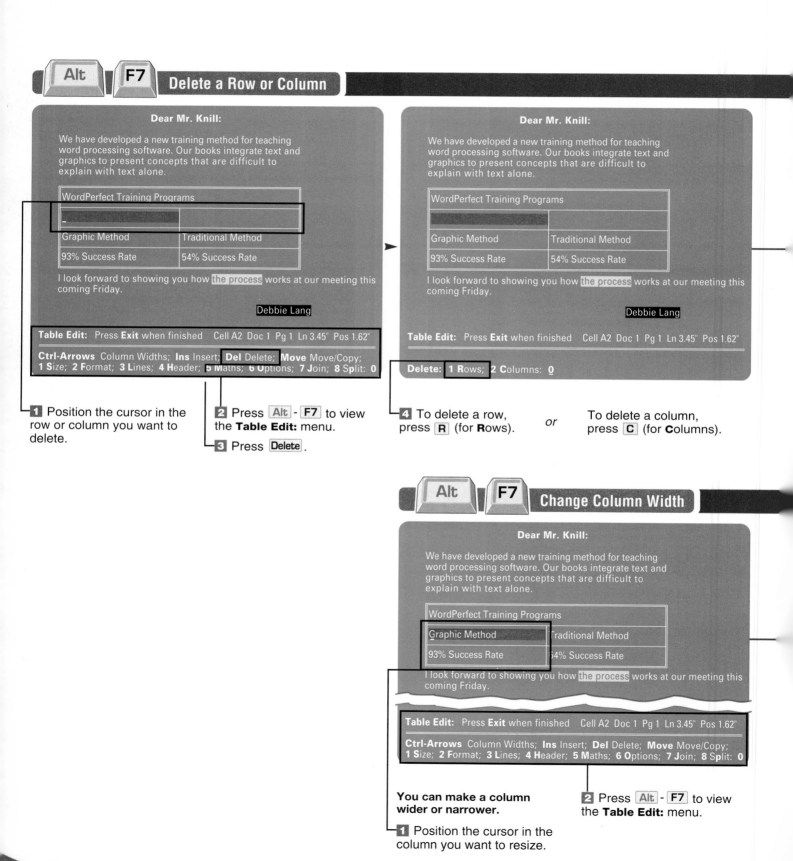

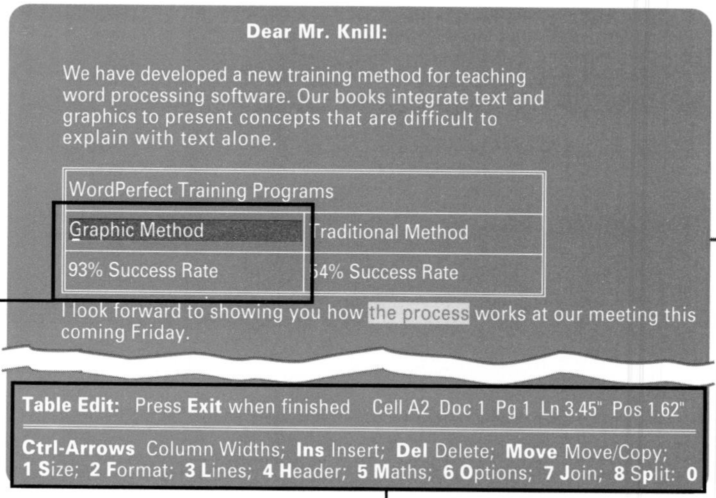

Dear Mr. Knill:
We have developed a new training method for teaching word processing software. Our books integrate text and graphics to present concepts that are difficult to explain with text alone.
WordPerfect Training Programs
Graphic Method
Traditional Method
93% Success Rate
54% Success Rate
I look forward to showing you how the process works at our meeting this coming Friday.
Table Edit: Press Exit when finished Cell A2 Doc 1 Pg 1 Ln 3.45" Pos 1.62"
Ctrl-Arrows Column Widths; Ins Insert; Del Delete; Move Move/Copy;
1 Size; 2 Format; 3 Lines; 4 Header; 5 Maths; 6 Options; 7 Join; 8 Split: 0

You can make a column wider or narrower.

1 Position the cursor in the column you want to resize.

2 Press Alt - F7 to view the **Table Edit:** menu.

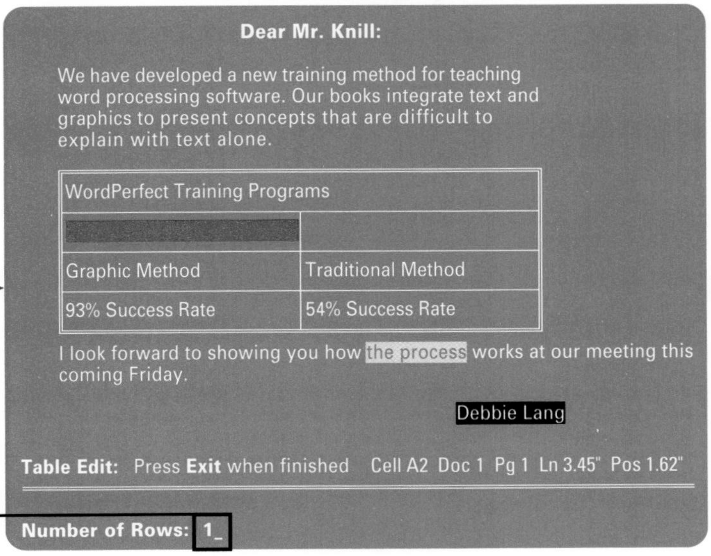

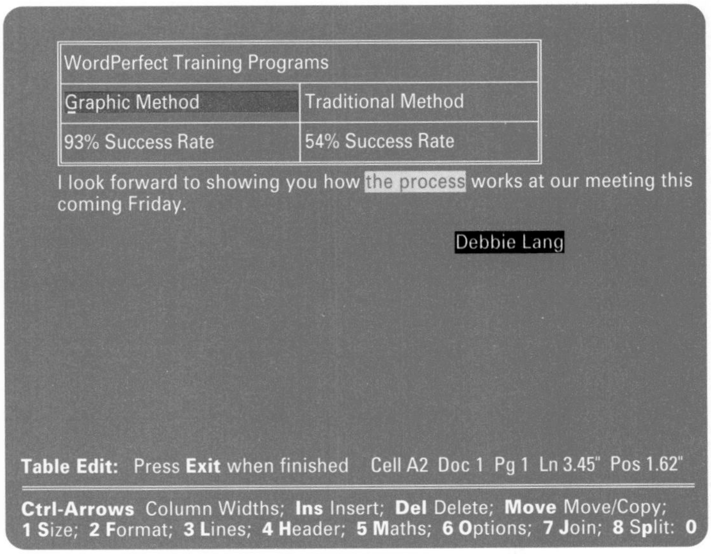

5 Type the number of rows (or columns) you want to delete (example: **1**). Then press Enter.

■ The row (or column) disappears.

6 Press F7 to return to the normal editing mode.

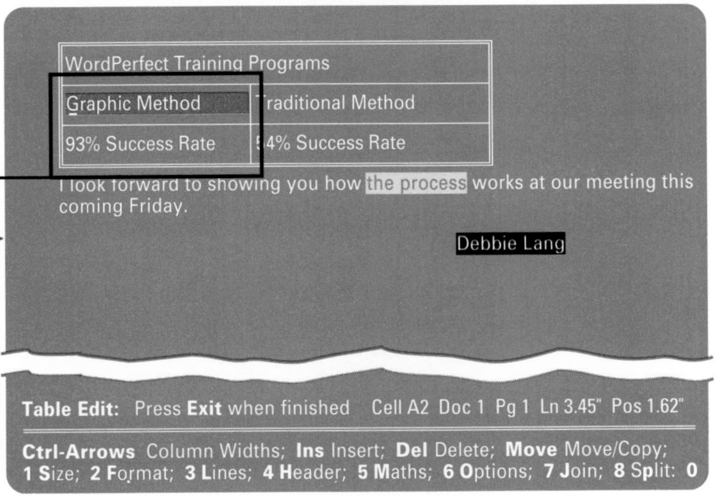

3 Press and hold down Ctrl as you press → or ←. Continue until the column is the desired size.

4 Press F7 to return to the normal editing mode.

CHANGE TABLE LINES

Alt F7 Change Table Lines

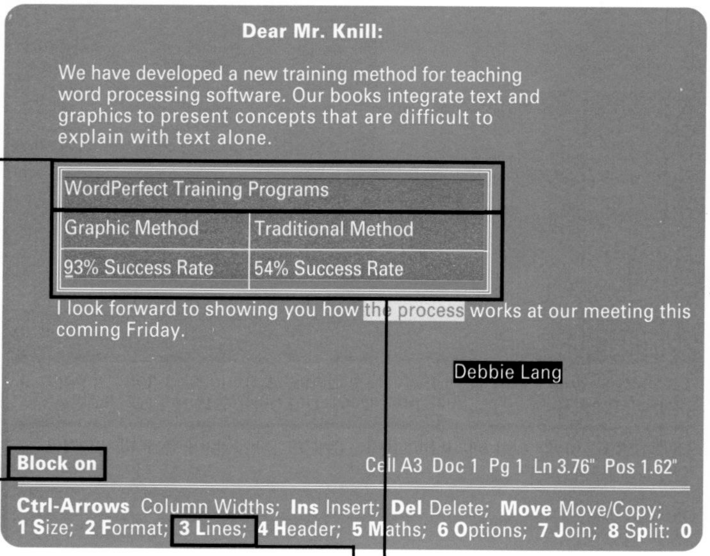
Dear Mr. Knill:
We have developed a new training method for teaching word processing software. Our books integrate text and graphics to present concepts that are difficult to explain with text alone.
WordPerfect Training Programs
Graphic Method
Traditional Method
93% Success Rate
54% Success Rate
I look forward to showing you how the process works at our meeting this coming Friday.
Debbie Lang
Block on
Cell A3 Doc 1 Pg 1 Ln 3.76" Pos 1.62"
Ctrl-Arrows Column Widths; Ins Insert; Del Delete; Move Move/Copy;
1 Size; 2 Format; 3 Lines; 4 Header; 5 Maths; 6 Options; 7 Join; 8 Split: 0

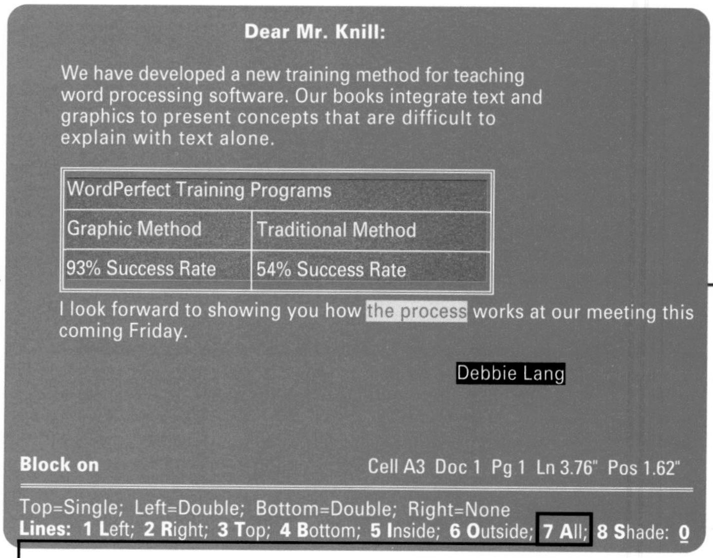
Dear Mr. Knill:
We have developed a new training method for teaching word processing software. Our books integrate text and graphics to present concepts that are difficult to explain with text alone.
WordPerfect Training Programs
Graphic Method
Traditional Method
93% Success Rate
54% Success Rate
I look forward to showing you how the process works at our meeting this coming Friday.
Debbie Lang
Block on
Cell A3 Doc 1 Pg 1 Ln 3.76" Pos 1.62"
Top=Single; Left=Double; Bottom=Double; Right=None
Lines: 1 Left; 2 Right; 3 Top; 4 Bottom; 5 Inside; 6 Outside; 7 All; 8 Shade: 0

You can change the type of lines used in a table.

1 Position the cursor in the first cell you want to change.

2 Press Alt - F7 to view the **Table Edit:** menu.

3 Press F12 or Alt - F4 and **Block on** flashes at the bottom of the screen.

4 Press →, ↓, ← or ↑ until you highlight the cells you want to change.

5 Press L (for **L**ines).

6 Press the highlighted letter that specifies the lines you want to change (example: A for **A**ll).

WordPerfect offers many different types of lines.

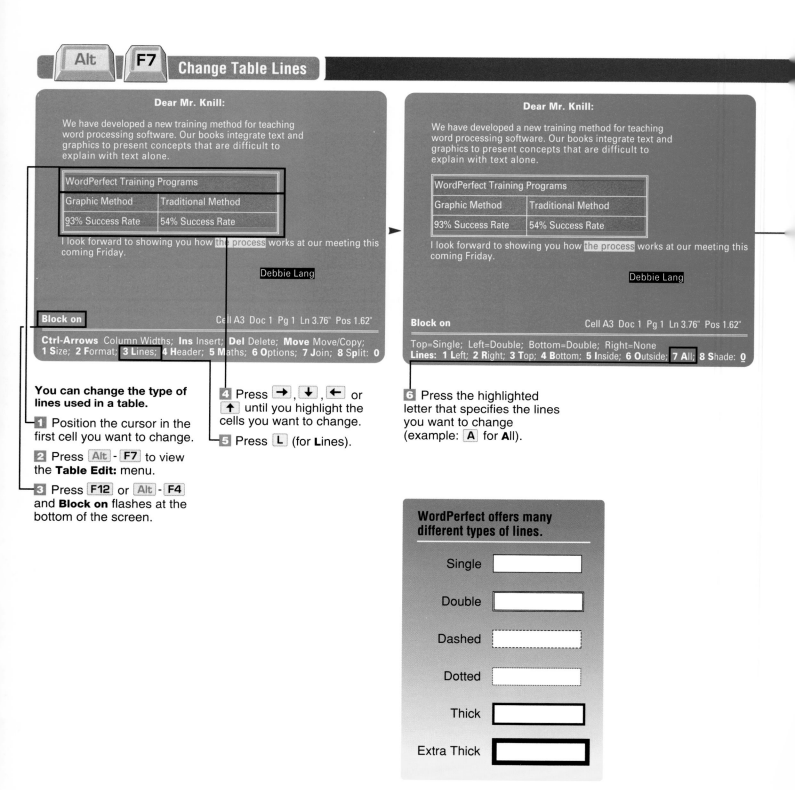

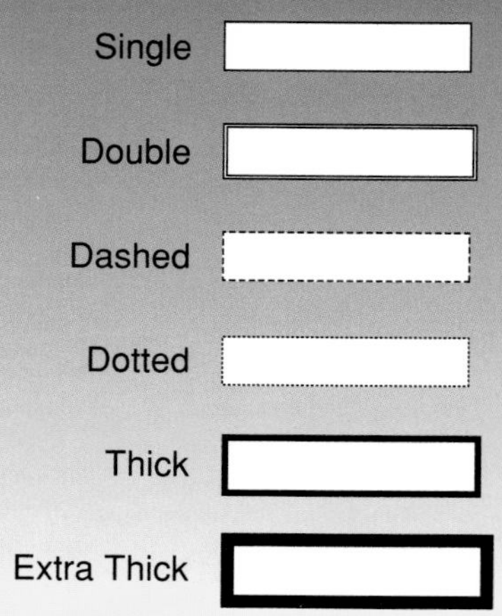
Single
Double
Dashed
Dotted
Thick
Extra Thick

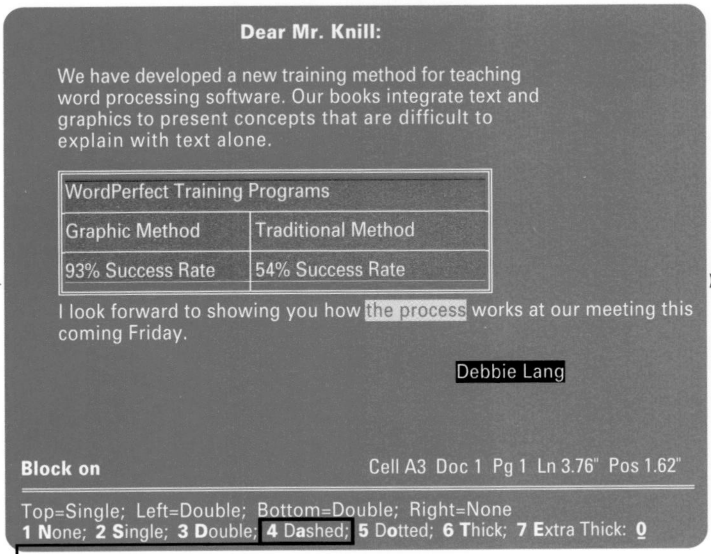

7 Press the highlighted letter that specifies the desired line type (example: A for D**a**shed).

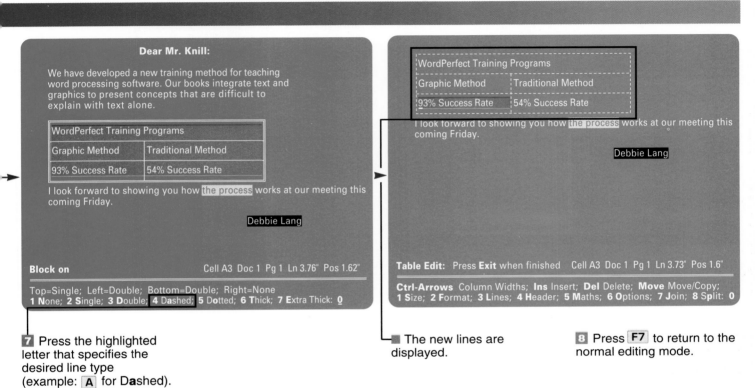

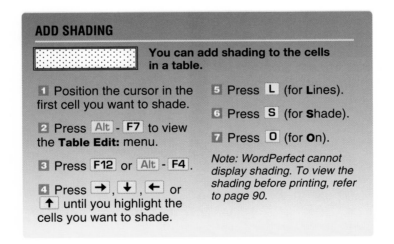

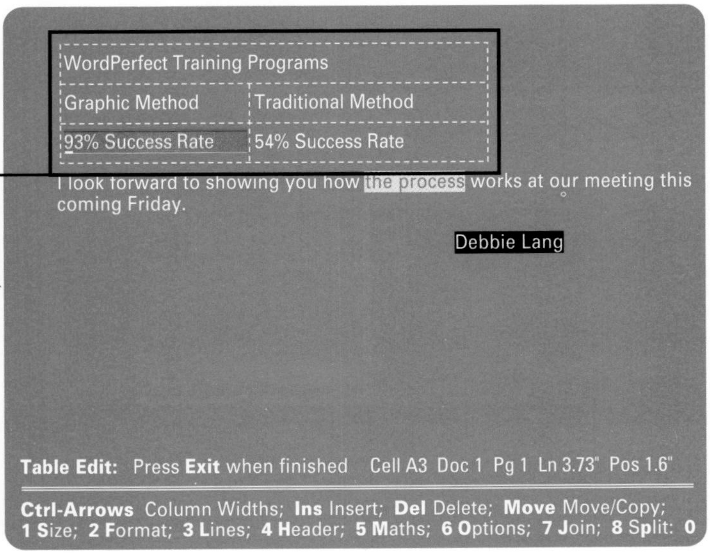

■ The new lines are displayed.

8 Press F7 to return to the normal editing mode.

ADD SHADING

You can add shading to the cells in a table.

1 Position the cursor in the first cell you want to shade.

2 Press Alt - F7 to view the **Table Edit:** menu.

3 Press F12 or Alt - F4.

4 Press →, ↓, ← or ↑ until you highlight the cells you want to shade.

5 Press L (for **L**ines).

6 Press S (for **S**hade).

7 Press O (for **O**n).

Note: WordPerfect cannot display shading. To view the shading before printing, refer to page 90.

VIEW A DOCUMENT

Shift F7 View a Document

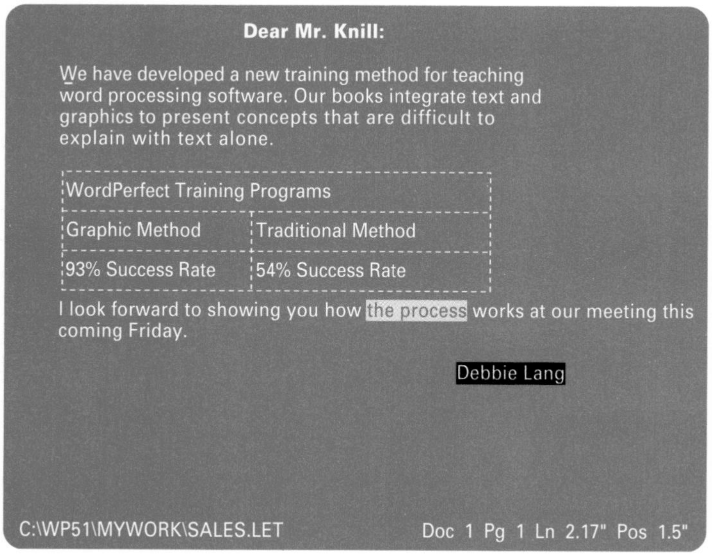

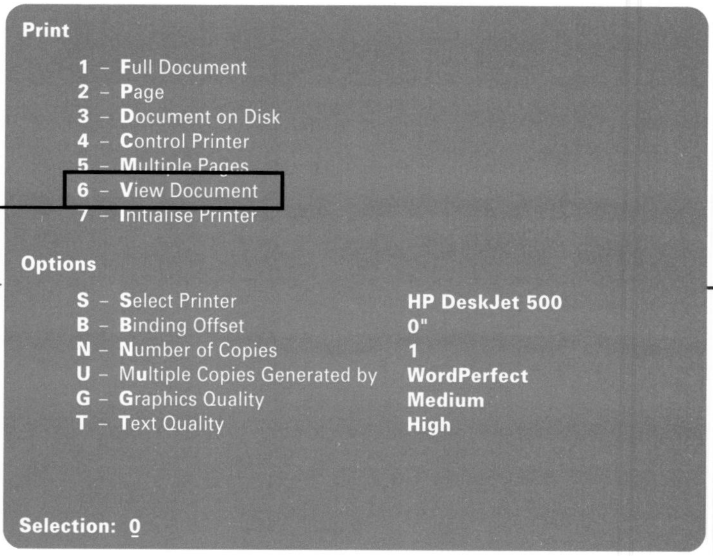

You have the option to see how a document will appear on a printed page. This is very useful for viewing features that do not appear on the screen but will print.

1 Press Shift - F7 and the **Print** screen appears.

2 Press V (for **V**iew Document).

Note: Assume that this document is three pages long.

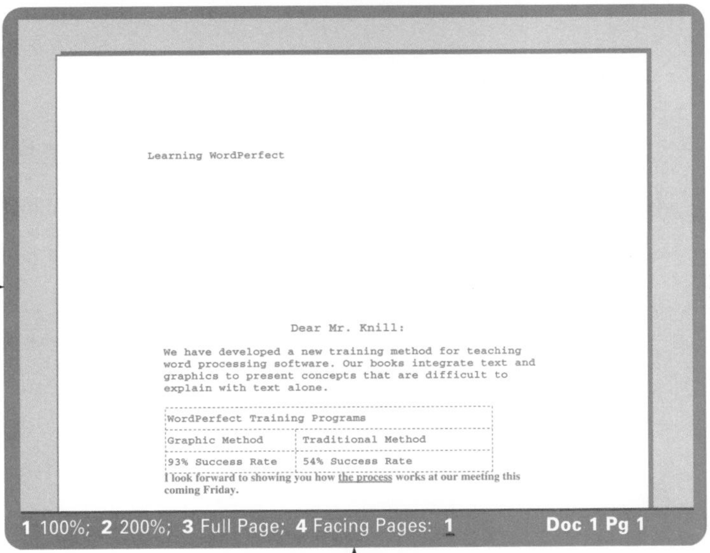
Learning WordPerfect
Dear Mr. Knill:
We have developed a new training method for teaching word processing software. Our books integrate text and graphics to present concepts that are difficult to explain with text alone.
WordPerfect Training Programs
Graphic Method
Traditional Method
93% Success Rate
54% Success Rate
I look forward to showing you how the process works at our meeting this coming Friday.
1 100%; 2 200%; 3 Full Page; 4 Facing Pages: 1
Doc 1 Pg 1

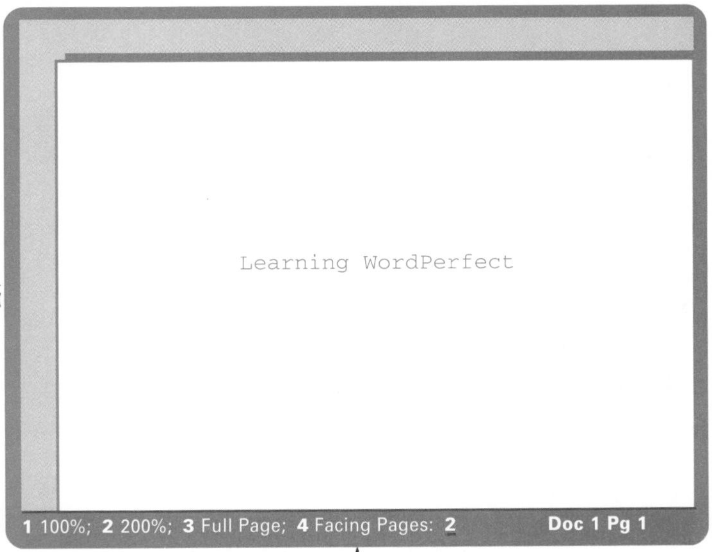
Learning WordPerfect
1 100%; 2 200%; 3 Full Page; 4 Facing Pages: 2
Doc 1 Pg 1

■ Press 1 to view the document at 100%.

■ To scan through the page, press ↓ or ↑.

■ Press 2 to view the document at 200%.

■ To scan through the page, press →, ↓, ↑ or ←.

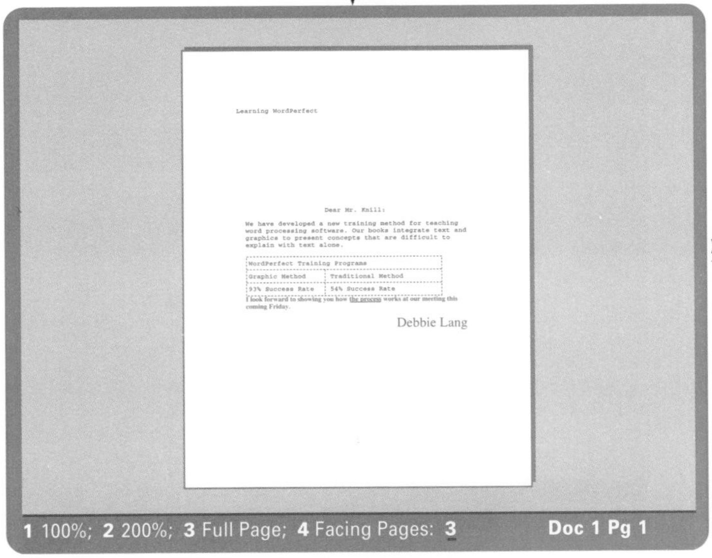
Debbie Lang
1 100%; 2 200%; 3 Full Page; 4 Facing Pages: 3
Doc 1 Pg 1

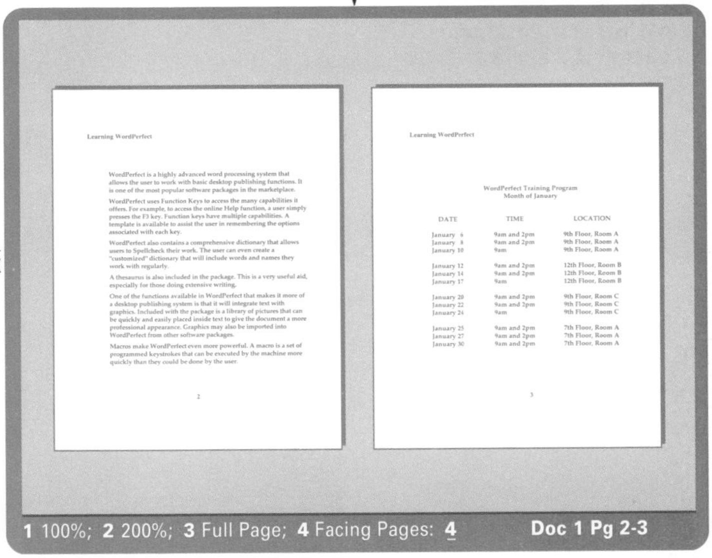
1 100%; 2 200%; 3 Full Page; 4 Facing Pages: 4
Doc 1 Pg 2-3

■ Press 3 to view the entire page.

■ Press 4 to view two pages side-by-side.

Note: If no facing page exists, only one page is displayed.

To view other pages in the document

Press PgUp or PgDn.

To return to the document

Press F7.

PRINT A DOCUMENT

Shift F7 Print One Page

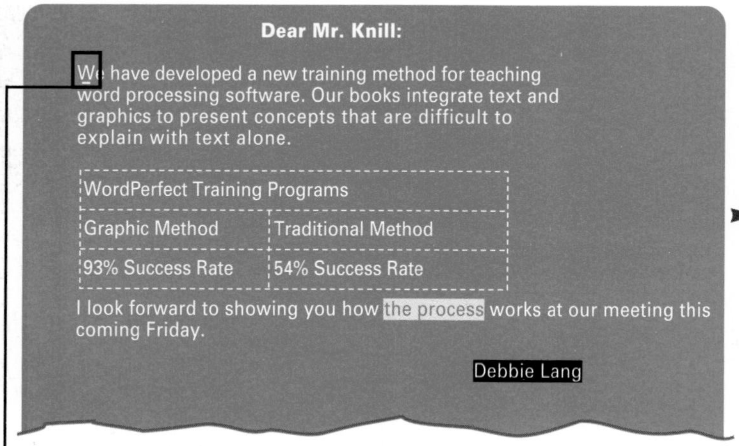

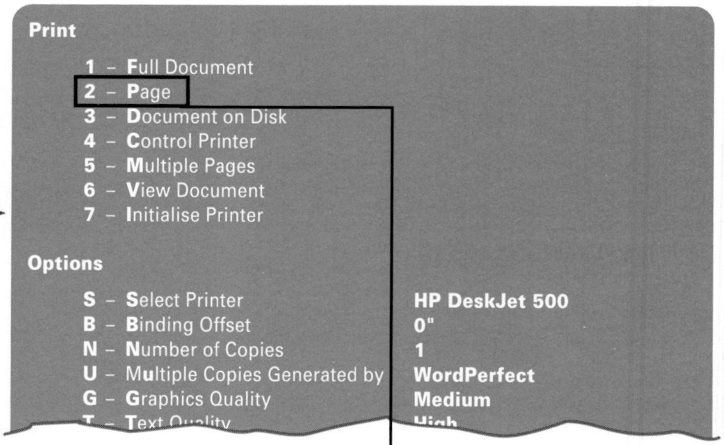

1 Position the cursor anywhere on the page you want to print.

2 Press Shift - F7 and the **Print** screen appears.

3 Press P (for **P**age).

Shift F7 Print Entire Document

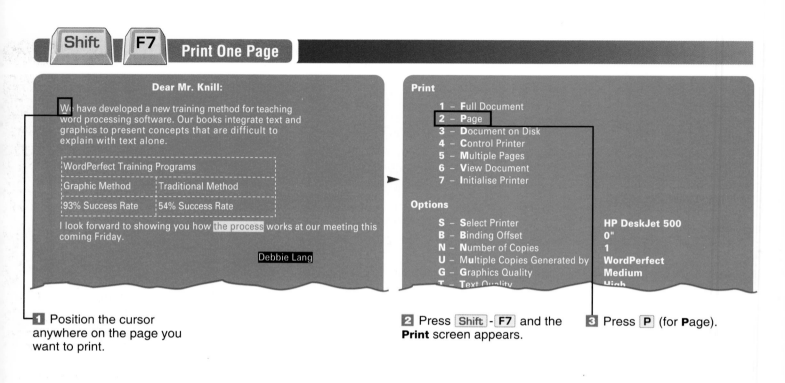

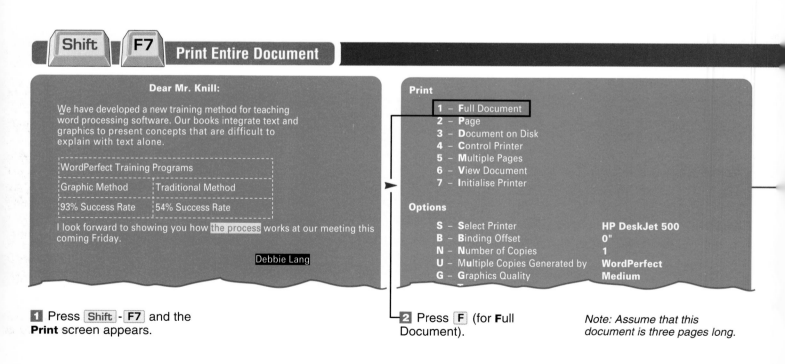

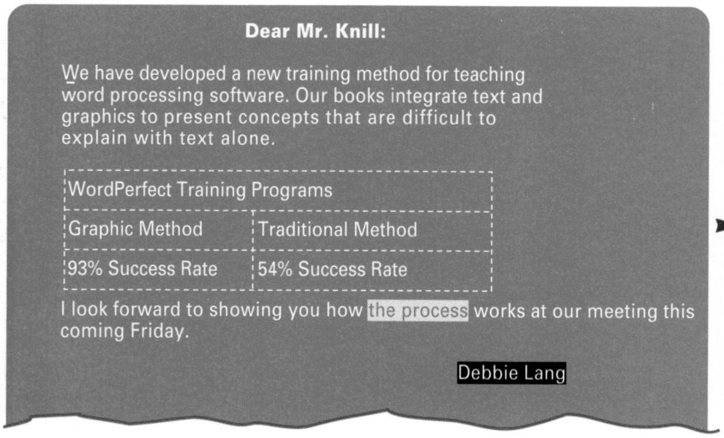

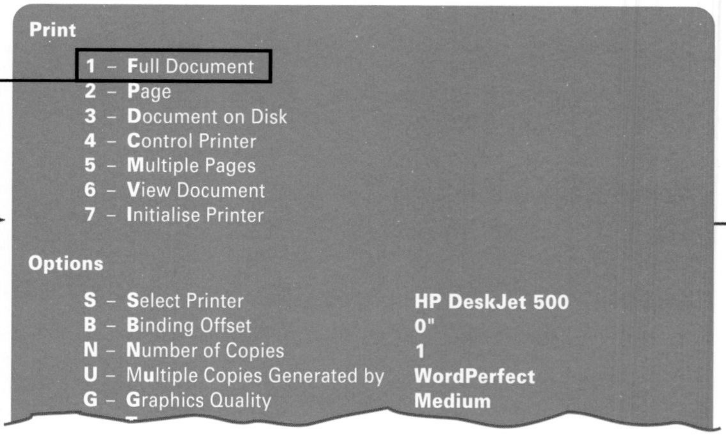

1 Press Shift - F7 and the **Print** screen appears.

2 Press F (for **F**ull Document).

Note: Assume that this document is three pages long.

Shift F7 Print Multiple Pages

Print

1 – **F**ull Document
2 – **P**age
3 – **D**ocument on Disk
4 – **C**ontrol Printer
5 – **M**ultiple Pages
6 – **V**iew Document
7 – **I**nitialise Printer

Options

S – **S**elect Printer   **HP DeskJet 500**
B – **B**inding Offset   **0"**

Page(s): 1 3 7_

3 To print random pages

Type the page numbers, separated by spaces (example: **1 3 7**). Then press Enter.

or

To print sequential pages

Type the first and last pages of the sequence, separated by a dash (example: **6-11**). Then press Enter.

1 Press Shift - F7 and the **Print** screen appears.

2 Press M (for **M**ultiple Pages).

Page 1

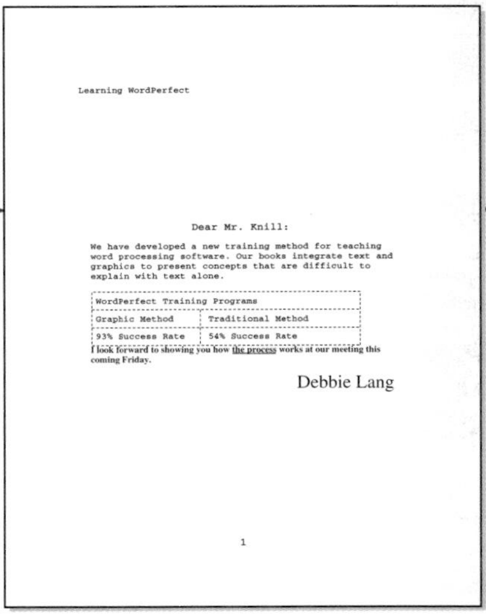

Learning WordPerfect

Dear Mr. Knill:

We have developed a new training method for teaching word processing software. Our books integrate text and graphics to present concepts that are difficult to explain with text alone.

WordPerfect Training Programs	
Graphic Method	Traditional Method
93% Success Rate	54% Success Rate

I look forward to showing you how the process works at our meeting this coming Friday.

Debbie Lang

1

Page 2

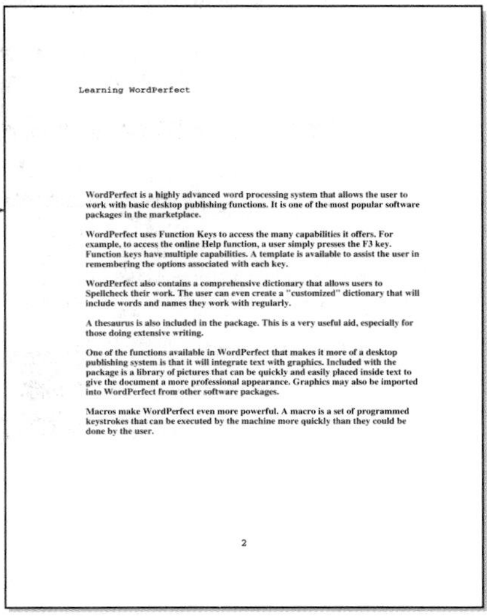

Learning WordPerfect

WordPerfect is a highly advanced word processing system that allows the user to work with basic desktop publishing functions. It is one of the most popular software packages in the marketplace.

WordPerfect uses Function Keys to access the many capabilities it offers. For example, to access the online Help function, a user simply presses the F3 key. Function keys have multiple capabilities. A template is available to assist the user in remembering the options associated with each key.

WordPerfect also contains a comprehensive dictionary that allows users to Spellcheck their work. The user can even create a "customized" dictionary that will include words and names they work with regularly.

A thesaurus is also included in the package. This is a very useful aid, especially for those doing extensive writing.

One of the functions available in WordPerfect that makes it more of a desktop publishing system is that it will integrate text with graphics. Included with the package is a library of pictures that can be quickly and easily placed inside text to give the document a more professional appearance. Graphics may also be imported into WordPerfect from other software packages.

Macros make WordPerfect even more powerful. A macro is a set of programmed keystrokes that can be executed by the machine more quickly than they could be done by the user.

2

Page 3 (Last Page)

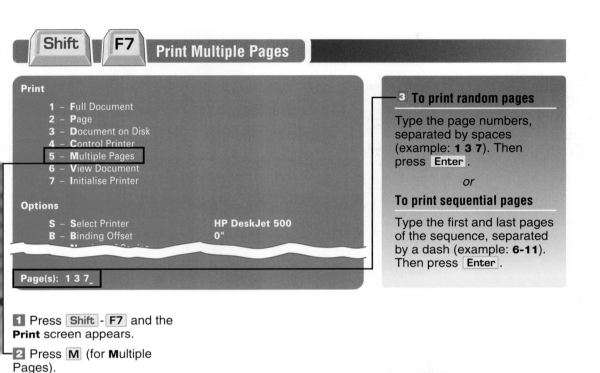

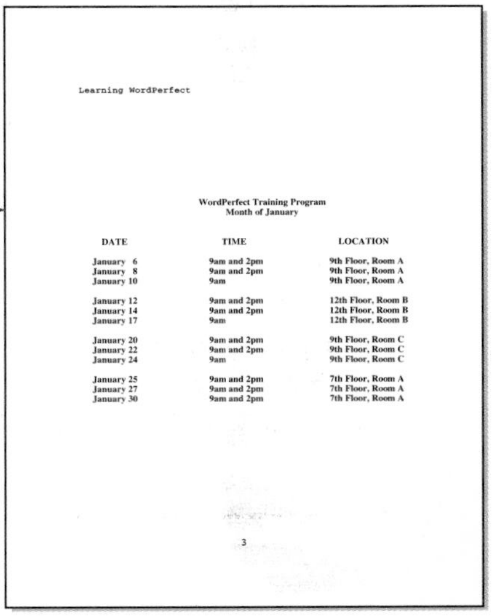

Learning WordPerfect

WordPerfect Training Program
Month of January

DATE	TIME	LOCATION
January 6	9am and 2pm	9th Floor, Room A
January 8	9am and 2pm	9th Floor, Room A
January 10	9am	9th Floor, Room A
January 12	9am and 2pm	12th Floor, Room B
January 14	9am and 2pm	12th Floor, Room B
January 17	9am	12th Floor, Room B
January 20	9am and 2pm	9th Floor, Room C
January 22	9am and 2pm	9th Floor, Room C
January 24	9am	9th Floor, Room C
January 25	9am and 2pm	7th Floor, Room A
January 27	9am and 2pm	7th Floor, Room A
January 30	9am and 2pm	7th Floor, Room A

3

DISPLAY THE LIST FILES SCREEN

The List Files screen allows you to perform many MS-DOS file management tasks within WordPerfect.

1 Some List File features do not work properly when a file is displayed on the screen. To prevent problems, clear the screen.

To Clear the Screen

1 Press F7.

2 Press N (for **N**o) if you do not want to save the document.

3 Press N (for **N**o) to clear the screen.

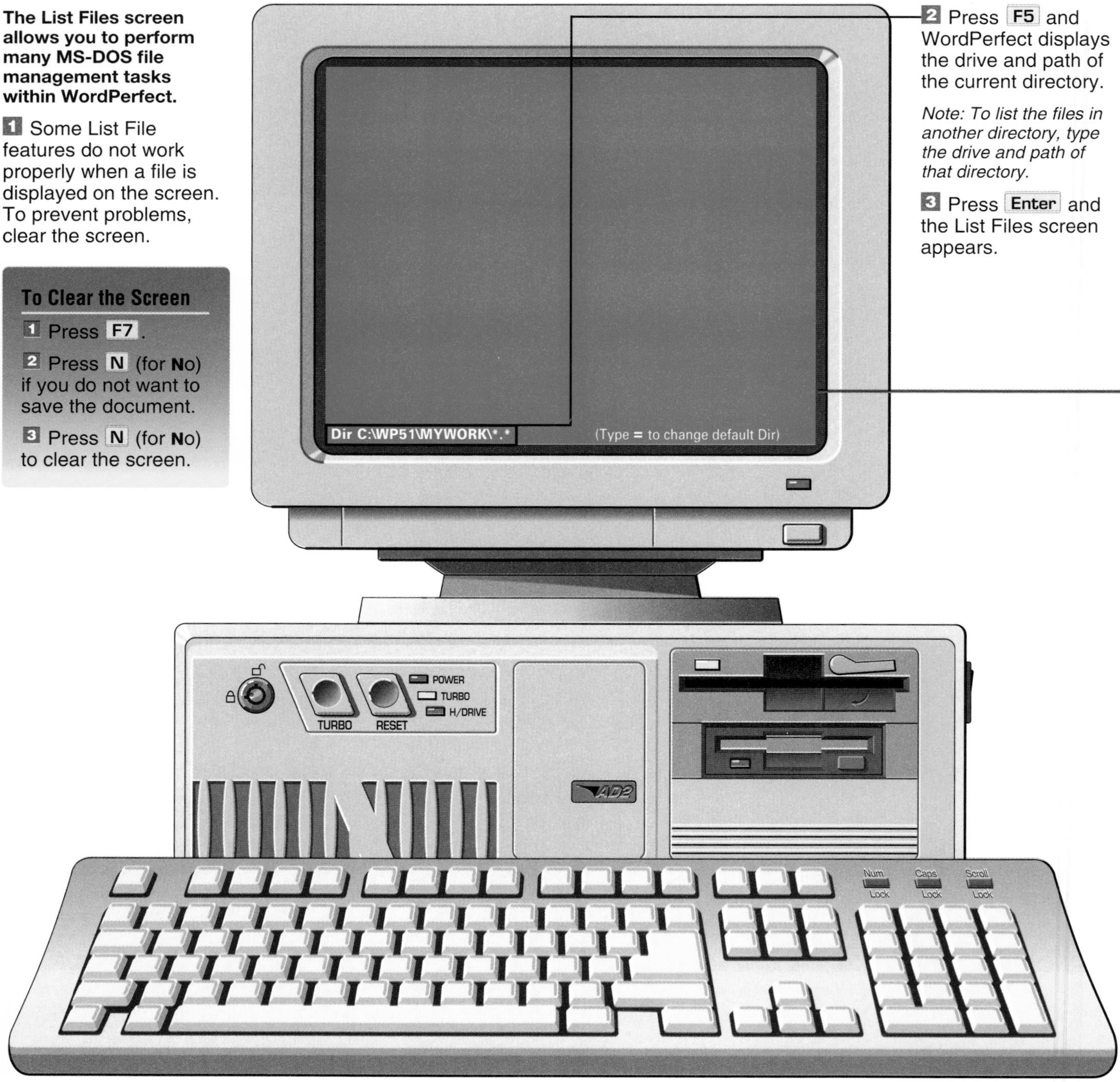

2 Press F5 and WordPerfect displays the drive and path of the current directory.

Note: To list the files in another directory, type the drive and path of that directory.

3 Press Enter and the List Files screen appears.

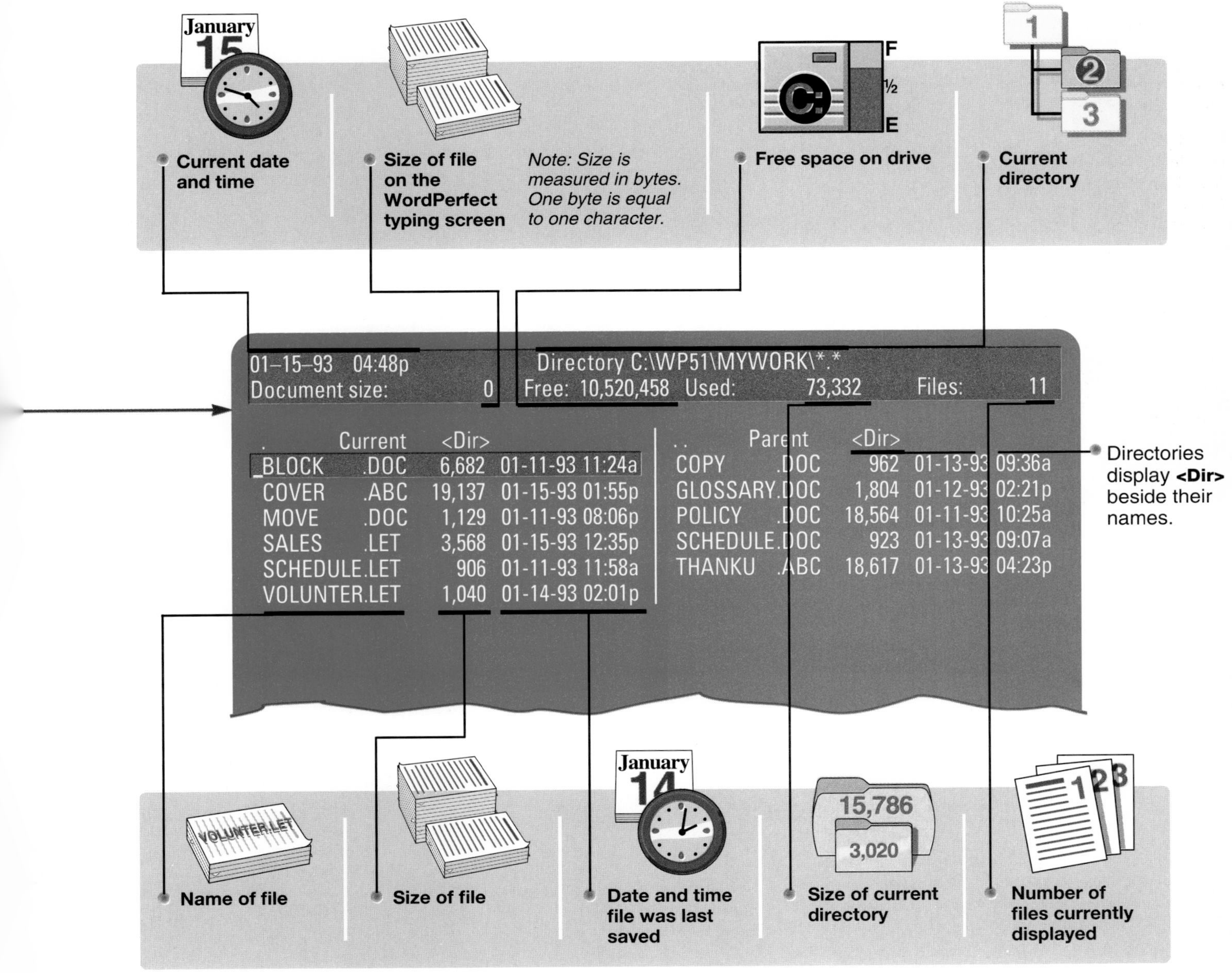

To exit the List Files screen

Press F7.

C Copy a File

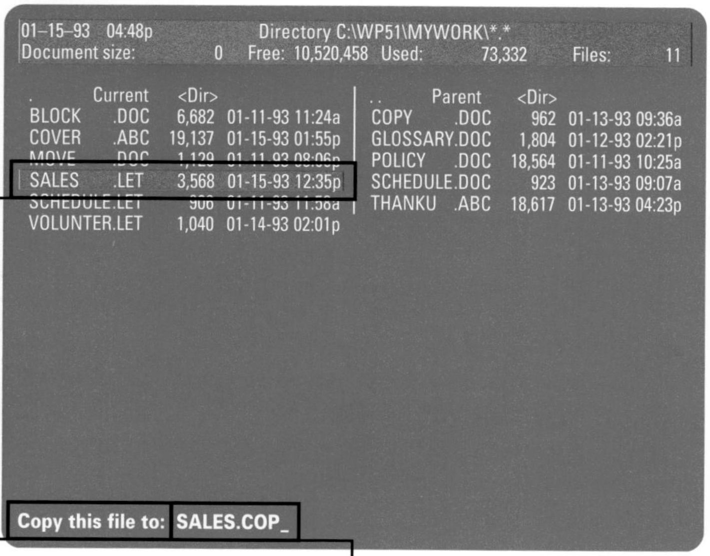

You can make an exact copy of a file and place it in the same directory or a different one. This does not affect the original file.

1 Press →, ↓, ↑ or ← until you highlight the file you want to copy.

2 Press C (for **C**opy) and this message appears.

Copy file to same directory

3 To copy a file to the same directory you must change its name. Type a new file name (example: **SALES.COP**). Then press Enter.

or

Copy file to different directory

3 Type the drive and path to indicate where you want to copy the file, then type the file name (example: **A:\SALES.LET**). Then press Enter.

M Move a File

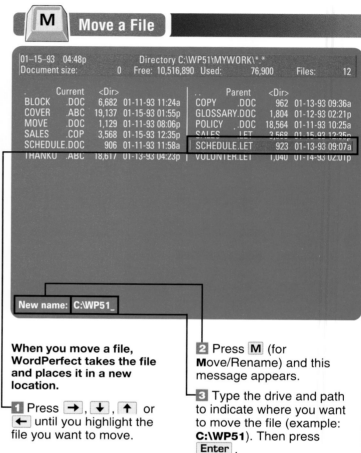

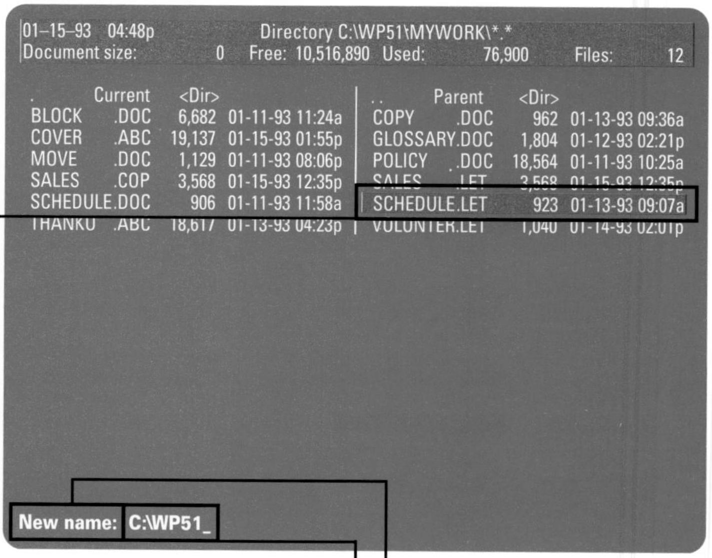

When you move a file, WordPerfect takes the file and places it in a new location.

1 Press →, ↓, ↑ or ← until you highlight the file you want to move.

2 Press M (for **M**ove/Rename) and this message appears.

3 Type the drive and path to indicate where you want to move the file (example: **C:\WP51**). Then press Enter.

DISPLAY THE LIST FILES SCREEN
COPY
MOVE
RENAME
DELETE
PRINT
NAME SEARCH
FIND
OTHER DIRECTORY

M Rename a File

```
01-15-93  04:48p             Directory C:\WP51\MYWORK\*.*
Document size:        0   Free: 10,517,813  Used:    75,977     Files:    11

 .        Current   <Dir>                   | . .      Parent    <Dir>
BLOCK    .DOC    6,682  01-11-93 11:24a    | COPY     .DOC      962  01-13-93 09:36a
COVER    .ABC   19,137  01-15-93 01:55p    | GLOSSARY.DOC    1,804  01-12-93 02:21p
MOVE     .DOC    1,129  01-11-93 08:06p    | POLICY   .DOC   18,564  01-11-93 10:25a
SALES    .COP    3,568  01-15-93 12:35p    | SALES    .LET    3,568  01-15-93 12:35p
SCHEDULE.DOC      906  01-11-93 11:58a    | THANKU   .ABC   18,617  01-13-93 04:23p
VOLUNTER.LET    1,040  01-14-93 02:01p

New name: KNILL.LET_
```

You can change the name of a file.

1 Press →, ↓, ↑ or ← until you highlight the file you want to rename.

2 Press M (for **M**ove/Rename) and this message appears.

3 Type the new file name (example: **KNILL.LET**). Then press Enter.

D Delete a File

```
01-15-93  04:48p             Directory C:\WP51\MYWORK\*.*
Document size:        0   Free: 10,517,813  Used:    75,977     Files:    11

 .        Current   <Dir>                   | . .      Parent    <Dir>
BLOCK    .DOC    6,682  01-11-93 11:24a    | COPY     .DOC      962  01-13-93 09:36a
COVER    .ABC   19,137  01-15-93 01:55p    | GLOSSARY.DOC    1,804  01-12-93 02:21p
KNILL    .LET    3,568  01-15-93 12:35p    | MOVE     .DOC    1,129  01-11-93 08:06p
POLICY   .DOC    3,568  01-15-93 12:35p    | SALES    .COP    3,568  01-15-93 12:35p
SCHEDULE.DOC      906  01-11-93 11:58a    | THANKU   .ABC   18,617  01-13-93 04:23p
VOLUNTER.LET    1,040  01-14-93 02:01p

Delete C:\WP51\MYWORK\SALES.COP? No (Yes)
```

Deleting a file permanently removes it from the disk.

1 Press →, ↓, ↑ or ← until you highlight the file you want to delete.

2 Press D (for **D**elete) and this message appears.

3 Press Y (for **Y**es) to delete the file.

```
01-15-93  04:48p             Directory C:\WP51\MYWORK\*.*
Document size:        0   Free: 10,517,813  Used:    75,977     Files:    11

          Current   <Dir>                   |          Parent    <Dir>
*BLOCK    .DOC    6,682  01-11-93 11:24a   | *COPY     .DOC      962  01-13-93 09:36a
 COVER    .ABC   19,137  01-15-93 01:55p   |  GLOSSARY.DOC    1,804  01-12-93 02:21p
*KNILL    .LET    3,568  01-15-93 12:35p   |  MOVE     .DOC    1,129  01-11-93 08:06p
*POLICY   .DOC    3,568  01-15-93 12:35p   | *SALES    .COP    3,568  01-15-93 12:35p
 SCHEDULE.DOC      906  01-11-93 11:58a   | *THANKU   .ABC   18,617  01-13-93 04:23p
 VOLUNTER.LET    1,040  01-14-93 02:01p
```

WORK WITH MULTIPLE FILES

You can copy, move, delete, print or search several files at one time.

1 Press →, ↓, ↑ or ← until you highlight one of the files you want to work with.

2 Press Shift - 8 and * appears beside the file name.

3 Repeat steps 1 and 2 until you mark with asterisks all the files you want to work with.

4 Proceed with the copy, move, delete, print or search command.

Note: To remove an asterisk beside a file name, press →, ↓, ↑ or ← until you highlight the file. Then press Shift - 8.

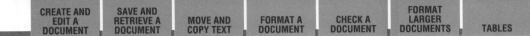

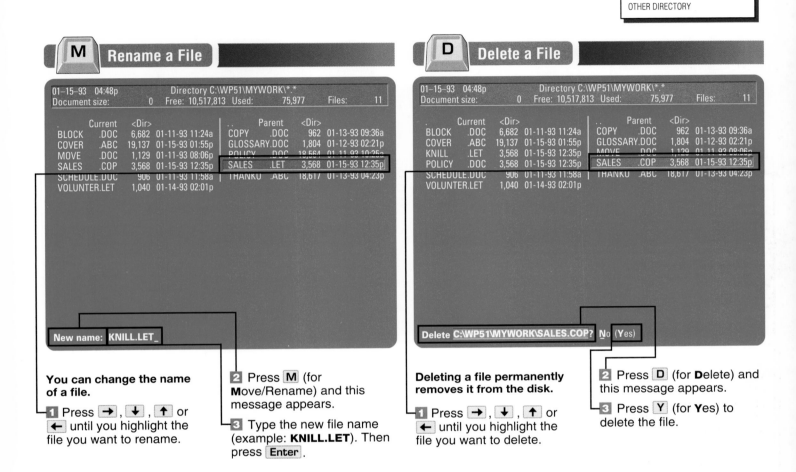

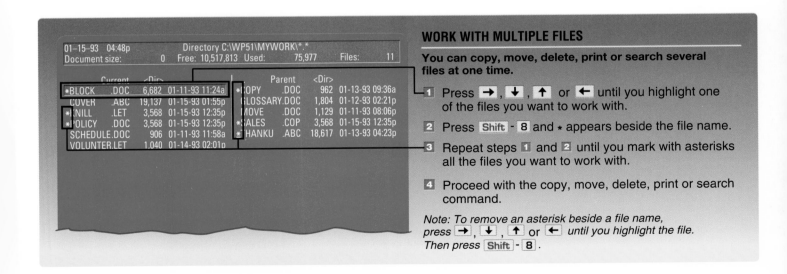

P Print a File

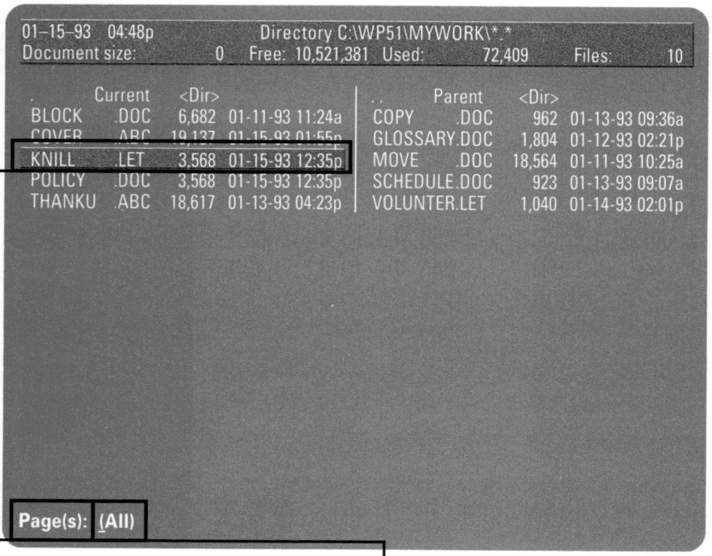

You can print a file without retrieving it.

1 Press →, ↓, ↑ or ← until you highlight the file you want to print.

2 Press P (for **P**rint) and this message appears.

3 To print all the pages in the document, press Enter.

Other Printing Options

Print one page
Type the page number (example: **3**). Then press Enter.

Print random pages
Type the page numbers separated by spaces (example: **1 9 22**). Then press Enter.

Print sequential pages
Type the first and last pages of the sequence separated by a dash (example: **6-11**). Then press Enter.

N Name Search

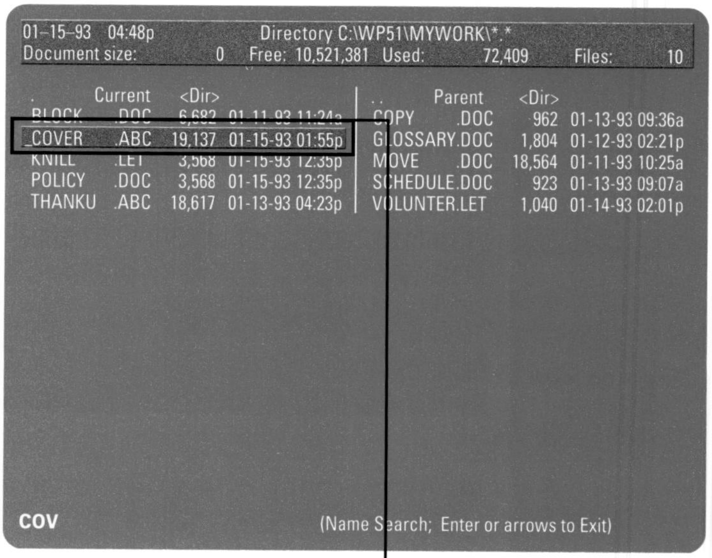

You can quickly locate a file if you know its file name.

1 Press N (for **N**ame Search).

2 Type the first letter of the file name (example: **C**).

■ WordPerfect highlights the first file name it encounters beginning with that letter.

3 Continue typing the letters in the file name until you locate the desired file (example: **COV** for **COVER.ABC**).

4 Press Enter to end the search.

F Find a File

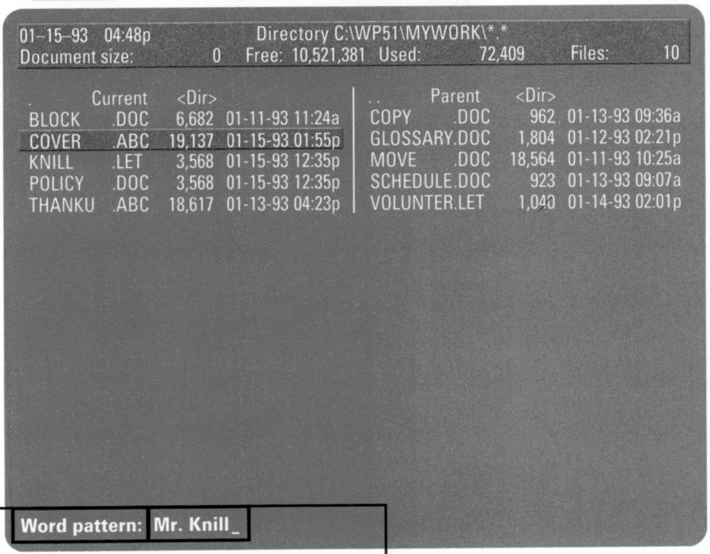

If you cannot remember the name of a file, you can find it by searching for a word or phrase in the document.

1 Press F (for **F**ind).

2 Press E (for **E**ntire Doc) and this message appears.

3 Type the word or phrase you want to search for (example: **Mr. Knill**).

4 Press Enter and WordPerfect displays the files that contain the searched text.

O Other Directory

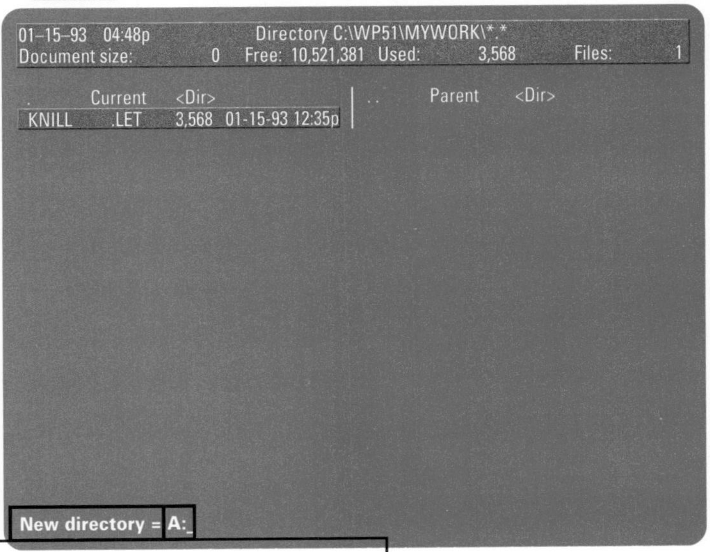

You can view the contents of a directory not listed on the screen.

1 Press O (for **O**ther Directory) and this message appears.

2 Type the drive and path of the directory (example: **A:**).

3 Press Enter twice and WordPerfect displays the contents of the directory.

Viewing Files

To view the contents of many files before retrieving a specific one, refer to page 34. This feature is useful if you cannot remember the name of the file you want to retrieve.

Retrieving Files

To retrieve a document from the List Files screen, refer to page 34.

Change Default Directory

You can instruct WordPerfect to always use a specific directory when saving and retrieving files. For more information, refer to page 28.

MERGE FILES OVERVIEW

Merge Files Overview

If you want to send the same letter to many different people, the merge feature can save you a lot of time.

Primary File

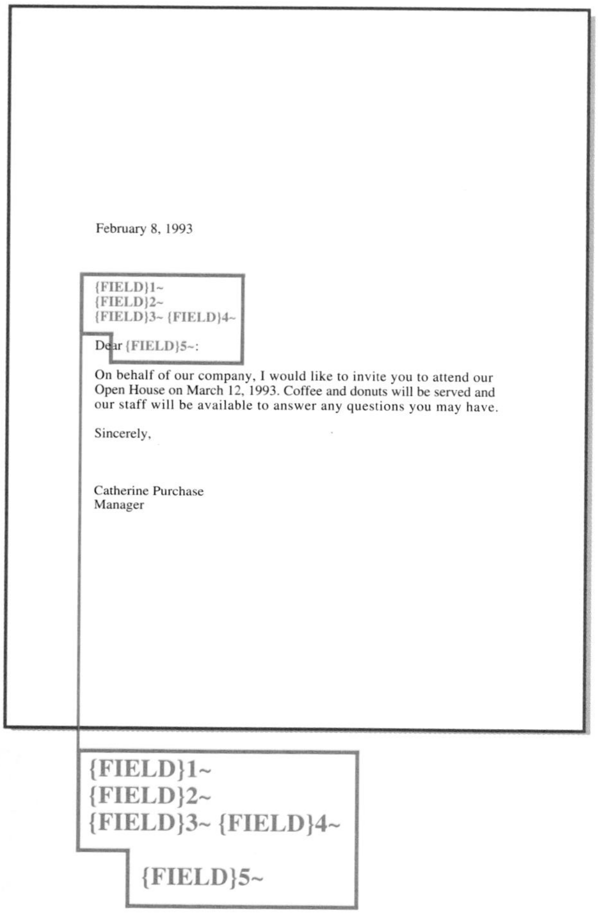
February 8, 1993

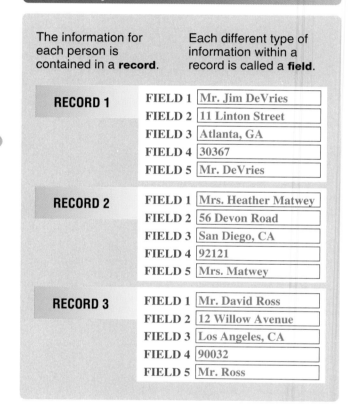

{FIELD}1~
{FIELD}2~
{FIELD}3~ {FIELD}4~

Dear {FIELD}5~:

On behalf of our company, I would like to invite you to attend our Open House on March 12, 1993. Coffee and donuts will be served and our staff will be available to answer any questions you may have.

Sincerely,

Catherine Purchase
Manager

Secondary File

The information for each person is contained in a **record**.

Each different type of information within a record is called a **field**.

RECORD 1	FIELD 1	Mr. Jim DeVries
	FIELD 2	11 Linton Street
	FIELD 3	Atlanta, GA
	FIELD 4	30367
	FIELD 5	Mr. DeVries
RECORD 2	FIELD 1	Mrs. Heather Matwey
	FIELD 2	56 Devon Road
	FIELD 3	San Diego, CA
	FIELD 4	92121
	FIELD 5	Mrs. Matwey
RECORD 3	FIELD 1	Mr. David Ross
	FIELD 2	12 Willow Avenue
	FIELD 3	Los Angeles, CA
	FIELD 4	90032
	FIELD 5	Mr. Ross

The primary file contains the text that will appear in each letter. It also contains **{FIELD}** codes that tell WordPerfect where to insert the information that changes from letter to letter.

Note: This file does not have to use all the fields in the secondary file.

The secondary file contains the information for each person you want to send the letter to. When merging the documents, WordPerfect inserts this data into the primary file.

Each field **must** contain the same type of information in every record.

For example, if the first field of one record contains a name, the first field of **every** record must also contain a name.

Note: The secondary file must contain all the fields used in the primary file.

Merged File

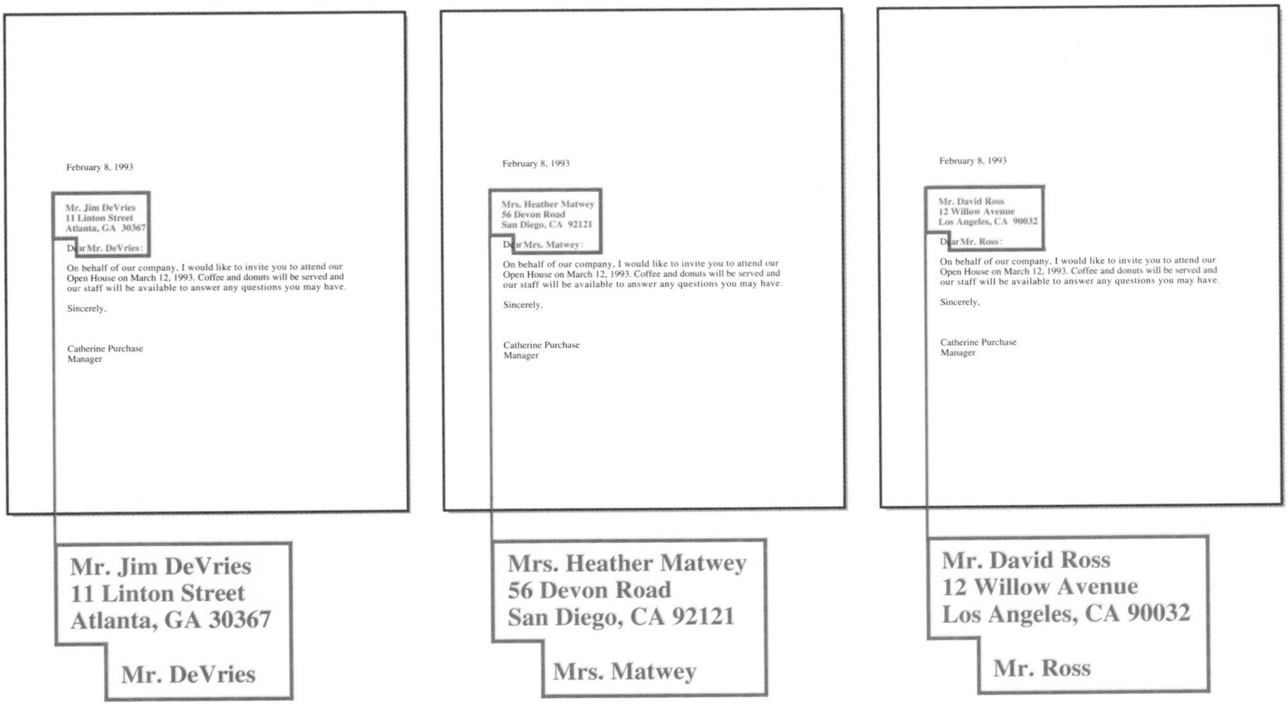
February 8, 1993
Mr. Jim DeVries
11 Linton Street
Atlanta, GA 30367
Dear Mr. DeVries:
On behalf of our company, I would like to invite you to attend our Open House on March 12, 1993. Coffee and donuts will be served and our staff will be available to answer any questions you may have.
Sincerely,
Catherine Purchase
Manager
Mr. Jim DeVries
11 Linton Street
Atlanta, GA 30367
Mr. DeVries
February 8, 1993
Mrs. Heather Matwey
56 Devon Road
San Diego, CA 92121
Dear Mrs. Matwey:
On behalf of our company, I would like to invite you to attend our Open House on March 12, 1993. Coffee and donuts will be served and our staff will be available to answer any questions you may have.
Sincerely,
Catherine Purchase
Manager
Mrs. Heather Matwey
56 Devon Road
San Diego, CA 92121
Mrs. Matwey
February 8, 1993
Mr. David Ross
12 Willow Avenue
Los Angeles, CA 90032
Dear Mr. Ross:
On behalf of our company, I would like to invite you to attend our Open House on March 12, 1993. Coffee and donuts will be served and our staff will be available to answer any questions you may have.
Sincerely,
Catherine Purchase
Manager
Mr. David Ross
12 Willow Avenue
Los Angeles, CA 90032
Mr. Ross

This file is the result of merging the primary and the secondary files.

WordPerfect inserts the information from the secondary file into the proper locations set by the **{FIELD}** codes in the primary file.

TIP

Before creating the primary and secondary files, decide how to split the information into different fields. For example, treat the address as one field, or break it down into separate "address", "city", "state" and "zip code" fields. This may be of help later on if only parts of the address are required in a merge.

CREATE THE PRIMARY FILE

Shift F9 Create the Primary File

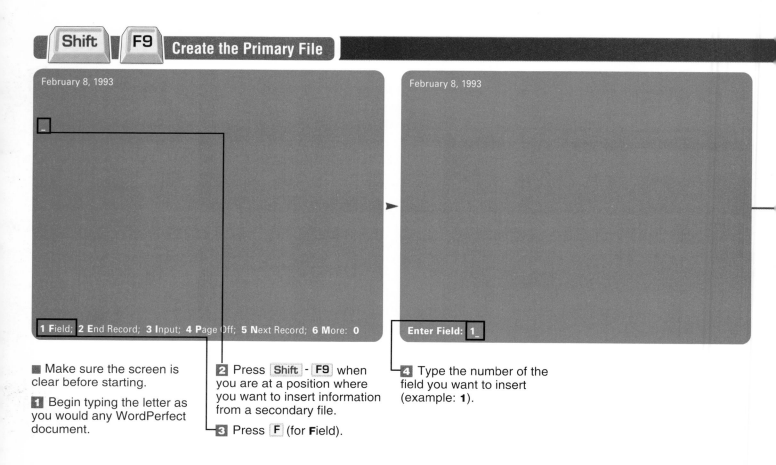

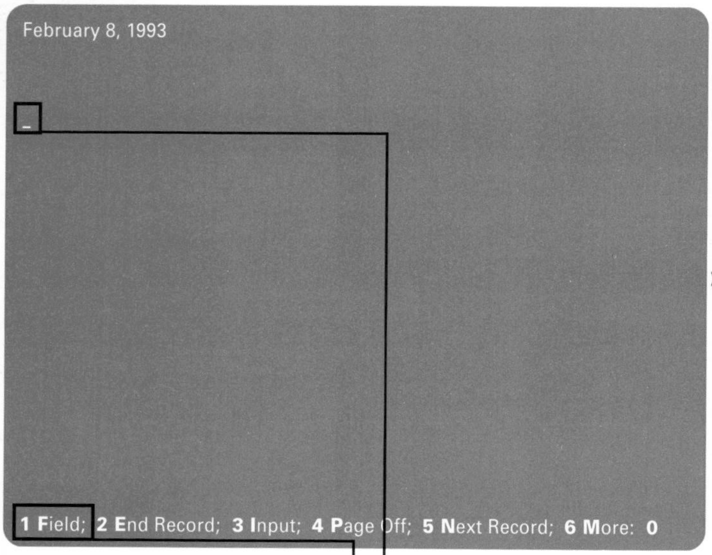

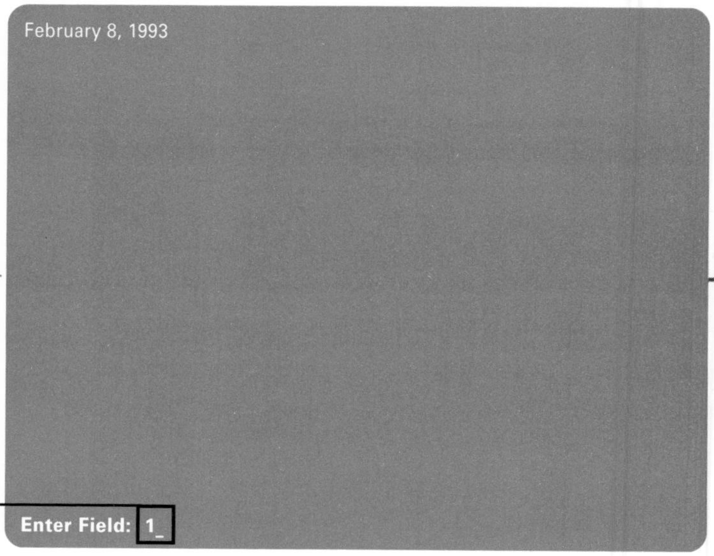

■ Make sure the screen is clear before starting.

1 Begin typing the letter as you would any WordPerfect document.

2 Press Shift - F9 when you are at a position where you want to insert information from a secondary file.

3 Press F (for **F**ield).

4 Type the number of the field you want to insert (example: **1**).

CLEAR THE SCREEN

1 Press F7.

2 Press N (for **N**o) if you do not want to save the document.

3 Press N (for **N**o) to clear the screen.

In this example, each record contains 5 fields.

FIELD 1	Name
FIELD 2	Address
FIELD 3	City, State
FIELD 4	Zip Code
FIELD 5	Salutation

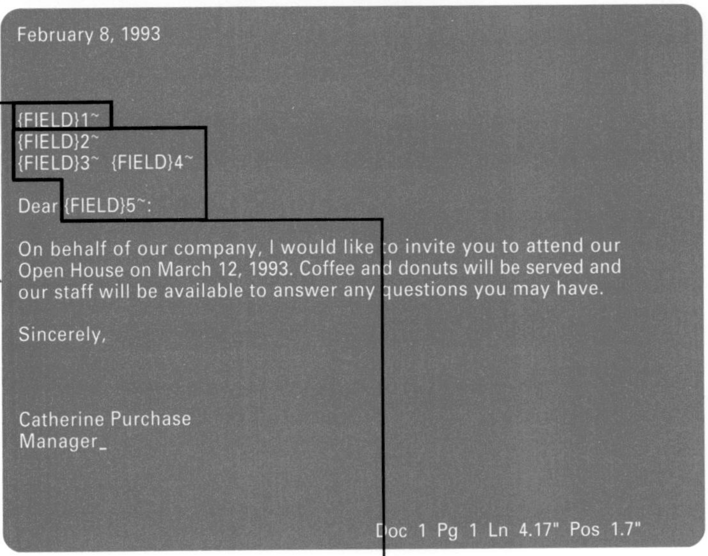
February 8, 1993
{FIELD}1~
{FIELD}2~
{FIELD}3~ {FIELD}4~
Dear {FIELD}5~:
On behalf of our company, I would like to invite you to attend our Open House on March 12, 1993. Coffee and donuts will be served and our staff will be available to answer any questions you may have.
Sincerely,
Catherine Purchase
Manager_
Doc 1 Pg 1 Ln 4.17" Pos 1.7"

5 Press Enter and a code appears (example: **{FIELD}1~**).

■ To start a new line, press Enter.

6 Continue typing the letter, repeating steps **2** to **5** for each field you want to insert.

SAVE THE PRIMARY FILE

1 Press F10.

2 Type a name for your document (example: **LETTER.PF**).

3 Press Enter.

■ When you merge the primary and secondary files, WordPerfect replaces the **{FIELD}** codes with information from the secondary file to create a letter directed to each person.

INSERT THE CURRENT DATE

If you insert the DATE code in the primary file, the current date will appear in its place each time you merge the primary and secondary files.

February 8, 1993

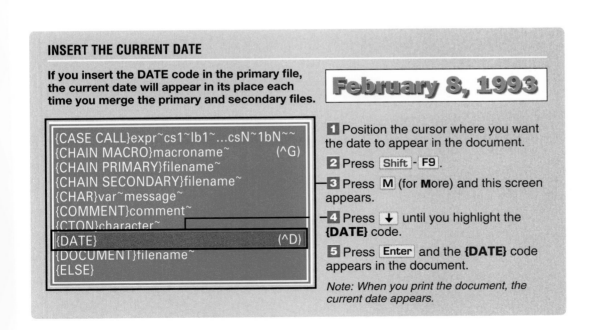

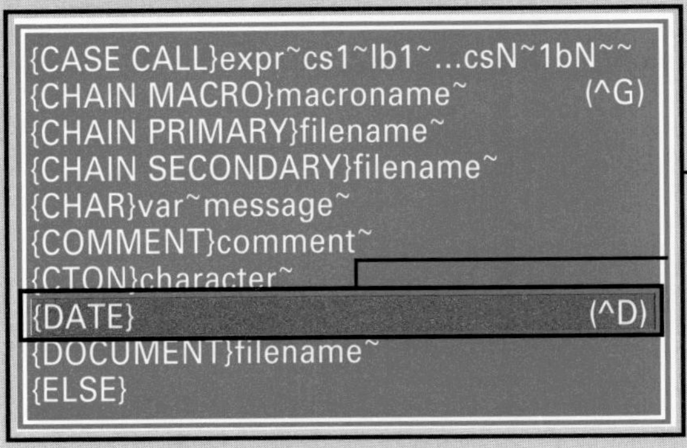
{CASE CALL}expr~cs1~lb1~...csN~1bN~~
{CHAIN MACRO}macroname~ (^G)
{CHAIN PRIMARY}filename~
{CHAIN SECONDARY}filename~
{CHAR}var~message~
{COMMENT}comment~
{CTON}character~
{DATE} (^D)
{DOCUMENT}filename~
{ELSE}

1 Position the cursor where you want the date to appear in the document.

2 Press Shift - F9.

3 Press M (for **M**ore) and this screen appears.

4 Press ↓ until you highlight the **{DATE}** code.

5 Press Enter and the **{DATE}** code appears in the document.

Note: When you print the document, the current date appears.

CREATE THE SECONDARY FILE

F9 Create the Secondary File

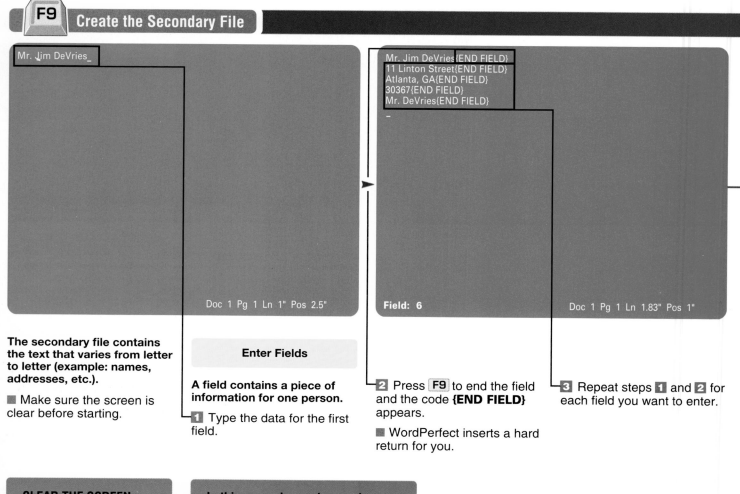

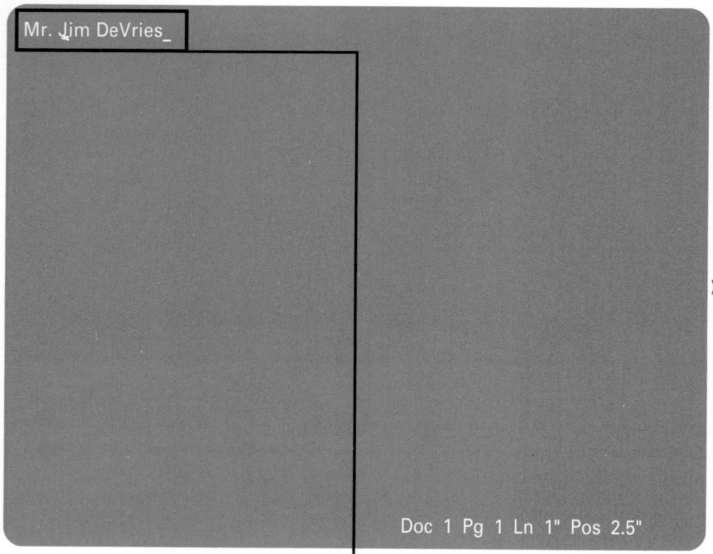

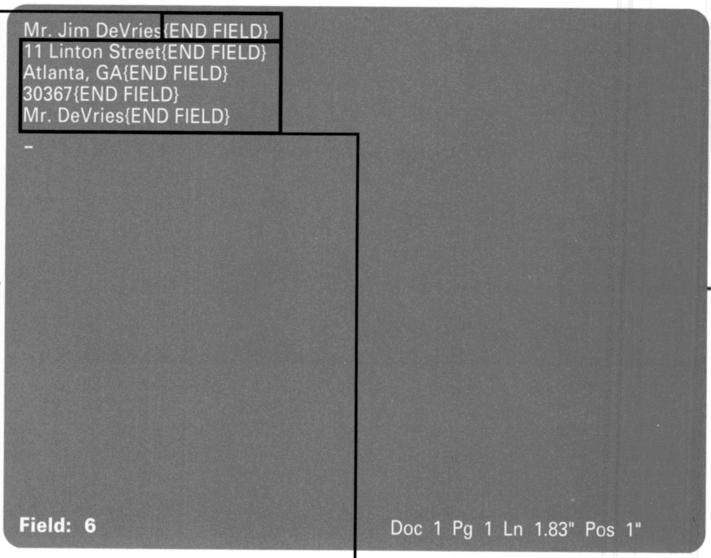

The secondary file contains the text that varies from letter to letter (example: names, addresses, etc.).

- Make sure the screen is clear before starting.

Enter Fields

A field contains a piece of information for one person.

1 Type the data for the first field.

2 Press F9 to end the field and the code **{END FIELD}** appears.

- WordPerfect inserts a hard return for you.

3 Repeat steps 1 and 2 for each field you want to enter.

CLEAR THE SCREEN

1 Press F7.

2 Press N (for **N**o) if you do not want to save the document.

3 Press N (for **N**o) to clear the screen.

In this example, each record contains 5 fields.

FIELD 1	Name
FIELD 2	Address
FIELD 3	City, State
FIELD 4	Zip Code
FIELD 5	Salutation

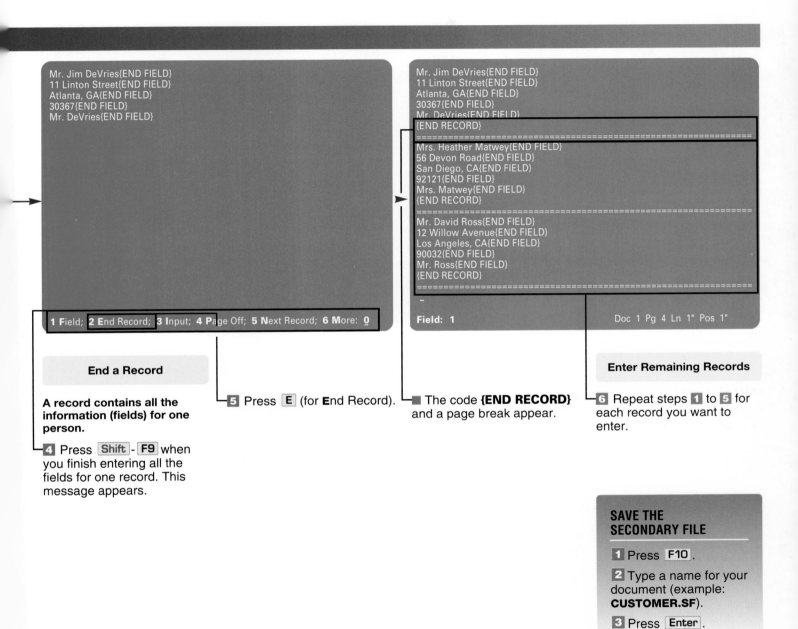

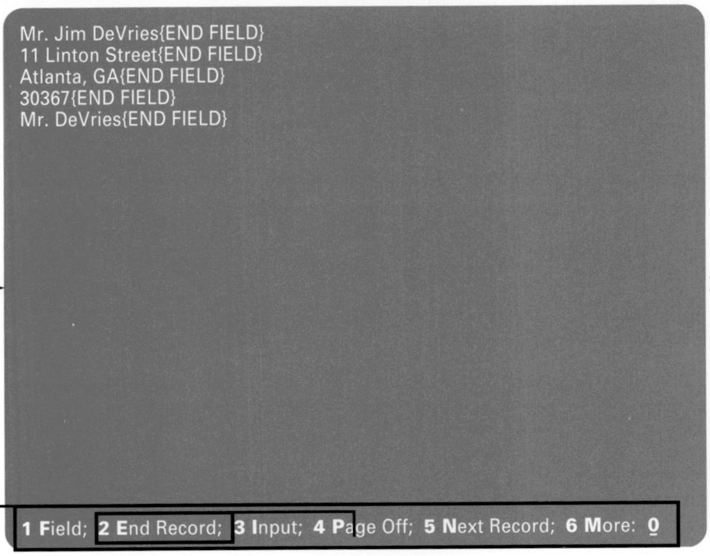

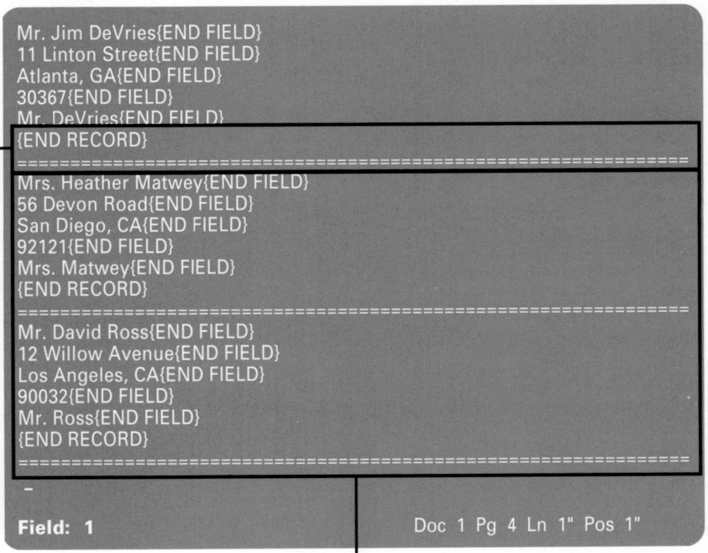

End a Record

A record contains all the information (fields) for one person.

4 Press Shift - F9 when you finish entering all the fields for one record. This message appears.

5 Press E (for **E**nd Record).

■ The code **{END RECORD}** and a page break appear.

Enter Remaining Records

6 Repeat steps 1 to 5 for each record you want to enter.

SAVE THE SECONDARY FILE

1 Press F10.

2 Type a name for your document (example: **CUSTOMER.SF**).

3 Press Enter.

MERGE FILES

Ctrl F9 Merge Files

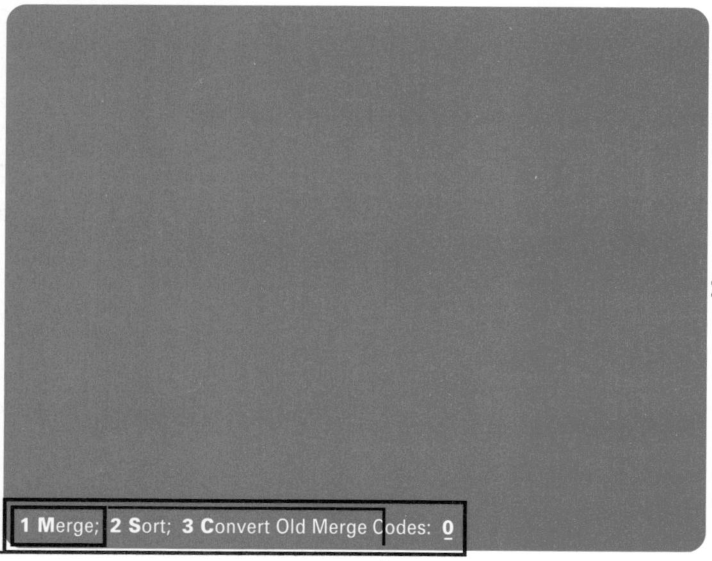

■ Make sure the screen is clear before starting.

1 Press Ctrl - F9 and this message appears.

2 Press M (for **M**erge).

3 Type the name of the primary file (example: **LETTER.PF**). Then press Enter.

USING MERGE TO CREATE ENVELOPES

Step 1: Set Dimensions of Envelope

■ Make sure the screen is clear before starting.

1 Press Shift - F8. Press P (for **P**age). Press M (for **M**argins).

2 Type 2 and press Enter to set the top margin. Type **.5** and press Enter to set the bottom margin.

3 Press S (for Paper **S**ize).

4 Press ↑ or ↓ until you highlight **Envelope**. Press Enter twice to return to the main **Format** screen.

5 Press L (for **L**ine). Press M (for **M**argins).

6 Type **3.5**, then press Enter to set the left margin. Press F7 twice to return to the typing area.

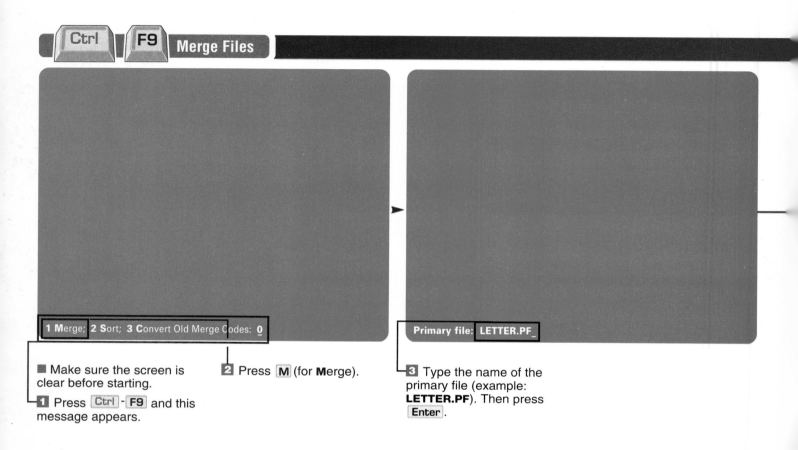

Step 2: Create a Primary File

1 Press Shift - F9. Press F (for **F**ield). Type the number of the field you want to insert and press Enter.

Note: The fields you insert depend on the setup of your secondary file.

2 Repeat step 1 for each field you want to insert.

Your screen may look as follows:

{FIELD}1~
{FIELD}2~
{FIELD}3~ {FIELD}4~

3 Save the file and clear the screen.

Secondary file: CUSTOMER.SF_

4 Type the name of the secondary file (example: **CUSTOMER.SF**). Then press Enter.

Catherine Purchase
Manager
==
February 8, 1993

Mr. David Ross
12 Willow Avenue
Los Angeles, CA 90032

Dear Mr. Ross:

On behalf of our company, I would like to invite you to attend our Open House on March 12, 1993. Coffee and donuts will be served and our staff will be available to answer any questions you may have.

Sincerely,

Catherine Purchase
Manager

Doc 1 Pg 3 Ln 4.17" Pos 1.7"

■ The result of the merged files appears on the screen.

5 Press ↑ to scroll through the document before printing to ensure no errors have occurred.

■ You can edit and print this file like any file in WordPerfect.

TIP After printing the merged document, you can erase the merged file from the hard drive to save space (as long as the primary and secondary files are retained).

Step 3: Merge the Files

1 To merge this new primary file with an existing secondary file, press Ctrl - F9. Press M (for **M**erge).

2 Type the name of the new primary file and press Enter. Type the name of the secondary file and press Enter.

Index